Heterick Memorial Library
Ohio Northern University

	DUE	RETURNED	DUE	RETURNED
1.			13.	
2.			14.	
3.			15.	
4.			16.	
5.			17.	
6.			18.	
7.			19.	
8.			20.	
9.			21.	
10.			22.	
11.			23.	
12.			24.	

Advance Praise for Integrated Direct Marketing

Ernan Roman pioneered the linking and sequencing of different communication tools to achieve high purchase impact. He demonstrates the impressive results of integrated direct marketing and points to where today's marketing thinking and practice are heading.

Philip Kotler
Distinguished Professor of International Marketing
J.L. Kellogg Graduate School of Management
Northwestern University

Integrated Direct Marketing (IDM) is an essential business tool for increasing revenues and managing costs. The results and logic of IDM are powerful forces for change. IDM presents a new way of thinking about customers. Focusing on serving customers, targeting communications and integrating resources will reshape sales and marketing organizations into a single cohesive unit. Ernan Roman is a leader in reengineering where it counts most, the customer interface.

Brian M. Gillespie
Director, Worldwide
Central Reservations Operations
ITT Sheraton Corporation

Ernan Roman has applied the principles of total quality management to direct marketing. Develop a process. Reduce waste. Improve response. Improve returns. These are the things every marketer is trying to do. It's a handbook on stewardship and accountability that every marketer should have.

Don E. Schultz
Professor of Integrated Marketing Communications
Medill School of Journalism
Northwestern University

Smaller, growth-oriented firms have a special reason to cheer the strategies outlined in Integrated Direct Marketing. *By focusing on methods that produce greater sales results from existing marketing budgets, Ernan Roman has developed a high-impact approach that works well even with limited resources. The powerful techniques of IDM show that being smart "can" make up for being small.*

Bryan St. Amant
Marketing Manager
BIW Connector Systems, Inc.

The old ways of marketing and selling just don't work like they used to. Today's tough business environment demands smart, results-focused marketers. In Integrated Direct Marketing, *Ernan Roman zeros in on the new marketing realities and offers "real world" solutions.*

Charles I. Tannen
Chairman
Direct Marketing to Business Conference

Ernan Roman has expressed his unique direct marketing visions in such a way that not only direct marketers but all marketers must read this latest book.

Eddy Boas
Chairman
Pan Pacific
Direct Marketing Symposium

The practice of direct marketing often mirrors folklore and widely held beliefs rather than precision methods. Ernan Roman's new book, Integrated Direct Marketing, *provides the methods and the "how to" examples that yield proven, measurable results . . . must reading for the serious marketing professional.*

Greg Lakin
Consultant and Former Director of Direct Marketing
Bell Atlantic

Integrated Direct Marketing *helps reengineer our approach to marketing communications in a practical, carefully orchestrated manner to achieve the results we all say we want. Ernan Roman's new book continues to include excellent examples and knowledge that is valuable to all marketing, sales, or business executives.*

John Hunter
Senior Vice President, Customer Services
QVC, Inc.

The concepts in Ernan Roman's Integrated Direct Marketing *are the basis for the evolution of more targeted business to business marketing efforts at DuPont—efforts that can finally be measured in terms of revenue generation. In the new edition, Mr. Roman offers skeptics a side by side comparison between a traditional business to business product launch . . . and one using the IDM philosophy. The difference in sales productivity per marketing dollar is dramatic, and clear proof that IDM works. That case alone is reason enough to buy the book!*

Gerald W. Hale
Manager
DuPont Customer Telecontact Center

Ernan Roman's approach to Integrated Direct Marketing is a breath of fresh air on a subject which is often misunderstood. This book is excellent. His practical, case-study-driven methodology for integrating and deploying the media makes this new book an invaluable resource for marketers throughout the world.

Ian J. Kennedy
Executive Chairman
K & D Bond Direct
Sydney, Australia

In this "Age of the Individual," marketers face the task of reducing the confusion surrounding the concept of direct marketing and understanding its true potential. They can learn a lot from Ernan Roman's philosophy—"the whole is greater than the sum of the parts"—and his practical, action-oriented guide to implementing it.

Jet Magsaysay
Editor-in-Chief
World Executive's Digest

INTEGRATED
▪ DIRECT ▪
MARKETING
▪

ERNAN ROMAN

NTC Business Books
NTC/Contemporary Publishing Group

Library of Congress Cataloging-in-Publication Data

Roman, Ernan.
    Integrated direct marketing: the cutting-edge strategy for synchronizing
advertising, direct mail, telemarketing, and field sales / Ernan Roman.
       p.   cm.
    Includes bibliographical references and index.
    ISBN 0-8442-3349-8
    1. Direct marketing.   I. Title.
HF5415.126.R65   1995
658.8'4—dc20   94-17508
                                         CIP

Dedication

*With love and thanks to my wife, Sheri, and our children,
Elias and Helaina, for they have provided the support and
encouragement to sustain this marketing zealot.*

Cover by Randall Smith, Bethel, Connecticut.
IDM is a service mark of Ernan Roman Direct Marketing Corporation.

Published by NTC Business Books
A division of NTC/Contemporary Publishing Group, Inc.
4255 West Touhy Avenue, Lincolnwood (Chicago), Illinois 60646-1975 U.S.A.
Printed in the United States of America
International Standard Book Number: 0-8442-3349-8
19   18   17   16   15   14   13   12   11   10   9   8   7   6

CONTENTS

Foreword   ix
Introduction   xi
Acknowledgments   xiii

CHAPTER 1

One-to-One Marketing: An Overview of Integrated Direct Marketing   1

The "Good Old Days" of Direct Marketing   2
Integrated Direct Marketing: A Definition   2
The Logic Behind the Process   4
The Five Principles of IDM   5
The Ultimate Success   8
How to Use This Book   8
Key Points   11
POSTSCRIPT: Why Do Organizations Resist Change?
   by Dr. Barry A. Farber   12

CHAPTER 2

The Face Behind the Data: What Do Customers Really Want?   15

The Integrated Database Is the Foundation of Customer-Driven
   Success   17
Strategically Speaking   18
Tactically Speaking: Where to Start   21
Building and Enhancing the Integrated Database   25
A Step-by-Step Process for Building an Integrated Database   34
Marketing's Role   38
The Role of Information Systems (IS)   39
The Integrated Database: Focused on the Customer   40
Key Points   41

CHAPTER 3

The Marketing Blend: Precision Deployment of Media for Double-Digit Response   43

Marketing Overview   44
Planning and Execution   44
Media Mix and Budget Allocation   46
Media Performance   46
Conversion to Sales   48
Internalizing the IDM Process Through Organizational
    Integration   49
Reengineering Marketing and Sales at IBM   50
Integrating Media for Profitability   51
The Principle of Response Compression   62
Initial and Ongoing Communications   63
Key Points   66
POSTSCRIPT: **Some Thoughts on Media** *by Greg Lakin*   66

CHAPTER 4

The IDM Creative Process: Customer-Driven, Market-Justified   72

Creating the IDM Campaign   73
The Creative Process at Work: IBM and USAA   77
Example 1: IBM's Lead Generation Program   77
Example 2: USAA Communicates to a Closed Market   101
Multi-Media Is the Message   105
Key Points   106
POSTSCRIPT: **Media Integration** *by Dan Majkowski*   106
POSTSCRIPT: **The Role of Direct Media**
    by Mitchell A. Orfuss   107

CHAPTER 5

Getting to Know You: Customer Contact Management   109

Customer Contact Management: A Definition   111
The Impact on Profitability   111
Getting the Most for Your Marketing Dollar   112
Relationships Instead of "Fishing"   113
Applying Customer Contact Management Principles at IBM   113
The Power of Shared Information   118
USAA: Customer Contact Management in Action   119
Making It Happen   122
Key Points   125

CHAPTER 6

The Proof Is in the Numbers: Measuring the Success of IDM   126

Measuring to Build Long-Term Relationships   127
IDM Quality and Performance Metrics   128
Planning to Measure   131
Budgeting for IDM   135
Budgeting Guidelines by Medium   140
Building the Business Case   145
Quantifying Customer Satisfaction   150
POSTSCRIPT: **Measuring an Actual Campaign Using a Traditional Media Allocation**   151

CHAPTER 7

Putting Together Your IDM Plan: Worksheets and Guidelines   154

Four Phases of IDM Planning   155
Phase 1: Developing the Initial Marketing Plan   157
Phase 2: Conducting IDM Depth Research and Developing the Final Marketing Action Plan   173
Phase 3: IDM Implementation   178
Phase 4: Ongoing Communications   183
POSTSCRIPT   183
POSTSCRIPT: **Fine-Tuning IDM Implementation— A Checklist** *by Scott Hornstein*   185

Epilogue   188

Appendix A Working-Week Calendar for IDM Program Implementation   189
Appendix B Calculating the Lifetime Value of a Customer by Richard J. Courtheoux   198
Appendix C Outbound and Inbound Telemarketing   203
Appendix D Checklist for Decision Making About In-House Versus Outside-Vendor Services   209
Appendix E IDM Quality and Performance Metrics   215

Index   218

"Revolutionary ideas don't usually start with a bang. They start with a whimper and sneak up on you. Before you know it, everybody not only has accepted the idea but claims to have been doing it all along ... Ernan Roman's Integrated Direct Marketing is just such an idea. Why? Because it works."

Al Ries
Chairman, Trout and Ries

In 1988, when I wrote that review of Ernan Roman's first book, Integrated Direct Marketing (IDM) was one of the most powerful ideas to come out of marketing in years.

A lot has happened since then. Markets and businesses have changed. Smart marketers want measurable results; not awards. Customers want value; not entertainment. Management expects cost effectiveness as well as profits. Mass media and mass communication are rapidly losing their appeal due to their decreasing effectiveness.

Meanwhile, Ernan Roman has taken his revolutionary idea and proven its worth in large and small corporations. Integrated Direct Marketing provides a strategic and tactical process for managing customer-driven communications. It is a way to focus sales and marketing on building strong, lasting relationships with customers. But, in spite of these benefits, there's still a lot of chaos and confusion out there.

This new book, *Integrated Direct Marketing,* clears up that confusion and explains, in simple terms, how you can implement IDM at your company. It details the major principles of IDM, explains how to take IDM from concept to reality at your own business, and demonstrates IDM at work with in-depth case studies of IBM, Citibank, Bell Atlantic, and Hewlett-Packard, as well as smaller companies.

Integrated Direct Marketing is practical – it faces the reality of the barriers that you're likely to come up against, and shows how to get around, over, or through them.

The first barrier is perceptual.   Just adding multiple media won't make your campaign integrated, nor will it produce IDM's double-digit results. IDM is a customer-driven process that's based on research, precision, and analysis. If you're ready to rethink your direct marketing and commit to a proven process, the guidelines are here.

The second barrier is organizational.   It exists among disciplines such as marketing, field sales, and advertising, that value their turf and are not used to working cooperatively.

To integrate your direct marketing, you have to integrate yourself. Roman's concept of the cross-functional team and step-by-step road map for roles and responsibilities will go a long way toward focusing everyone on the customer and increased results.

The third barrier is implementation.   Anytime you send a message that diverges from your core message, you create confusion. Not only doesn't it help you; it can hurt you. Too many people in communications believe the more the merrier. The more messages you have, the more programs you run, the more money you spend, the more successful you'll be. The truth is quite the contrary.

Media and messages must be integrated and managed so your company speaks with one voice – carrying a message of value, as defined by the customer. The case histories in the book illustrate this point beyond a shadow of a doubt.

I wish you the best in bringing the IDM revolution to your own marketing organization. This new book is a powerful tool. And as you read it remember, that the future of your company may well be in your hands.

Al Ries

This book has been a joy to write. It has given me and my colleagues the opportunity to share the experiences and impressive results of companies who are using the process of Integrated Direct Marketing in very special ways.

Our excitement in writing this new book is that we can build on the solid foundation established in our first book, *Integrated Direct Marketing: Techniques and Strategies for Success*, published in 1985, and continue the journey towards developing a truly customer-driven direct marketing and field sales process. The goal of this process is simple: Significant increases in qualified response, increased profit, and reduced waste through the precision deployment of relevant and targeted communications.

The blending of two factors got us here. The first is technology, with its ability to accumulate and analyze tremendous amounts of customer and prospect data quickly and inexpensively.

But technology is only a tool—often misused to create generic mass-produced communications diluted to the lowest common denominator.

The second factor is the recognition by many companies that the focus on the customer must be the driving force. We must compel ourselves to abandon the "make and sell" manufacturing mind-set which has devastated the effectiveness of most marketers. Instead, we must rapidly evolve to the customer-based commitment of "listen and serve."

These are not new concepts. What's new is the recognition that companies can't get away with the same old "B-52" saturation bombing techniques they use for their marketing efforts.

And what are the results from Integrated Direct Marketing? Innovative marketers consistently find that customer-focused, integrated deployment of media, message, and field sales channels works! When customers see that your company is committed to their needs and is communicating in value-added, responsive, integrated ways—they respond!

When you read the success stories from the companies profiled in this book, you will see how Fortune marketers like IBM, AT&T, Hewlett-Packard, and a small company like Adept Technology Inc. have taken the leap to customer-driven, precision marketing. And you will learn how they have reaped substantial profits as a result of achieving double-digit response rates versus the usual 1 to 2 percent mail response—reducing cost per sale and increasing customer satisfaction.

The focus is simple—your customer. Integrated Direct Marketing provides you with a battle-tested, thoroughly documented process for integrating your media and field sales channels with precision, accountability, and value.

Adhere to the discipline of the IDM process we have documented, and you are certain to achieve astounding results!

As you read this book, we hope that you will let yourself embark on an adventure and prepare yourself to challenge status quo dragons flaming fears of change, traps of territoriality, and feuding fiefdoms.

Your reward will be the vision and process for building value-based, long-term relationships and reducing cost of sales through the precision deployment of high-quality marketing media and field sales. It is a battle well worth fighting because, at the end, you and your customers win. The only losers are those afraid of embracing change: they fight against the tide.

Good luck on your marketing journey.

Ernan Roman
Douglas Manor, NY

ACKNOWLEDGMENTS

As consultants, our job is to create new visions and strategies. However, we depend on our clients to embrace the visions and commit themselves and their resources to implementing the marketing and sales change process.

The following executives deserve special mention. Mike Lawrie, IBM US Vice President and Area General Manager, and Curt Gillespie, IBM Business Unit Executive, have demonstrated the vision and the commitment to implementing Integrated Direct Marketing with a passion and focus that has been a pleasure to see. Judie Neiger, Marketing Communications Specialist, and Garry Dawson, MARCOM Manager at Hewlett-Packard, are among the earliest converts to IDM. Their tenacity and perseverance in driving the sales and marketing change process at H-P has been remarkable. Greg Lakin, former Director of Direct Marketing at Bell Atlantic, brought valuable insights and creativity to the way he implemented IDM at Bell Atlantic.

A very special acknowledgment is due Scott Hornstein, Senior Partner, ERDM, who has devoted his considerable intellect and passion for innovation to the task of refining and strengthening the IDM process. His contributions to IDM and this book are significant, and I owe him a heartfelt thanks. No one could ask for a more dedicated and generous colleague.

A warm thanks also to my mother, Eva Haller and her husband, Yoel Haller, for their insightful contributions and critiques of this manuscript. Eva also deserves special mention for having introduced me to this industry in 1972!

The following people have made important contributions to this book and to ERDM. Marija Bryant provided creative skill, patience, and stamina in helping to shape this book. Randy Smith contributed his considerable design skills to the graphics and the elegant cover. Carol Hamilton applied her unswerving patience to ensuring that the word processing and formatting of this manuscript were excellent.

A final thanks to Anne Knudsen, Executive Editor, NTC Publishing, for her encouragement and insightful editorial guidance.

One-to-One Marketing
An Overview of Integrated Direct Marketing

Direct marketing as I have described, practiced, and predicted it for more than 30 years is over.

Lester Wunderman
Chairman Worldwide,
Wunderman Cato Johnson
(Opening remarks at 76th annual
Direct Marketing Association Conference)

American business was built on the principle of "make and sell"—manufacture a large volume of the same product, advertise that product to a mass audience, and let the sheer numbers generate profitable sales. That was fine while it lasted. But sometime in the '80s, markets began to fragment, competition intensified, and differentiation through product attributes wasn't an advantage for very long.

These changes in the marketplace have only accelerated and intensified through the '90s and will continue into the second millennium. Outspoken consumers and enabling technology are the principal drivers of these changes. Customers demand more choices in buying precisely what meets their wants and needs, and they expect individualized attention. Further, the technology of both production systems and marketing systems has made it possible to tailor products, service, and communications to meet those expectations.

1

This market evolution mandates the following changes for all marketers:

- A new emphasis on longer-term relationships versus short-term sales. Said differently, marketing is evolving from "hunting and gathering" of immediate sales to the nurturing and tending of customers to create repeat business.
- A reconceptualization of the customer as a partner and not a target. Focused efforts to create and sustain these partnerships are built and deployed based on an in-depth understanding of customers' unique and ever-changing sets of needs and requirements.
- Reengineering the corporate structure to merge current islands of specialization and information to create consistent, customer-oriented response to market needs and requirements.

In short, the basic goals and measurements of marketing and direct marketing are evolving from "find the customer and sell the product we have" to a true partnership of "how can we serve your unique needs?"

THE "GOOD OLD DAYS" OF DIRECT MARKETING

Many of us remember that time not so long ago when direct marketing was a corporate cash cow. Get a list, mail a letter or a brochure, and sales came in with each ring of the phone. Or, if a field sales force was involved, generate leads, throw the leads over the wall, and wait for the sales to come rolling in.

The definition of success was based on who was doing the measuring. Marketing defined the gross volume of leads as "success." Meanwhile, sales defined success as revenue and commissions. And all the time the customer was measuring us based on value, satisfaction and commitment over time. Customers were seeing fragmented, sales-oriented messages that fostered the perception of "commodity," with price as the major differentiating factor. Few, if any, direct marketing efforts looked at success from a total company, long-term customer partnership perspective.

Clearly, this divergence between marketers and customers had to change, and the decreasing response rates and sales figures provided companies with the wake-up call.

INTEGRATED DIRECT MARKETING: A DEFINITION

It was in this environment of change that, in 1983, my company, Ernan Roman Direct Marketing Corporation (ERDM), developed Integrated Direct Marketing (IDM^{sm})* as a process for customer-focused marketing. At the time, it was revolutionary.

*IDM is a service mark of Ernan Roman Direct Marketing Corporation.

IDM is a process for the precision deployment of multiple media and sales channels including:

- Publicity and public relations
- Advertising
- Direct mail
- Telemarketing
- Field sales channels

IDM seeks to maintain contact with the customer at multiple points during the sales cycle and throughout the long-term relationship to ensure ongoing, effective communication, including (1) **pre-sale** contact to determine the needs, interests, and preferences of prospects and customers; (2) precise, integrated **communications during the sales process** that are designed for ever-increasing focus on customers' requirements; and (3) **ongoing communications** to maintain the customer relationship—as customers' needs change—whether a sale has been closed or not.

IDM has become accepted as a proven, highly effective process for customer-focused marketing. The results from years of careful measurement have proven that IDM will:

- Generate double-digit qualified responses, with a focus on quality, not tonnage
- Provide leads that result in timely, tenacious follow-up and closure by the sales force
- Often decrease cost of sale by redeploying budgets and resources for greater productivity
- Increase customer satisfaction and lifetime value
- Increase efficiency and productivity of both direct marketing and the sales force

These results have been tested time and again against stringent benchmarks.

◆ Reaching People, Not Targets

Don Schultz, professor of Integrated Marketing Communications at Northwestern University, describes the changes to marketing in "The Natural Evolution of Direct Marketing" (*Beyond 2000: The Future of Direct Marketing,* Lincolnwood, IL: NTC Business Books, 1994). "Manufacturers developed products; mass produced them. Sent them into distribution channels such as mass retailers and merchandisers. Then they mass advertised and mass promoted to mass audiences, which they believed they could reach with various forms of mass communication. Mass marketing worked in the middle to late 20th century because there were lots of new products, increasing populations, instant and easy credit, increasing availability of products and services, sophisticated communication channels.

"But in the 1970s and 1980s, all this mass marketing broke down. Technology in the form of UPC codes, point of sale scanners, and sophisticated new research techniques combined to give the retailer and the marketer more and more specific information on their individual customers. New media forms developed. Databases were constructed and filled with purchase behavior data. Micro-marketing was in. Mass marketing was out. That was true whether you sold men's slacks, women's perfume, automobiles or potato chips. Technology, just as it had been used to create the mass market, destroyed it."

THE LOGIC BEHIND THE PROCESS

The basic idea behind IDM—that a good mix of media will improve results—has been around for as long as the follow-up phone call. What's new about IDM is that it goes far beyond an intuitive mix of media to a true integration of the methods of communicating with your customers. It is not just advertising, direct mail, or telemarketing but rather it is an integrated communications approach that is strategic, research-based, and targeted to the ever-changing customer needs and preferences. IDM is implemented through the precision deployment of media and sales channels to achieve a significant increase in the quality and quantity of response while establishing ongoing value for the customer.

Therefore, IDM is:

- **Strategic** in that all sales and marketing channels operate according to a precise plan and are synchronized to maximize results
- **Research-based** in that the success of the process depends on in-depth knowledge of the customer—knowledge that goes beyond demographics and database marketing
- **Targeted to customer needs** in that all your communications to the prospect or customer—no matter what the media—must be judged relevant and provide true value

The precision integration and deployment of marketing and sales channels is the "magic" of IDM—if magic there is. IDM requires no new media but rather a careful, strategic orchestration of existing media—publicity/public relations, advertising, direct mail, telemarketing and field sales contact. By synchronizing the media, you are deploying a cohesive, sustained message rather than the fragmented scattershot often experienced by customers or prospects. The objective is to "personalize" the message to the needs of individuals and to sustain that communication over time and across multiple media and sales channels.

THE FIVE PRINCIPLES OF IDM

Our audience made us successful.

George Burns

Integrated Direct Marketing is based on five basic principles:

1. Start with the Customer
2. Listen to the Field Sales Force
3. Synchronize Media with Laser Precision
4. Develop Creative that Provides Value to the Customer
5. Continue the Process Throughout the Sales Cycle and Beyond.

1. Start with the Customer

The customer must become our partner, and we must listen carefully to what the customer has to say. IDM provides a systematic process for listening to the customer's needs and preferences, and driving action that provides value and satisfaction.

To enhance customer response and long-term satisfaction, you need to understand your customer base—not as undifferentiated mass markets or targets but as people and businesses with decision makers who have a unique set of needs, media preferences, and concerns. You need, also, to be able to track those needs and concerns as they change over time. The answers can mean the difference between a direct marketing campaign that gets results and one that winds up in the wastebasket. IDM depth research helps you to achieve that understanding.

Depth research does not require a large sampling to generate needed information about your market. The focus is on depth rather than breadth. Careful selection of interviewees with a tightly organized questionnaire can validate and determine:

- The decision-making process
- Roles and responsibilities of key contacts
- Positioning of the creative
- Appeal of the offer
- Media preference
- Media mix

2. Listen to the Field Sales Force

One of the cornerstones of IDM is the importance of field sales involvement from day one. Since sales shares responsibility for meeting goals of long-term relationships and profitability, they must be at the planning table and involved throughout. After all, sales will be following up on the leads. They are the ones who know the face-to-face realities of the customers, who are out in the marketplace every day. Listening to your field sales can pay immediate dividends.

Field sales should be included in these critical activities in the planning process:

- Development of the marketing strategy (near term and long term)
- Selection of lead generation events (seminars, teleconferences, trade shows, follow-up calls, etc.)
- Definition of "qualified" leads
- Review of creative materials
- Analysis of results
- Determination of follow-up events.

Traditional lead follow-up rate averages 30 percent with an average closure rate of only 10 percent. By integrating the field sales force and nurturing their buy-in and ownership of the IDM program, a lead follow-up of 60 percent can be achieved, with average closure of 25 percent.

There's no mystery here: the more sales involvement in the planning, the more input on what constitutes a qualified lead, the better the leads and, as a result, the more tenacious the follow-up. Higher closure rates follow as a natural result.

3. Synchronize Media with Laser Precision

You probably use more than one medium already. But orchestrating the media to meet your objectives requires asking yourself some key questions: What's the role of each medium? How has it performed historically? What mix will build the sense of "event"? What's the optimal timing for each medium? What are the media preferences of my target markets?

Remember that each medium has strengths and weaknesses. Depth research can help you determine how to best match the medium and the message. By redeploying the media according to a precise plan, you can be sure to reach the market in the most persuasive and cost effective way.

Be careful to control the double-edged sword of telemarketing. The purpose of your outbound call can be as varied as the objectives of your marketing campaign—to generate a sale, confirm an offer, or provide additional information. However, the call must have clear value to the prospect and a context that links it to the other communications. Then, the prospect knows what your call is about, is more willing to spend the time with you, and is in a better position to make an informed decision.

Plan and pace all your media to work together to create synergy with each other as opposed to simply coexisting. Look beyond single events. Avoid the all-too-common mail or phone blitzes. Build on the strengths of each medium to make a positive impact on your prospect and generate increased response. Over time, your direct marketing will become more targeted, as information obtained through ongoing communications drives increasingly personalized messages.

4. Develop Creative that Provides Value to the Customer

A key part of the IDM process is creative that is driven by the customer and prospect depth research. The objective is to provide an offer, information, or action point that meshes with the prospect's buying process and decision-making requirements. Just because your communication conveys what you, your management, engineering, or researchers believe is important doesn't mean that the customer sees any value in it. The key question to answer is the customer's unspoken one: "So what? What does this do for me or my business?"

Call existing customers and test ideas or copy lines; ask if the offer or event has value. Use your salespeople and their contacts to hone the creative message until it has impact, relevance, and urgency to the people you are hoping to reach.

5. Continue the Process Throughout the Sales Cycle and Beyond

The terms "customer" and "prospect" represent two aspects of the same person. Every decision maker is both, at different times during a relationship. Therefore, let's take our eyes off those terms and concentrate on the relationship, on providing the value and satisfaction that will strengthen and lengthen the relationship.

IDM takes direct marketing beyond beating the bushes for short-term sales and recognizes that customers live in a continuum with ever-changing needs and requirements that we should be positioned to satisfy (see Exhibit 1-1).

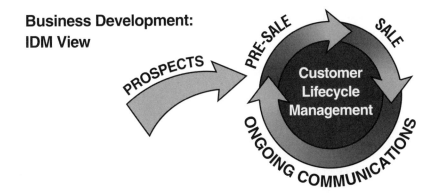

Exhibit 1-1. IDM is a carefully orchestrated process that delivers targeted, customer-driven communication over the entire customer life cycle.

THE ULTIMATE SUCCESS

What will separate the winners from the losers over the next critical years is the ability to make the changes needed to get closer to the customers. According to Don Schultz (professor of Integrated Marketing Communications at Northwestern University), there are certain rules that hold true when implementing any change, including IDM:

- Quit looking at product. Products are irrelevant. Get away from how many units did we sell or what's our market share and start looking at it as income flows. What's a customer worth? Is that customer more profitable to me this year than last year? The problem with that is that every organization is focused on feeding the plant. I'm going to make a bunch of these things and I'm going to find someone to sell them to. That's what creates the problem.
- Stop communicating to the masses. The organizations that are in difficulty are those who are caught in mass production and mass communication simply because that's what they're set up to do.
- People do what they are rewarded for doing. So change the compensations system. Reward people for serving customers and increasing customer value. There's no reward for serving customers in organizations today. As long as you give them quotas, they're going to treat customers like targets of opportunity.
- It's got to come from the top down—from leadership with vision and commitment to change.

According to a business leader who has brought IDM into one of the world's largest enterprises, "It starts with a leap of faith. And that leap of faith can be helped by senior management," says Curt Gillespie, IBM Business Unit Executive, speaking of a major reengineering of marketing and sales along IDM lines. "But pretty soon there have to be results. We've got to be able to give concrete examples of how we've produced revenue with very high customer satisfaction at a lower expense rate than with traditional methods. And if we can't prove that with hard numbers, we shouldn't be doing business this way."

HOW TO USE THIS BOOK

The marketing scene today may go down as the year of the straddle—one foot planted in the fertile soil of direct interaction with known customers, the other stuck in the rut of bombarding the marketplace with one-way communication to gain "share of mind" among unknown customers and prospects.

Stan Rapp
"One Foot In, One Foot Out"
Direct, February, 1994

This book is intended to help you use IDM to communicate more effectively with customers and prospects. Following is a brief overview of each of the subsequent chapters.

Chapter 2 The Face Behind the Data: What Do Customers Really Want?

Focus

The need for in-depth customer information and ongoing, personalized contact to update our understanding of each individual customer hasn't changed—whether we're in business-to-business or consumer marketing. But the process for managing that information has; we call it the integrated database.

This chapter provides a step-by-step process for building and enhancing the integrated database.

Case Histories

- How Hewlett-Packard has:
  - Reduced mail quantity from 70,000 pieces to 10,000 pieces
  - Reduced budget
  - Increased response
  - Increased lead follow-up and conversion to a higher average sale
- Recent depth research results challenge the way we do business: a strong customer bias against outbound telemarketing

Chapter 3 The Marketing Blend: Precision Deployment of Media for Double-Digit Response

Focus

Depth research, prior history, testing, and analysis continually bring us closer to understanding the needs and requirements of our customer and prospect base. This evolving understanding is the basis for the process of integrated budget allocation and media deployment.

Case Histories

- How an A/B test of the IDM methodology produced:
  - a 300 percent increase in qualified leads with a 300 percent reduction in the cost of lead
  - an increase in conversion of 250 percent
  - a 1300 percent improvement in revenue
  - an E:R of 4.4 percent

- How a catalog start-up used publicity to establish effective positioning and response
- How Citibank tested and proved the value of telemarketing scripting and IDM Total Quality Control (TQC)
- How a national telecommunications provider achieved
  - a 67 percent increase in sales rate
  - a 43 percent reduction in cost of sale
  - enhanced customer satisfaction as measured by a 50 percent reduction in "do not call" requests

Chapter 4 The IDM Creative Process: Customer-Driven, Market-Justified

Focus

Jazz—good jazz—is a blend of player and instrument. It's part structured and part improvisational. It's hard to define, but you know it when you hear it. That's the kind of synergy IDM creative demands—separate media, working together in harmonious congruence to make the audience take notice.

Case Histories

- How IBM successfully integrated both media and message to reposition a product line and create strong response
- USAA's success in a closed market: providing a value-add in creative execution matched to life-cycle stages and events

Chapter 5 Getting to Know You: Building Relationships for the Long Term

Focus

Technology—databases, computer lists, personalization—has given direct marketing the tools to send more messages to more people more efficiently. But the results have been a kind of "shell shock"—the aftereffects of being the "target" for multiple direct marketing messages. The key to eliminating that shock is synchronized management of the contact with the customer—across media and throughout the life cycle.

Case Histories

- How and why USAA has been a leader in building and maintaining long-term customer relationships

Chapter 6 The Proof Is in the Numbers: Measuring the Success of IDM

Focus

The process of measuring the results of an IDM program is more complex than traditional direct marketing because you are tracking and measuring responses to the whole, integrated program as well as the component parts. What's the impact of this? For one, you are measuring how well your program achieved your shared objectives. For another, you need to demonstrably show the value of customer retention over customer acquisition. Traditional measures of effectiveness—leads and sales—may not be appropriate in gauging the value of a customer relationship.

Case Histories

- How Adept Technology, a growth company that designs, manufactures and sells industrial robots for assembly processes implemented IDM and
  - More than doubled their response rate
  - Reduced cost per lead from $150 to $30 with no loss of quality
  - Doubled lead follow-up rate because of the improved lead quality and field sales integration
- How a large manufacturer of telecommunications equipment analyzed current IDM results (response = 129 percent of forecast, leads = 116 percent of forecast, sales = 169 percent of forecast) to learn how to further improve performance, return and customer satisfaction.

Chapter 7 Putting Together Your IDM Plan: Worksheets and Guidelines

Focus

Now that you've read what IDM can do, here are the guidelines to help you do it in your business. The step-by-step process covers the critical issues and will help you to organize your thinking and assign resources.

KEY POINTS

- IDM is a cross-functional process and operates with a shared vision.
- The five basic principles of IDM:
  1. Start with the customer.
  2. Listen to the field sales force.

3. Synchronize media with laser precision.
4. Develop creative that provides value to the customer.
5. Continue the process throughout the sales cycle and beyond.
- IDM is a strategic, precise process of customer contact that redeploys media and sales channels in nontraditional ways. This results in quality responses that lead to sales.
- Many years of benchmarking have proven IDM in the trenches.

POSTSCRIPT

Why Do Organizations Resist Change?
Barry A. Farber, PhD
Chair, Department of Clinical Psychology,
Teachers College, Columbia University

Organizations, like individuals, typically resist change. Indeed, many of the issues underlying organizational resistance to change are analogous to factors explaining individual resistance. Like individuals, organizations invariably prefer the status quo to the unpredictability of new ways of behaving or viewing the world.

It is the rare company, much as it is the rare individual, that is truly a risk-taker. Notwithstanding statements affirming an organization's "broad consensus for change" and commitment and openness to new perspectives, most businesses would prefer to make only the slightest alterations in the way things work. Sometimes such alterations are sufficient to truly turn things around; more often, they become quickly assimilated into old patterns, providing validation to the French proverb, "The more things change, the more they remain the same."

Just as the traits and behavioral patterns of individuals define, predict, and limit new ways of thinking and behaving, the long-standing norms and mores of a business organization serve to constrain innovative changes. Organizations, like individuals, become invested in certain ways of doing and thinking. These patterns become part of the individual psyche or corporate ethos. In most organizations, employees, as well as management, have become comfortable–often too comfortable–working in a predictable environment. In fact, businesses most often hire people who are likely to do things "the company way" and unlikely to upset tradition. Even downturns in business that spur management's hiring of outside consultants may be interpreted by the majority of employees as temporary aberrations best fixed by patience and a renewed commitment to the standard, once effective policies of the past. In fact, it is not even unusual under such circumstances to discover that management harbors a wish for consultants to confirm the wisdom of what management has always done. Specifically, the wish is for experts to confer a "seal of approval" on past policy and, at most, to suggest minor changes to the usual practices.

Thus, standard operating procedures are often seen by both management and labor as the only rational means to do business, the "one best way." "We have gotten this far and done reasonably well," so the thinking often goes, "and it would be foolish, indeed dangerous, to change things too much and risk disaster."

Another set of circumstances that affects resistance to change is, that despite management's reassurances, a number of key individuals within any given organization will feel threatened by proposed changes. These threats may occur on a number of dimensions: that is, individuals may feel that their jobs will be eliminated or reduced in status as a result of change; they may feel their expertise undermined by suggestions of better ways of doing things; they may feel angry and insecure over the perception that upper management has listened far more attentively to outside consultants' suggestions than their own; similarly, they may feel manipulated by their sense that upper management has given one set of "conservative" directives to those within the organization (e.g., "Play it safe"; "Don't take too many risks"; "We're doing pretty well as is") and another, more challenging and exciting message to outside consultants (e.g., "Let's shake things up, even at the expense of hurt feelings"); they may even feel that the established, albeit informal, social network will be altered in ways that preclude old friendships and cooperative patterns; and they will almost certainly feel that outside consultants do not really understand the ways things work in this particular organization.

All of these dynamics may well lead to the possibility of sabotaging the efforts of consultants or the management change agents. Such actions may not take the form of overt hostility or interference; rather, more commonly, what occurs is apparent cooperation and agreement that is offset by passive-aggressive attempts to ensure that the consultants or management change agents will fail. "Forgetting" to tell a key player what to do; "losing a memo"; becoming "too busy" to attend a meeting; subtly questioning the wisdom of some proposed action to other important personnel; failing to complete key documents in a timely fashion–all these maneuvers may quite effectively bring the change process to an impasse.

Long before recognizing organizational resistance to change, psychologists were aware of how highly resistant individuals are to change. Even in a psychotherapeutic situation where individuals have sought help in modifying their behavior and are often paying a great deal for such help, they tenaciously cling to comfortable, familiar patterns. Indeed, even when these patterns are recognized as nonproductive and perhaps even destructive, individuals generally prefer to continue acting in ways that confirm their long-held sense of the world. Typically, individuals must be confronted time and again with their maladaptive ways of thinking and behaving before they change; often, they must be challenged to take risks. Even so, change is often slow and nonlinear. Moreover, of all the variables that affect the probability of therapeutic change, it is the quality of the therapeutic relationship (as perceived by the patient) that is most salient. That is, the technical skills of the therapist are decidedly less important in effecting change in individuals than is his or her ability to enter into a trusting and safe therapeutic relationship.

All of this has important implications for those attempting to modify long-standing organizational patterns or policy. Most critically, change agents must become deeply aware of the culture of the organization–the formal and informal networks of an organization, as well as its rules, history and traditions.

It is frequently the case that organizational interventions or marketing ideas are technically brilliant but unsuccessful. These interventions fail because the proponents of these ideas have not adequately understood the meaning and implications of change for those involved. Thus, those who come into organizations with recommendations and innovations must speak to key players not only about the technical aspects of their ideas but the psychological implications as well. For example:

- How do you feel about this new idea?
- Do you see any problems in gaining cooperation from important individuals?
- Who else do you think we should speak with?
- Whose toes am I stepping on?
- Is my timeframe realistic or should I give people more time to adapt to these new proposals?
- What about this change will be most difficult for the company to accept?
- Does this strategy fit in with the way the company usually operates?
- Is there something else we should be doing to help people understand or accept these ideas?

Failure to address these issues invariably compromises effectiveness. As Sarason (1982) has observed, "to the extent that the effort at change identifies and meaningfully involves all those who directly or indirectly will be affected by the change, to that extent the effort stands a chance to be successful" (p. 27).* The organizational change leader, like the psychotherapist, may need to be not only creative, smart, and challenging but empathic, self-aware and sensitive as well. These latter qualities create the context for change to be accepted and maintained.

*S. B. Sarason. *The Culture of the School and the Problem of Change,* 2nd ed. (Boston: Allyn and Bacon, 1982).

The Face Behind the Data

What Do Customers Really Want?

"Hello. Is this the person to whom I am speaking?"

Lily Tomlin, as Ernestine

When we talk to a customer or a prospect, what's the message we're sending? Do our communications have value and relevance? How do we know?

A 2 percent response may mean we're making money. But 98 percent of our market trashed our communication.

This message is clear. We must refocus our efforts to communicate greater relevance and deliver greater value. Information is the enabler; it is the tool we need to achieve double-digit response and leverage the lifetime value of a customer.

Customers go through a life cycle with a product or service. They begin as prospects, or "not interested now." As need arises, the prospect decides on a purchase and becomes a customer; as that need changes, the purchase continues to satisfy; or if it no longer satisfies, the customer once again becomes a prospect.

This life cycle can be seen as a relationship with the company that produces the product or service. The relationship can be short or long, and can span one purchase or many. It's a function of the company's commitment to staying current with its customers, to understanding and providing what customers and prospects want and need. It's a two-way street, an interactive communications process. The database is the center, the driver of these communications.

Once upon a time, all the information about a customer relationship was in the sales person's head and on 3" x 5" cards. By knocking on doors, shaking hands, and having lunch, a sales person learned the customer's needs. Customer satisfaction and a long-term relationship were based on how well the sales person knew the customer and what he or she did to help the customer be successful.

Today, few companies can afford a reliance on face-to-face selling. Current realities, such as increased competition and shrinking margins, are forcing companies to place greater emphasis on lower cost, interactive communications.

Customers and prospects may understand the economic realities and the need for change, but they continue to judge us on our ability to listen to their needs and address their concerns.

The foundation of customer-focused communication is the database: it contains the names and addresses of all customers, and possibly much more. The type of information we have on our customers and prospects (for example, transactions and response behavior) and how accurate it is are our tools in building the relationship.

As we build that critical set of information, we should ask how each piece of data can be used to create and nurture the relationship. What can we learn about our customers' needs and issues? How can we use that information to shape the communications process?

To answer these questions, we must adopt a customer-driven view and expand the role of the database. We refer to this enhanced database as the **integrated database,** because it now must contain and integrate the financial or transactional information—the basis of any business relations—with "behavioral" or lifestyle information. What are the needs a customer has that drive the purchase decision? How have the customers behaved in looking for the solutions to their needs?

This body of information is the basis for forming a conversation, and then a relationship. But to be successful, both sides must be listening. The conversation between the company and the customer must be interactive. And each side must learn and respond to changing needs.

A simple case in point concerns a national retail brokerage firm. Its database was built to gather transactional information, because that is the basis of its business. And its marketing efforts, using that database, focused on creating more transactions. Communications were broad and based on the theory that investors are investors and they can't invest unless we give them the opportunity. So virtually everyone was sent every offer, and it worked, to a degree.

However, there came a time when the company was faced with two imperatives:

1. Increase the quality and quantity of response.
2. Increase sales force follow-up of leads and conversion of leads into sales. (The sales force was not following up on leads because of poor quality.)

As part of implementing the IDM methodology, the brokerage firm took a hard look at its database, and took some important actions:

- The financial, transactional database was preserved, and a new entity, the integrated database, was created using the financial information as its foundation.
- The basic information about each account was corrected and standardized. Inspection showed that information central to a relationship, such as your name and address, appeared many different times (sometimes once per transaction) and in many different forms.
- The information was analyzed to indicate the financial vehicles purchased (need), and customers were surveyed to capture their investment strategy, goals, and time frame.
- Demographics, which had not been a priority ("I don't need to know your age, I need to know whether you pay your bills") were built through cross-referencing with outside lists.
- Behavior was added
  - Internally—what communications each customer had responded to, as a clear indication of interest.
  - Externally—how else these customers had behaved in their search to satisfy their investment needs (for instance, subscribing to an investment newsletter specific to the stock market).

This collection of information allowed the company to successfully test communications strategies that were based on customer need. Instead of arbitrarily promoting a stock, bond, or fund, they were able to promote specific benefits and target communications to the group of customers who expressed the need that the benefits addressed.

The company mailed less and phoned less, but to a more interested segment. Results: a higher volume of more qualified response. The sales force, and the company, were delighted.

THE INTEGRATED DATABASE IS THE FOUNDATION OF CUSTOMER-DRIVEN SUCCESS

According to the Direct Marketing Association, the quality of your database contributes about 60 percent to the potential success of your direct response efforts. No news here—it's intuitive.

We as marketers must take this to heart and assume a leadership position regarding the integrated database. Yes, it is certainly a partnership between the Information Systems (IS) department and Marketing, but the data is a strategic marketing tool that Marketing must own.

We must also recognize that the database is in a constant state of change. Industry averages, as reported in the July 1994 issue of *Target Mar-*

keting, state that consumer lists change about 2 percent a month, and business-to-business data goes out of date at approximately 1 percent a week!

Thus, the database will require both initial and ongoing investment and allocation of resources to fulfill it's critical role. Scott Hornstein, Senior Partner, Ernan Roman Direct Marketing (ERDM), offers the following field-tested advice on integrated database building. Starting from scratch, it may be helpful for us to divide the building of an integrated database into two phases: Strategic and Tactical.

STRATEGICALLY SPEAKING:

Who Is our Target Market?

Questions to consider:

- Who can benefit by responding/purchasing this product or service?
  - What is their demographic profile (e.g., age, education, income, annual sales, industry, number of employees, etc.)?
  - What psychographics should be considered (e.g., subscriptions to publications that discuss these types of products and services, membership in certain associations)?
- How can they benefit by responding/purchasing this product or service?
  - State these benefits simply, as decision-drivers such as: enhance basic telephone services, save money, increase competitiveness, improve profitability.
- Who has bought before?
  - Whether it's the actual product/service, a line extension, or a new concept, what can we learn about existing customers in terms of demographics, psychographics, needs, and requirements?
- How big is the potential target market?
  - How many opportunities do we think there are for sales? Are all the customers and prospects on our current database? What potential outside sources will add additional decision makers?
- What is the buying cycle?
  - Are there specific stages to the buying cycle (e.g., needs assessment, investigation, evaluation, negotiation, installation) and which decision makers and influencers are involved at each stage? What are their information requirements at each stage?

Answers to these questions begin to form the foundation of the database file structure, which is the list of definable, sortable information fields in the database. We'll discuss this further under tactics.

What Do We Want the Integrated Database to Do?

Strategically, we want the integrated database to perform two basic functions:

- Help us to identify opportunity
- Drive the communications process to address that opportunity

To help us identify opportunity, let's think of our customers and prospects as falling into four categories:

1. The 10 percent to 20 percent of customers who generate 80 percent to 90 percent of revenue

   This should be our highest potential market segment and deserves the greatest concentration of resources. This group represents the highest customer lifetime value.

2. The 80 percent to 90 percent of customers who generate 10 percent to 20 percent of revenue

   Next in line, this segment holds great potential. It is comprised of customers who buy, but because they have less purchasing power, fewer needs, or are someone else's loyal customer, they represent a smaller revenue base.

   Also, we must prioritize within this group. First, to better understand and service their needs. Then, to cost-efficiently allocate our resources.

3. Qualified prospects: decision makers who have exhibited interest in our company, product, or service

   Decision makers who have responded to our offers, but have not yet become a customer

4. Suspects

   Decision makers who fit the demographic/psychographic profile of a customer but have not yet responded to our offers

Driving the communications process is a two-way street. The integrated database must supply information, as well as absorb and process feedback to enable continuous improvement. Some of the key steps are:

- Reports that seek to identify the commonality of customers who have bought before, which is the simplest form of regression analysis
- Reports that analyze current response to help us understand how customers' needs and requirements are changing
- Generating output necessary to drive direct mail and telemarketing, processing input that will help to continuously improve these media, and facilitating the lead management process

- Direct Mail
  - *Output:* Generation of mailing tapes
  - *Input:* Response, sales, name/address corrections, profiling and qualitative information updates to drive future contacts from BRC, fax, inbound and outbound telemarketing, and field sales
- Telemarketing
  - *Output:* Generation of outbound calling tapes
  - *Input:* Response, sales, name/address corrections, profiling and qualitative information updates to drive future contacts from BRC, fax, inbound and outbound telemarketing, and field sales
- Lead Management
  - *Output:* Lead management forms, update reports analyzing opportunity
  - *Input:* Information on qualified leads (including key profiling data), classification of leads, feedback from the sales force on lead disposition
- Tracking key indicators

  We mentioned an analysis of the commonality of who has bought before. Necessarily, this analysis must revolve around the sortable information on the integrated database. For instance, if your consumer database consisted of basic demographic data, such a report might be able to tell you that previous purchasers were within a certain age range, were head of household, have owned a home for 5+ years, etc. If behavioral information is included, the description might be more finite and include need—such as the desire to screen inbound telephone calls, to collect rare books, to save for a child's education.

  These points of commonality can be viewed as key indicators. We should ask ourselves: If these points of information were common to responders/purchasers, to what extent will their presence indicate or predict future response or purchase?

  Two action items emerge:

  1. The integrated database should contain demographic, psychographic, and behavioral information in sortable fields to enable in-depth segmentation. We'll discuss both Basic Information and Extended Information/Relationship History under tactics.
  2. Key indicators should be tracked to determine if a predictive model can be built. This model, which might be conceived as a point scoring system, can be a powerful tool in increasing the profitability of your direct marketing efforts. The model can be used in allocating resources, either as a planning tool or to determine channel of distribution (e.g., field sales follow-up or third-party distribution). The model can also be used in determining the viability of outside list sources or enhancements.

◆ **What Do Customers Expect of Us?**

Customers, in conversation or through Depth Research studies say one thing: Communicate with us as individuals, relative to our individual needs, and show us the value you bring.

An executive recently put this all in perspective during a depth research interview. The question was, "What advice can you offer (the company) as it communicates its announcements and offers to you. The respondent said:

> Talk to me. I'll tell you who should get what message at our company. Sit down with me for a half an hour every six months to discuss my needs and who in my organization should get what information. The organization changes, the staff changes, the needs change. But if I do this, you must live by my rule: do not bother my people with unwanted solicitations.

It's an offer you can't refuse.

Customers have specific information needs according to their interests and job responsibilities and they see a focused communications stream as a benefit. It's a mandate for you to collect information on needs and to stratify media, message, and offer per those needs.

◆

TACTICALLY SPEAKING: WHERE TO START

In most cases, a database exists within an organization and comes complete with various computer systems and a host of turf issues. It's likely the corporation relies on this database to perform specific functions, aside from any direct marketing. A typical example would be the financial database. The corporation must get billing out, or no money comes in. Thus, change may be difficult, if not impossible, in the near term.

Think about piloting the integrated database outside the organizational structure. Free of preconceived notions and limitations, this database pilot can concentrate on the customer, on building all the elements that your organization needs to be successful. Prove its functionality and its worth and transfer the information to the existing database. The successful pilot then becomes the model for your future internal, integrated database.

What Information Do We Need on the Integrated Database?

The following discussion divides information requirements into two categories: Basic Information and Extended Information/Relationship History. This is the information that should be in sortable fields within your database.

Of course, you can go to market with less information, and certainly there is more information you can compile given time and budgets. However, this basic information will give you an idea of a workable integrated database:

Basic Information.   Exhibit 2-1 constitutes the short list of basic information we should know about all our customers, prospects, and suspects. These are facts that are available from many different sources, and they constitute the basis of a relationship. Given its importance, it is surprising how often the information is taken for granted, and how inaccurate many databases are. Accurate demographic data gives you an edge over your competition.

Exhibit 2-1.   Basic Information for the Integrated Database

Business to Business	Consumer
Category (e.g., customer, prospect, etc.)	Category
Source (e.g., list, multibuyer status—did the name appear on more than one ist source?)	Source
	Name
	Genderization
Name	Address
Genderization (e.g., Mr./Mrs./Ms.)	City, state, zip
Title	Direct telephone number
Company	Marital status
Address	Age
City, state, zip	Number of children
Direct telephone number	Head of household
SIC	Occupation
Characteristics of the company	Education
(e.g., annual sales, number of employees)	Home ownership
Credit rating, as applicable	Credit rating, as applicable

Extended Information/Decision Drivers and Relationship History. What are customers' information requirements and media preferences? What are their product or service requirements? Are they doing business with your competitor? Who makes the decisions and per what timeline? What offers have they responded to in the past?

This data, which covers needs, events, and interactions, allows you to understand the uniqueness or individuality of every customer, prospect, and suspect. This behavioral, lifestyle information is critical to crafting a communications plan that brings messages of value, which enhances and deepens the relationship.

The information to answer these questions and populate these database fields comes from within and outside your own organization. And it is gathered and refreshed over the course of the relationship, with every interaction. Our goal is the actionability of the information, and thus it must be accurate and current. The information is about people and people change.

Business to Business

- Identify decision-making units (d.m.u.s).
  Are purchase decisions about your product or service made at this location? If not, what role does this location play in the decision-making process (e.g., end-user or specifier). This information can help you to select and integrate the message, as well as prioritize media, such as telemarketing and sales channels.
- Understand the role of the d.m.u. within the corporation.
  For example, the d.m.u. may be corporate headquarters or a remote branch office responsible for research and development. This can influence both the media and the content of your message.
- Understand the characteristics of the d.m.u.
  Is it appropriate to list the annual sales or number of employees?
- What is installed and when was it installed? Was it purchased (new or used) or was it leased?
  Was your product or service installed by this d.m.u., and when? Are competitive products and services also installed? Do we know when?

Business-to-Business and Consumer

- Who is involved in the decision-making process and what are their individual information requirements?
  Are decisions made alone, or are others consulted (e.g., a husband may consult his wife before making a large consumer purchase)? If others are consulted, it is helpful to understand their role in the decision-making process (e.g., end-user, financial buyer, technical specifier) and what information they need from you to fulfill their responsibilities.
- What problem or circumstance can be addressed by your product or service?
  Examples for Businesses:
  - Improving international competitiveness
  - Enhancing communications and cooperation with vendors
  - Shortening the time from an idea to profitability.
  Examples for Consumers:
  - Shopping for nonessentials, such as music or clothing, from home for two-career couples
  - Enhancing basic telephone service, such as call waiting, conference calling, or caller ID
  - Saving money on the purchase of financial instruments, such as mutual funds, by buying direct and not paying a broker's commission

- How have customers demonstrated their interest in satisfying this need?

  Have these decision makers subscribed to a publication focusing on this issue? Do they belong to an association? Have they attended a seminar?
- Where are customers in the decision cycle?

  The decision cycle may be viewed as having four stages:
  - Needs assessment
  - Budget allocation/securing funding
  - Market evaluation
  - Negotiation and purchase

  Which step is the customer about to take?
- What is the customer's direct response history?

  Has the customer demonstrated direct marketing responsiveness with other companies? (This information can come from outside lists and enhancements.)

  Has the customer recently responded to any of your offers, such as participation in an event, request for sales follow-up, purchase? When did they respond?

    This data must be viewed along with the offer: If the customers recently attended an event, they may be good candidates for a lead-generation campaign. However, if they recently purchased, they should be suppressed from the lead-generation effort.

  What was the medium of response?
  - 800 number/Inbound
  - Outbound
  - Fax
  - BRC

  What is the customer's media preference?
  - For instance: This decision maker prefers to get information, followed by outbound telemarketing to answer questions and, if appropriate, handle the lead or the order. The best time to reach him or her is between 8:00 am and 8:30 am.
- What is the service record?
    - Are there quality issues of which we should be aware?
- How has customer satisfaction trended?

◆ IDM Depth Research as a Contributor to Database Strategy

The process of IDM depth research was developed to personalize the messages coming from large-scale quantitative surveys and research studies—to hear more clearly what individual decision makers have to say regarding key issues, away from the peer influences and dynamics often associated with techniques such as focus groups.

Central to the depth research process is a highly structured interview guide that engages decision makers in a conversation to elicit their views on specific topics. Development of the interview guide is a cross-functional effort. As part of the methodology, interviews should include current customers, wins, and recent losses. Thus, we look to the sales force to generate the decision-maker names, and to gain their cooperation.

It may be useful to think of IDM depth research as a highly structured telephone "test" of customer response *before* committing time and money to your campaign. It is an important addition to your integrated database, generating directional, qualitative sales and marketing information. For a detailed discussion of depth research and its role in the development of an IDM campaign, see Chapter 4.

IDM depth research can answer a number of key questions about your customers and prospects.

- Who are the decision makers?
- What business issues keep them awake at night?
- What values do they associate with your company? With your competition?
- Which media best reaches them?
- What is their perception of print? direct marketing? telemarketing? PR?
- What influences their buying decision?
- How should mail packages be designed so that they'll be opened (given the flood of mail)?
- What information has real value?
- In short, what do you need to do to get the right message to the right person at the right time?

The questions asked, and the information gathered, are critical input to the file structure of the integrated database—the qualitative information that is important to the decision-making process.

BUILDING AND ENHANCING THE INTEGRATED DATABASE

There are a number of internal and external resources to consider as you build your integrated database.

1. Assess Your Internal Sources

There may be pockets of information in your company that can substantially enrich the knowledge you have about your customers and prospects. For example:

A. Financial Records. One asset may be your company's financial file, or the historical record of all transactions. This will give you a good picture of what a decision maker or a decision-making unit (d.m.u.) has bought and when they bought.

However, it usually requires some clever programming to make the information truly useful to the direct marketing; some demographic information (e.g., decision maker's name and address, SIC, annual sales) on these files is often inaccurate because its maintenance has not been a priority.

Billing has been the priority, so what is usually on the file is the accounting department and the d.m.u.'s address. Also, these files frequently have an entry for each transaction, with slight variances to the name and address at each entry. Your first activity may be to find out which name and address is correct and to standardize all entries. Then "household" the file, or combine all recent transactions with a company or individual to get a picture of their purchase history.

◆ Take a Look at Your Database from a Customer's Perspective

Let's start with the basics: are you treating these people like important decision makers? Check some sample records:

- Are there the familiar forms of names? (For example, have we earned the right to have letters and telemarketing calls addressed to "Bill" instead of "Mr. Clinton"?)
- Are all company names spelled correctly, including punctuation? (How sure are you? Most customers react quickly and negatively to misspellings of company name.)
- Are there abbreviations? (USPS abbreviations for states are acceptable, but everything else should be spelled out.)
- Do all decision makers in one location have the same telephone number? (Direct or "reach" phone numbers will enhance telemarketing productivity, along with "best time to call.")
- When was the record last updated, and how? By merge/purge, rep review, direct marketing survey, or telemarketing scrub?

B. Cross-Reference Internal Data. Check other profit centers within your company that also market to your customers. Take a look at their financial files and/or marketing databases.

Combining selected information about important customers can give you a better picture about what they are purchasing and their pattern of purchasing. This may give you some insight into their decision-making needs and cycle. (What products or services have been purchased, in what sequence and what time of year? Are supplies purchased in a predictable pattern?)

Don't forget the customer service and warranty/maintenance databases. (Who has called for technical assistance or a house call?) These customers may require new information, products or services to meet their expanding needs.

By reviewing and combining data, you'll not only get a better idea of the relationship each customer has with your company, you'll also start to get an idea of what kinds of promotions the other profit centers are doing, and thus the direct marketing "noise" aimed at a particular customer.

One of the key findings from over a dozen ERDM depth research studies is the almost unbelievable avalanche of direct mail that decision makers—business and consumer—report receiving. Business people report that they get as much as 40 to 50 mail packages every day. Even if it's half that, marketers are overwhelming the decision maker. In this volume, communications of benefit are most certainly lost.

Often, that avalanche of mail includes offers from different profit centers within our own corporation. Your customer can get simultaneous, separate messages urging him or her to:

- Upgrade equipment
- Take a maintenance contract
- Register for onsite training
- Buy a new software package

To avoid creating customer dissatisfaction, we must prioritize and reduce these communications. This is discussed in Chapter 5, Contact Management.

Now, with some clever programming and some "eyeballing" of records, you can begin to concentrate on the 20 percent of our customer base that generates 80 percent of the revenue. These are your key customers and are responsible for the long-term financial viability of your organization. They are your loyal customers who have proven their worth over time, so a dollar spent here is more likely to generate a high return than anywhere else.

This is not to say that we ignore everyone else. Rather it's a matter of understanding market needs and responding with the appropriate level of investment.

The top 20 percent of customers represent your current and future profitability. It is worth concentrating more resources on them. And, in turn, they have every right to expect more from you than from your competitors. And while you should never ignore the rest of your market, it makes sense to build alternate avenues of communication and distribution that satisfy them, but at significantly lower cost.

C. Field Sales Call Report Systems.   Another asset may be the call report system your sales force uses. Designed to keep a record of contacts with customers and prospects, it is likely to be the most current and accurate source concerning company information and decision makers. The top

20 percent of customers are usually well tracked, as presumably the sales force would have the most frequent contact with them.

The downside is that the field's system is usually not compatible with your current database resource, and some of the anecdotal information, which indicates need, may be in the "comments" section and thus is not sortable. However, these problems are small and easily overcome given the richness of information.

D. Telemarketing Database Scrub.   Another database strategy is the telemarketing database scrub.

The integrated database is composed of information about people— their names, address, titles, preferences, etc. And as people move and change the information changes, in most cases more quickly than the database can respond.

The most accurate, thorough, and cost-efficient way to stay current is to continuously sample the status of your basic database information by an outbound telemarketing database scrub. However, confine the call to basic information, and do not undertake a scrub to a market more than once a quarter because, in the customer's eyes, this is not a value-added call.

Information the database scrub can gather and verify includes:

- Decision-maker name (and spelling)
- Correct mailing address (and spelling) for the decision maker
- Direct or "reach" telephone number and best time to call
- If a business, the role of the location (e.g., headquarters, branch office) and whether the location is a decision-making unit

E. Data Verification through Customer Contact.   Take the time to double-check all of your information with the decision maker.

Each telemarketing script (inbound and outbound) should include questions to verify elements of the database record: Is this how the decision maker spells his or her name? Is this the correct address? Is this the "ship to" address? Would you still categorize this as the most important issue you are trying to solve?, etc., as appropriate to the promotion. Similar verification "checks" can be included on business reply cards and fax forms, which, at the very least, should ask for name and address corrections.

We can also learn from efforts that do not reach the decision maker.

"Nixie" is the direct mail industry term for undeliverable mail returned to us by the USPS. Something was incorrect or missing in the name, address, apartment or suite number, city, state, and/or zip. The USPS was unable to deliver the mail and returned it.

Check with your local postmaster, but most frequently, the only mail that is returned is First Class, or Second or Third Class when the return of undeliverable mail is requested (under the meter or indicia) with a promise that the sender will pay the cost of that delivery.

Most often, nixies are gathered in a box. First, everyone gets upset—
"How did we get so much undeliverable mail?"—and looks for someone to
blame it on. Later, the box is thrown away.

We take issue with both scenarios and suggest that nixies are an important metric and tool for improvement.

The basic metric of lists and databases is deliverability. And it is a
widely held belief that up to 5 percent nondeliverability of a list or database is acceptable. In fact, most list rental agreements include that clause.

If it's your database, nixies should be looked up and the information
corrected. If it's a rented list, keep track—you'll learn about the quality of
the list first-hand, and maybe qualify for a credit with the list owner/man-
ager. Either way, there is no reason to tolerate money thrown away.

It's no different with telemarketing, except that, when a customer's telephone number doesn't connect or turns up as disconnected or out-of-business, it is usually lost in the shuffle of numbers. You, the marketer, should
take action.

◆ Telemarketing's Role in Relationship Building

IDM Depth Research on media preferences showed that decision makers have a strong bias against one of the most powerful and most often
misused mediums—telemarketing.

Telemarketing is a sharp double-edged sword. Properly integrated
into the media mix, telemarketing is the most powerful medium for
generating response, leads, and sales. But—and it's a serious caution—telemarketing also has the greatest potential for eroding customer satisfaction. Witness the disturbing growth of "do not call"
requests.

Intensive planning before deploying your telemarketing is of prime
importance. Your telemarketing strategy must be market-justified and
provide value to your customers and prospects. Database selection criteria should include need as well as demographic profile. And selection
criteria will help in the stratification of message by decision-maker
requirements.

There must be strong rationale to deploy telemarketing against
customers who have stated they are telemarketing-averse, and who
have a history of not responding to the medium. Given the proper
selection criteria and message, suppressing these names will cut the
waste factor, decreasing expenditure and increasing percent
response—delivering a message of greater value to a smaller, more
focused group.

We put it under the heading of list ecology—making sure your database stays fresh and responsive over time. We'll discuss telemarketing
in more detail in Chapter 4.

◆

2. Assess Your External Sources

Resources you should consider outside your organization include lists and databases rented to enhance your integrated database. These can answer critical questions such as:

> *Coverage:* How do you know you have each decision-making unit in your geographic territory on your database?

> *Demographics:* How large is the company, what is the SIC, what were their annual sales, and how many employees do they have? Who is head of household, what is his or her occupation, and what is the annual household income?

> *Additional decision makers and influencers*

> *Product or service previously purchased:* Is this d.m.u. using my competitor's product or service.

A. Outside Lists and Enhancements.   Outside lists can be very useful in building, refreshing, and enhancing the integrated database. Here are some guidelines as you evaluate outside lists and enhancements.

Source

First, take a look at how this list came into being—the source of the information. What will it add to your database?
Some of the potential sources:

> *Responder lists* tend to be the most actionable, because a prime element of these lists is demonstrated direct response behavior. As we have said, past behavior is a strong predictor of future behavior, and one of our goals is response. And because the individuals on this list have purchased something through mail or phone, the basic demographics tend to be more accurate. A good example of a responder file is a subscription list—but make sure you're discriminating between a paid subscription and a controlled circulation publication. Controlled circulation publications, which are free to qualifying individuals, tend to be less highly regarded by the individuals and thus the demographics are not as consistently accurate.

> *Membership or association lists* involve individuals who have declared a specific interest through membership in an organization or association. However, these lists are often closely and fiercely guarded by the association. Negotiation and reasonableness will usually gain direct mail access; however, outbound telemarketing to this list is usually not an option.

> *Compiled lists* were put together based on commonality and are often the best for gaining coverage. They may be a compilation of all auto-

motive parts dealers from the Yellow Pages or lists of consumers sorted by ethnic origin. Additionally, there are lists that are exhaustively compiled through survey and regular telephone contact by organizations such as Computer Intelligence. These higher-level lists are excellent sources of customer information.

Financially based lists can provide more accurate data on income, annual sales, number of employees, and (most importantly), credit worthiness. Examples include TRW, Equifax, and D&B.

Reference lists are compiled for exactly that, reference. Use them to add extra dimension to your integrated database. One example is the NCOA (National Change of Address) list, which is compiled by the USPS and made available to subscribing service bureaus. The USPS estimates that consumer lists change 11 percent to 12 percent every year. By matching your database against this NCOA file, you will pick up a good percentage of the changes.

Value

Other criteria in assessing the value of a list:

How recently was the information on the list updated? Quarterly updates are desired. Many lists, for an extra charge, will offer you only those new, updated names that are part of the quarterly update.

What "sorts" are available? A sort is defined as additional information that is available for an increased charge. For instance, say you are evaluating a responder list, which is the subscriber list of a prominent direct marketing publication. The base cost is for all subscribers. If you want only presidents, CFOs and vice presidents of marketing in advertising agencies with billings over $5 million a year, each of those pieces of information will come at a premium. Your list will be smaller and more focused, but you'll pay more per thousand (see the discussion of utilization below).

Who's mailing what? Here's where a good list broker can really help. It's unethical for list brokers to reveal exactly who is using what list when and for what offer. However, they can steer you to lists that are used repeatedly by similar organizations with similar goals. The supposition is that organizations do not repeatedly use resources that do not achieve their goals. And since their goals are similar to yours, this constitutes a good recommendation.

Utilization

You can use outside lists in a number of ways:

Rental. Most lists are rented for a one-time usage. The rental fee is based upon the quality of the list, the value of the information to direct marketers, and its historical performance. Fees for a high-performing list may range from $100 to $200 per thousand names, before sorts. Direct mail is defined as one usage. Outbound telemarketing, as allowed by the list owner, is another usage. Thus, if the list rents for $200 a thousand (sometimes expressed as "per M") and you are negotiating for both mail and telemarketing rights, your base rental fee would be $400 per M. There is usually a 5,000 name minimum for a test.

The list owner or manager will also ask to see a sample of your mail piece, or telemarketing script as appropriate, before agreeing to the rental. And, you may request "protection" for a set time period around your mail date, usually two weeks to a month. This agreement with the list owner or manager states that they will not allow competitors who are renting their list to mail (or phone) within that protection period.

It is important to recognize that after you mail or phone a rented list, the responders become yours and are no longer governed by any rental agreements.

There are three situations that may affect or change the basic rental agreement. Each is beneficial to you, but is subject to negotiation:

- *Enhancement or new names only.* Your objective is to access and use some, not all, of the information on the list. For instance, you may wish to use the file to add or enhance important demographic information to your database. Or, you might be using a rented list to increase your coverage. You only want to rent the names that are not currently on your database.
- *Unlimited Usage.* Instead of renting for one-time usage, your objective is to secure unlimited rights for a set time period. For instance, your objective is to negotiate a deal that allows you to mail and/or phone the list as many times as you wish for, say, a six-month period.
- *Exchange.* Many list owners are themselves in the direct response business—for instance, publications that generate subscriptions through direct marketing. They have put their list, or portions of their list, on the rental market to establish a passive income stream. However, because their primary income stream is through direct marketing, they may be just as interested in your database as a source of names as you are in testing or using their list. If both sides are noncompetitive and see mutual benefit, a deal can usually be arranged.

Processing

The process for the incorporation of outside lists into your database is called "merge/purge." It's a batch process in which elements of each list are matched and information is selected for inclusion according to your specific instructions. Some benefits of merge/purge:

Deduplication: This process will identify duplication within your own file, as well as identify duplication between files. But, you have to tell the computer what to do once it finds the duplication. Internal duplication should be removed. Inter-file duplication gives you the opportunity to select which information from what list goes into the database.

Inclusion of information per a predetermined hierarchy: Which list has the best information? Here's a case in point: We just stated that the merge/purge will identify duplicate names. Let's say your objective is to enhance your database with additional information on decision makers. The merge/purge finds that Jane Sample is on your database and the outside list. The database record has ten information fields.

You have a choice as to which information goes on the final database. You can instruct the computer to accept your database for name and address, age, and number of children, but to use the outside list for education, home ownership, income, etc.

Identification of multibuyers: Let's say that your merge/purge consists of your database and three carefully selected lists. In theory, decision makers who appear on all four files should be your best candidates for response/sale. It's an indicator that should be tracked over time.

B. Modeling and "Cluster" Systems.   In an effort to develop new, more effective tools for targeting consumer communications, allocating resources, and approaching predictive modeling, some companies have developed "cluster" systems which are offered to direct marketers under names such as Prizm, Cluster Plus, NDL/Lifestyle Selector, and many others.

These systems are based in geographic behavioral patterns—founded on the theory that people who live near each other have similar characteristics and will behave similarly. There is great truth to this theory. Plus, these systems often allow you to work with areas that are significantly smaller than a zip code. These companies have done a great amount of research analyzing demographics, psychographics, and sometimes response patterns to determine these geographic "pockets" or clusters of similar decision makers.

The benefit to the marketer, in a quick overview, is an enhanced ability to:

- Segment the database according to marketing potential
- Develop marketing and communications plans by segment
- Allocate resources by segment and marketing potential

Two words of caution:

- *Do your homework.* Make sure your database is in excellent shape. Do your own studies to find out who is buying and why they are buying. Develop and test your own theories first, perhaps even progressing to your own predictive or scoring model. Cluster systems developed by outside corporations are a tool and not an answer. They were developed to service many corporations; thus their methodology must include generalizations that may or may not apply to you. Plus, they are only as good as the data you have. Cluster systems used in concert with your own good database thinking, testing, and developing is the best of all worlds.
- *Realize there are limitations as well as benefits.* These cluster systems traditionally work best with large databases, in the millions of names. If your database is smaller, the cluster system may not produce the return on investment you were seeking. And, the way some of the cluster systems work is that they first go in and code your database. Thus, outside lists must be "precoded" by the same cluster system to mesh with your database and give you full value.

A STEP-BY-STEP PROCESS FOR BUILDING AN INTEGRATED DATABASE

Here's where you start and how you proceed:

- Based on depth research results, response, and analyses of purchase patterns, segment your market place according to customer need.
- Determine the information fields you need to target these customers, prospects, and suspects and drive the communications process.
- Identify in-house data and information resources and assess their strengths and weaknesses.
- As appropriate, use the financial database as your foundation (but be careful to "clean-up" the data, e.g., one record per customer with standardized name, address).
- Determine what additional information cross-referencing to other in-house data sources will provide (for instance, the services database, which will have records of customer service calls, may have information concerning customer changes or moves, which may indicate changing needs).

- Now look outside, to determine what sources will enhance the data on the customers/prospects/suspects you have now, and which will provide new prospects and suspects. Assess the strengths and weaknesses of each.
- Establish your data hierarchy for the merge/purge, according to the strengths and weaknesses of each list source. This hierarchy may look like this:

Priority	List
1	In-house financial file for name, address, phone number, and purchase history
2	In-house services file for changes to current installation or to customer needs
3	Outside financial file for income, home ownership, and age
4	Outside subscription list for interest
5	Outside association list for membership

- Conduct a telemarketing database scrub to bring data up to the highest degree of accuracy.
- Before any promotion, have the field review the relevant database segments. They have the most current customer information. And, they must have confidence in the database to have confidence in the promotion.
- Add data verification portions to each telemarketing script and reply device.

◆ The Integrated Database Improves Communication Efficiency at Hewlett-Packard

As an illustration of how one company uses a relationship-oriented database, we have included a case study from Hewlett-Packard. Hewlett-Packard, a world leader in computers and electronic test equipment, saw the potential of IDM to improve both the quantity and quality of leads early on. HP has been using IDM to:

- Create executive preference for HP by establishing multiple value-based contacts at the highest executive levels rather than the usual MIS contact.
- Enhance relationships with the traditional MIS contacts and reinforce HP's image as a value-added supplier of computer hardware and software systems.
- Capture new information to update the HP database, such as current decision-maker names and titles, key business issues, brand

and model currently installed, timing and budget for planned systems upgrades and changes.

To achieve the first objective, HP focused on CEOs, CFOs, vice presidents of finance, and MIS within a target industry. Given marketplace
factors, a nontraditional strategy and offer were essential for breaking
through to these hard-to-reach, senior-level decision makers. A series of
strategic, executive audio teleconferences was chosen. The teleconferences addressed timely, critical business issues, as determined through
depth research, faced by these key executives. The convenient audio
teleconference required no travel by the executives and encouraged
participation by several executives at the same location.

Based on previous ERDM programs for HP, media were precision-
timed to deliver a synchronized message to heighten impact. Ongoing
awareness and interest were sustained through continued communications by phone and mail (see Exhibit 2-2).

The results not only met all objectives but exceeded expectations:

- Registration rate was 163 percent of forecast.
- Qualified leads were 222 percent of forecast, with more than
  12.5 percent of the mailed universe registering for the conference.
- In addition, 82 percent of confirmed registrants participated,
  with an average of 3.5 executives attending from each partici-
  pating company.

Perhaps most important, the HP sales force rated the responses as
high-quality leads of senior-level executives who had previously eluded
them. Because of the involvement of the sales force in all phases of the
development and implementation, leads that were generated met realistic qualifying criteria and were actively followed up.

A key element of the program was reaching the right people in
the targeted businesses. This required list management beyond the
usual "merge and purge." A telemarketing scrub assured accuracy of the
information and obtained critical profiling information that became
part of the IDM database.

"In fact, the HP database is now an ongoing objective," says Judie
Neiger, HP Marketing Specialist. "It has gone far beyond simply com-
piling the names of key executives in our target markets. The database
is now an increasingly sophisticated tool that identifies functional
responsibilities, competitive installations, and critical success factors as
well as response history.

"Now, before we even start our campaign, we invest time and
energy to bring our database up to date. We incorporate outside databases and conduct a telemarketing scrub to get specific names and

titles and make sure that the company has an application that can use the solution we're promoting. The temptation in the past was just: Let's get out a mailer and tell people about our new product. That's not a smart use of our resources."

To those who see IDM as an expensive effort, Neiger comments, "I can show a real cost/benefit advantage of an integrated approach versus separate phone, separate mail, or just a seminar. Through the use of IDM, we have reduced the average mailing from the 60,000 to 70,000 range down to 10,000, while garnering higher response and higher revenues. I have really embraced the concept of an Integrated Direct Marketing approach."

IDM: A Market-Proven Process

In HP and the other companies mentioned later in this book, IDM has proven itself beyond our most optimistic projections. In large and small companies, the discipline and precision of IDM have achieved double-digit results that go far beyond the traditional 2 percent.

The next decade will see dramatic changes in many areas: more electronic media in customer's homes and in businesses, and more business conducted through computers, telephones and cable as the "communications' highway" gains ground. Exciting as all this is, we must never forget that the technology is simply the facilitator; it cannot form the relationship that business must establish with the customers. These relationships are the result of managing the entire customer life cycle, not just a series of quick-hit sales calls.

The ability to link customer needs with sales, marketing, and business objectives is the power of Integrated Direct Marketing. The idea is simple and logical, the process is disciplined, and the results are proven. IDM is an important strategy for any business making the structural and philosophical changes needed to grow and thrive in the new marketing world.

> You can't be all things to all people . . . but you can be all things to the people you select.
>
> Donald Neuenschwander
> Chairman,
> Medical Center Bank of Houston

In summary, let's review the roles and responsibilities of our key database constituents: Marketing, Information Systems, and Field Sales. It is the successful partnering among these three that will enable a fully-functional, evolving, integrated database.

7- Step IDM Lead Generation Process

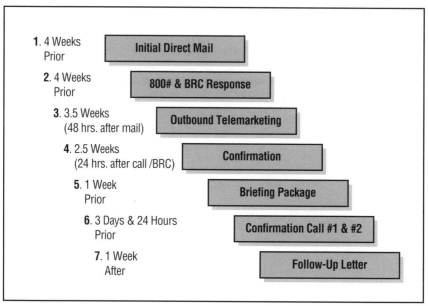

1. 4 Weeks Prior — **Initial Direct Mail**
2. 4 Weeks Prior — **800# & BRC Response**
3. 3.5 Weeks (48 hrs. after mail) — **Outbound Telemarketing**
4. 2.5 Weeks (24 hrs. after call /BRC) — **Confirmation**
5. 1 Week Prior — **Briefing Package**
6. 3 Days & 24 Hours Prior — **Confirmation Call #1 & #2**
7. 1 Week After — **Follow-Up Letter**

Exhibit 2-2. Hewlett-Packard followed the 7-step IDM lead-generation process to stimulate executive participation at a technology workshop and set the stage for ongoing communication.

MARKETING'S ROLE

Marketing must take ownership of the data and provide database leadership. Often, departments view the data as a hot potato, tossing the responsibility around. Absolutely no one wants it, it falls outside of existing organizational lines. Marketing does not have the requisite systems knowhow; Information Systems does not have the marketing expertise; and if it's customer information, it must belong to Sales.

The result of this data aversion is that the corporation suffers. Direct marketing efforts do not perform to expectation, and everyone wonders why—and looks around to place fault. The database becomes the whipping post.

What's needed is leadership.

The data is a marketing tool and should be owned by Marketing. Marketing has, or must have, the direct marketing subject matter knowledge. But without cross-functional cooperation to a common goal, the database is unlikely to get the nurturing it needs to become robust; the database cannot grow and prosper with Marketing's input alone. It must have the contribution of: IS, with its hands-on knowledge of computers and software;

Sales, with its field experience; Telemarketing, for instant market updates, and so forth.

In the best of all worlds, Marketing will assign a Database Manager or strategist—a direct marketing specialist with expertise in your industry and experience in database strategy and implementation.

THE ROLE OF INFORMATION SYSTEMS (IS)

IS must take ownership of the systems and provide leadership. They have the computer know-how, and we need them to hold up their end of the bargain.

The database accepts and provides information through systems. It accepts input from other internal and external database sources, as well as from customer contacts. It generates output in the form of mailing and calling tapes, reports, and analyses.

What do we want these systems to do? Here's a systems checklist:

- Generate mail tapes, to specification, to timeline
- Generate telemarketing call lists, to specification, to timeline
- Incorporate new information, as generated by customer contact
- Incorporate new information from outside sources
- Provide us with formatted or ad-hoc reports to provide us with market intelligence
- Facilitate the lead management system by providing the field with easy access

These action items seem logical and intuitive. However, many direct marketing programs have gone off the track because of their not being accomplished.

There are a number of reasons for this. Understandably, these requirements may be new additions to your company's already taxed IS department. The focus of IS may be elsewhere, and so these action items may receive low priority. IS may not have the direct marketing subject matter knowledge or experience.

It is critical that Marketing review the system requirements with IS as soon as possible, to identify dependencies and establish the necessary procedures. Once we're past these hurdles, IS can take the leadership role by contributing to the development of regression analyses and the predictive or scoring model just discussed.

The Outsourcing Alternative

There is another option—outsourcing—which for some corporations may be a good deal. Given the structure of the corporation, you may get more service for fewer dollars by going to a service bureau. The service bureau already has the subject matter knowledge and can perform both database maintenance and traditional service bureau tasks (such as merge/purge). But the question of priority remains: Are you a small fish in a big pond?

And the question of leadership remains. Who will make sure your output is to specification and on time? Who will partner with you to get you to the analyses and modeling?

THE ROLE OF FIELD SALES

The field shares responsibility for updating the database. Marketing takes the lead, but the field must contribute.

It is critical that Field Sales review the database periodically, at least once a quarter as part of the database update process, and certainly before any big campaign, for two reasons:

1. The field is calling on our most important customers every day. They have access to timely information that would not be available anywhere else (for example, shifts in corporate focus, new responsibilities for branch offices or executives), which will generate additions and deletions to the data.
2. Field Sales must have confidence in the database we use, or they will not have confidence in the results.

THE INTEGRATED DATABASE: FOCUSED ON THE CUSTOMER

The integrated database is the single greatest lever for success. It must drive the communications process, lengthening and enriching the customer relationship.

J. Walter Thompson Direct bases its integrated strategies on a sophisticated, continually evolving database. According to Mitchell A. Orfuss, president of JWT Direct,

> Integrated communications puts the database in the middle of the customer/company relationship. Before the sale, the job is to collect the data; after the sale, the job is to drive the data. Feedback is used to refine the message and to build closer relationships over time. Integration is not an afterthought. Integrated marketing efforts create the one-on-one dialog that reinforces and rewards behavior, which tends to improve lifetime value.

This chapter has given hints, processes, and insights into constructing and testing an integrated database. But what do we do after the testing and construction period?

The answer is to continue to build, continue to test, continue to enhance. We must devote continual energy and resources to database development. There is only one sure thing, the marketplace is continually changing and moving.

And if we rest on our laurels, we are most certainly sitting still.

KEY POINTS

- Per the Direct Marketing Association, the quality of your database contributes about 60 percent to the potential success of direct marketing efforts.
- The integrated database contains and integrates the financial or transactional information, with "behavioral" or lifestyle information.
- The integrated database drives the communication process, which is instrumental in forming a lasting relationship in which both parties learn and respond to changing needs:
  - Marketing must own the data and provide database leadership.
  - Information Systems must own the systems.
  - Field Sales shares responsibility for data update.
- There are strategic and tactical components to building the integrated database:
  - Strategic questions:
    - Who is our target market?
    - What do we want the integrated database to do?
  - Tactical moves:
    - Determine the basic information that should be in defined, sortable fields. Much of this basic information is demographic.
    - Determine what extended information should be collected in defined, sortable fields (this information is based in psychographics and behavior) to help us determine the customer or prospect needs and requirements.
      - IDM Depth Research can help define the psychographic and behavioral elements that contribute to response, and should thus be tracked on the integrated database.
- The steps to building and enhancing the integrated database:
  1. Assess your internal resources
     A. Financial records are usually the best place to start.
     B. Cross-reference internal data to get a better picture of the relationship customers have with your company.
     C. Field sales call report systems can contribute up-to-the-minute information on selected companies and decision makers.
     D. A telemarketing database scrub keeps the overall database current.
     E. Use each point of customer contact to verify and update database information.

2. Use lists and databases external to the corporation to provide further depth to the database:

   A. Assess outside lists and enhancements carefully, by category, method of compilation, recency of information, and utility. View the merge/purge, or electronic compilation of information, as your opportunity to pick and choose what's best about each list and include that in the database.

   B. Modeling and "cluster" systems may be of assistance, but only after you've done your homework in making sure your database is in excellent shape and in knowing who buys and why.

The Marketing Blend:

Precision Deployment of Media for Double-Digit Response

Direct marketing must intercept the consumer as close as possible to the point and moment of sale and affect the outcome not just once, but over and over again.

Lester Wunderman
Speech at 1993 Direct Marketing Association Conference

The process for integrating and deploying media is, in its final analysis, customer-driven. Depth research, testing and analysis continually bring us closer to understanding the needs and requirements of our customer and prospect base. This evolving understanding is the basis for budget allocation and media deployment.

If we have done our job well, we are rewarded first with sale, and then with our goal: a relationship that continues beyond the sale.

To illustrate how IDM can help you build relationships, let's review an actual case history of media integration, which was a head to head A/B test of the IDM process, versus the traditional media and budget strategies used in many companies. This case should provide you with a quantitative illustration of the benefits of reallocating existing budget and redeploying media to achieve:

- Increased quality and quantity of response
- Decreased cost of lead and cost of sale

- Increased revenue
- Decreased expense to revenue

This case history focuses on the introduction of a telecommunications product by a major U.S. manufacturer. The "A" test is the traditional media plan deployed by this corporation. The "B" test was the media plan per the IDM methodology. The results of IDM, in direct comparison to "traditional" media deployment, will show you the efficiency and yield of IDM, given the same market with the same budget.

MARKETING OVERVIEW

Following are the parameters for the A/B test:

- Target market: 25,000 small- to medium-sized businesses nationwide
- Marketing budget (total = $500,000):
  - $250,000 for Test A (Traditional)
  - $250,000 for Test B (IDM)
- Average sale: $10,000
- Program objective: Generate highly qualified leads for the sales force.

PLANNING AND EXECUTION

Test A: Traditional

In planning this major product introduction, the company focused on deploying media to create awareness, a big "splash," to:

- Clearly differentiate their company, and this product, due to its innovative technology
- Create heightened interest in the marketplace for this new product, and the company's other products
- Create a rallying point for the company, especially the sales force (large expenditures in highly visible media would generate enthusiasm within the sales force)

Seventy percent of the marketing budget was allocated to broadcast, Free Standing Inserts (F.S.I.s) in national publications and selected local radio, with the majority devoted to producing and placing commercials for a nationally televised sporting event.

The balance of the budget, 30 percent, was allocated to direct mail. Plans were for an initial postcard mailing as a preannouncement, followed in two weeks by the direct mail package. Both would be mailed via U.S. Postal Service, First Class.

Inbound telemarketing (a toll-free 800 number), as a powerful response medium, was included in the budgets for advertising (TV, print, and radio) and direct mail (postcard and mail). Additional response media included a return card attached to the Free Standing Insert, and a return card and fax options for the direct mail.

Outbound telemarketing was not budgeted at this stage for the following reasons:

- The focus of this campaign was primarily on the national TV exposure, the costs of commercial production, and spot placement.
- The company had a strong history of response from advertising (TV, print, and radio) and direct mail. Executives did not want to "cannibalize" the expected return from these media.

Test B: IDM

IDM media and budget expenditures were concentrated on the target audience of business decision makers as well as the objective of generating highly qualified sales leads for this product introduction.

Broadcast, radio, and national publications were not included in the media mix. These media would hit the target market, but this market would be only a small percentage of their total "reach" or circulation; hence, they would be too inefficient. Therefore, only 10 percent of the IDM budget was devoted to advertising—carefully selected, vertical industry publications to create awareness in support of direct mail and telemarketing, and to generate some response.

IDM testing has shown that business-to-business direct response advertising will typically generate about 10 percent of the overall response. However, response from advertising is somewhat "softer" or less qualified than response from direct mail or telemarketing. Because advertising has less room or "real estate" to contain benefits and facts, decision makers are responding to less information.

Highly personalized direct mail began approximately one week after the first advertisements appeared.

Experience and testing have shown that the workhorse team of direct mail and outbound telemarketing, with message and timing carefully integrated, can generate 80 to 90 percent of all qualified responses in an IDM program. Thus, 90 percent of budget was allocated to mail and phone, of which 65 percent of this allocation was devoted to telemarketing, to ensure the ability to reach decision makers. For greater impact of mail and phone, outbound telemarketing was timed within 24 to 72 hours after prospects received their mail package. (This Response Compression strategy is discussed in greater detail later in this chapter.)

The goal of the IDM test was not gross response; rather, it was the generation of highly qualified leads for sales force follow-up. So, to ensure tenacious follow-up we asked the field sales representatives to detail the information they required to consider the response a lead. They said that a respondent must:

- Be a decision maker
- Be actively looking for this type of product to solve a current business issue
- Have a sufficient budget allocated
- Be ready to make a purchase decision within a predetermined time
- Agree to a timed appointment with a sales representative

These criteria were included in the inbound and outbound telemarketing scripts. The only leads that went to the field met the above criteria.

As our goal was the quality and quantity of leads, our measurement focused on the total response. Though the contribution of individual media is measured and leveraged, IDM's goal is clearly the combined response from all media. The notion of "cannibalization" is not applicable.

The following charts and discussions illustrate the media mix and budget allocations, media performance, and conversion to sales for Test A and Test B:

MEDIA MIX AND BUDGET ALLOCATION

	Test A: Traditional Budget Allocation		Test B: IDM Budget Allocation	
	%	$	%	$
Advertising	70%	$175,000	10%	$25,000
Direct mail	30%	$75,000	25%	$62,500
Telemarketing	—	—	65%	$162,500

MEDIA PERFORMANCE

Test A: Traditional

	Results by Media		
	% Budget	# Leads	% Leads
Advertising	70%	438	35%
Direct Mail	30%	812	65%
Leads		1250	
Cost per lead		$200	

Advertising generated 35% of all leads. To understand the cost-efficiency of the advertising media deployed (gross response versus qualified response), following is an analysis of 800-number "misdirects."

Inbound telemarketing was the primary response vehicle for TV, radio and print. Misdirects are inbound calls that do not relate to the promotion, such as billing problems, and idle chatter (e.g. "Where are you? How's the weather there?"). They are calls that we certainly pay for, but have no productive outcome.

Analysis of Inbound Misdirects by Media

Media	% Inbound Misdirect
Television	42%
Radio	—
Print	15%
Direct mail	10%

Seventy percent of the budget was devoted to this advertising media mix. Fifty-seven percent of all response generated by these expensive media was unusable.

Direct mail generated 65 percent of all leads. However, the initial plan of a postcard to preannounce the direct mail was changed. IDM analysis of a "direct mail only" market test showed that the postcard as a "pre-announcement" actually depressed lead generation. The postcard generated a great deal of response, but because these executives were responding to very little information (not much more than the name of the product and an 800 number), the response was largely unqualified. Direct mail, following the postcard, generated a much lower level of response than anticipated (executives in the "buy cycle" had responded to the postcard). Thus, the direct mail was deployed first in the nationwide test, with the postcard deployed after the mail, as a reminder. *The cost of a lead was $200.00.*

There is no direct measurement to determine whether or not this large expenditure satisfied the incremental goals of clearly differentiating the company and its product line and generating increased overall sales due to sales force enthusiasm.

Test B: IDM

Results by Media

	% Budget	# Leads	% Leads
Advertising	10%	375	10%
Direct Mail	25%	750	20%
Telemarketing	65%	2625	70%
Leads		3750	
Cost per lead		$66.67	

The IDM test was focused on the primary goal of generating a quantity of highly qualified leads for the sales force. By design, response was driven to the highly interactive telemarketing channel to enhance lead quality.

Direct mail was deployed approximately one week after the first ads appeared in targeted, vertical trade publications. Outbound telemarketing, per Response Compression, was timed 24 to 72 hours after mail receipt. Decision makers were presented with a great deal of qualifying information prior to response. And, with 70 percent of response generated by outbound, decision makers had an interactive conversation, with the opportunity to ask questions and challenge benefits prior to response.

Thus, the results of media deployment are more in line with budget expenditures. IDM generated a 300 percent improvement in qualified leads and a 300% reduction in cost per lead.

CONVERSION TO SALES

Test A: Traditional

Test A generated 1250 leads at a cost per lead of $200. These leads were sent to the sales force for follow-up. Thirty-two percent of those leads, or 400, were actually followed up.

Test A: Traditional

Leads	1250
Sales force	
Follow-up	400 (32%)
Conversion	40 (10%)
Marketing cost per sale	$6,250

Our research with field organizations, from Ford to IBM, consistently shows that only 30 to 34 percent of all leads generated by direct marketing are actually followed up by the sales force. Reasons include the following:

1. What is sales' previous experience with leads generated by direct marketing? Usually, sales is the outsider. Few organizations recognize and treat the sales force as a customer. One reason is different measurement systems. Marketing is measured by the quantity of leads produced. Once that's done, their job is done. The field is measured by sales. In many cases, sales does not feel that their interests are being satisfied, since marketing has different goals.

2. Does the sales force feel a sense of "ownership" and "buy-in" to the campaign? Organizational silos and divergent measurement work against sales being a part of the process from planning through execution.

3. What happened with the first leads from this campaign? In this instance, the first leads came from advertising—television specifically. The spots on nationally televised sporting events ran far ahead of all other media. And because these decision makers who responded did not have much information to base their response on, most of the response was "information only."

Given that these leads were of lower quality, sales force follow-up suffered. Ten percent of the leads converted, yielding 40 sales. Marketing cost of sale was $6,250—over half the sales price of the product ($10,000).

So, on an initial marketing expenditure of $250,000, traditional media and budget deployment generated $400,000 in sales, for a 62.5 percent expense-to-revenue ratio. We still have to figure in the cost of sales, product cost, etc. to determine true profitability.

Test B: IDM

IDM generated three times as many qualified leads, 3750, at one third the cost per lead, or $66.67. These leads were sent to the sales force for follow-up. But of these IDM leads, 60 percent, or 2250, were followed up, and because of the higher quality, 25 percent, or 563, converted to a sale.

	Test B: IDM
Leads	3750
Sales force	
Follow-up	2250 (60%)
Conversion	563 (25%)
Marketing cost per sale	$444.05

With the IDM process, the sales force is totally integrated into the marketing activity, contributing to strategy, offers, and the criteria for defining a tightly qualified lead.

Each lead that was sent to the field met their own stringent criteria for "qualified lead." Thus, there was a high degree of ownership and buy-in from the field. And because these screening questions were part of inbound as well as outbound scripts, even the early leads that resulted from print ads were qualified.

An important recommendation for you: All copy (from the ads to the telemarketing script) must emphasize the high quality and consultative nature of the sales force. Responders who say "yes" to a sales call must be serious, and attach real benefit to meeting with the sales representative.

The IDM process of field sales force integration, and the precision deployment of media, yielded a 300 percent increase in the number of qualified leads, and almost doubled the follow-up rate. Leads met field requirements. Thus, conversion increased by 250 percent. The bottom line was a 1300 percent improvement in sales, versus the traditional program.

The results speak for themselves: 563 sales were closed yielding $5,630,000 in initial revenue. Expense-to-revenue was 4.4 percent.

INTERNALIZING THE IDM PROCESS THROUGH ORGANIZATIONAL INTEGRATION

Organizational integration, and the alignment of goals and objectives across the organization, is substantially more difficult to achieve than strong results from a pilot or test. However, this integration is critical as an organization seeks to internalize the IDM process, to make it business as usual.

Often, seemingly insurmountable organizational barriers exist between Publicity, Advertising, Direct Mail, Telemarketing, Marketing, Sales Promotion and Field Sales functions. Their responsibilities and growth are insular and vertical, creating silo-like focus that works against a truly integrated strategy in which media and message are consistently focused on the customer, on providing value, and on managing and enhancing customer lifetime value.

The barriers are often as much mental as organizational, with deep roots in corporate culture:

- Advertising thinks "image" and entertainment, which encompass TV and glossy publications.
- Direct marketing managers think letters and lists.
- Telemarketing, all too frequently, is outside the culture, and viewed as a manufacturing environment.
- And sales, of course, thinks face-to-face to win and keep "their customers."

This is a snapshot of corporate culture, and the current business as usual. Each function goes off in its own direction, and the power of the marketing is dissipated rather than strengthened.

Each medium, channel, and department has individual goals and measurements, which compete. Image has devised its own standard of measurement. Marketing activities are judged by the gross volume of response and leads; sales is measured by revenue and commissions. The customer measures you in terms of value, responsiveness, and commitment over time.

We will never realize the true potential of direct marketing until all measurement systems are aligned, and until those measurement systems are customer-driven.

REENGINEERING MARKETING AND SALES AT IBM

IBM, in reengineering its sales and marketing strategies, has taken this to heart and has structured a more customer-focused organization and marketing approach, seeking organizational, sales channel, as well as media and message integration.

Mike Lawrie, IBM US Vice President and Area General Manager, provides an inside look at some of the goals, strategies, and pitfalls that arise when a corporate giant makes such a major course correction:

> One of the greatest impediments we face is the notion of ownership. The direct sales force believes that they own the customer. However, we all have to recognize that those days are gone—no single part of IBM "owns" the customer. IBM has a relationship with the customer that takes on many different aspects. We must utilize our different distribution capabilities based on the needs of the different buyers that exist in the account. We will be making telesales calls to the "Glass House" very soon.

I look at distribution in two ways:

First, we must develop competitive direct access to the marketplace through client teams, product specialists and services people. They are more and more geared to providing "solutions" and higher "value-add" business because of their expertise. This channel is also very costly, and the value must be there for both IBM and the customer.

The other mode will be IBM's lower-cost, highly efficient, internal integrated marketing organization. They can retain current customers with a high level of service which is far more cost effective, and can also acquire new customers through lead generation and campaign management.

A key issue is getting everyone focused on the true profitability of the transaction. Part of it is, of course, measurement systems. As long as you pay people just on revenue, there is no incentive to use alternate forms of distribution. Once you begin to pay people on profitability, there's a big incentive to take a look at alternate channels. That's more important than organizational issues. Change how you pay them and the heart follows. In our area, every person is paid on profitability.

INTEGRATING MEDIA FOR PROFITABILITY

Remember that each medium has a unique role. For example: Television can appeal to emotions on a broad, general level. Radio, on the other hand, can localize the message, complementing television and bringing the message closer to home. Print advertising puts a compelling spin to the message and provides more information on a less emotional level than either television or radio. Mail personalizes the message, describes it in detail, and provides a compelling call to action. Telemarketing reinforces the other media and adds an interactive dimension of its own.

Following are some insights about media from Scott Hornstein, Senior Partner, ERDM, based on experience implementing IDM programs at a wide range of businesses.

Publicity/Public Relations

Publicity and public relations is, in its simplest form, information about your product, service, or company that is communicated via electronic and print news media. It's difficult to incorporate into your media mix because:

- Lead times are extremely long, usually about three months prior to actual publication.
- There is no guarantee that your story idea will appear in the media, or that it will bear any resemblance to your idea.

However, there is no stronger form of awareness. If your idea does appear in the media, it is generally accepted as true, and there is the implied endorsement of editorial. Publicity is a very powerful persuader, and absolutely translates into response.

◆ An Example from ERDM's Experience

According to Hornstein, the following is a very important case study illustrating the power of publicity as a direct response medium. As consultants to a start-up catalog company, we knew that to succeed, print ads and direct response lists had to work. The decision makers who read those publications and were on those lists had to have confidence in this new catalog and view it as an important, reliable supplier of quality merchandise. And for the catalog to do more than succeed, it had to be seen as different and unique, as providing a "value-add."

Through IDM depth research, decision makers told us that what was missing in the field, and what they really needed, was an expert—someone, some person or organization, with experience and insight, who was willing to share that expertise to help select among seemingly undifferentiated products.

Publicity presented a strong addition to our media mix and could provide that "expert" voice.

We researched and wrote a series of releases, each based on a different newsworthy story. The stories were not about our client's catalog, but about problems our common target market was facing. Each release started with a question asked by decision makers during Depth Research (e.g., What is the difference between product A and B? When should I use product C ? When shouldn't I use it?). The question was then answered by the founder of the catalog, our resident expert, in simple, clear, declarative terms.

Each release carried information on the company's breadth and depth of experience, and ended with a free offer: Call our toll-free Information Hotline and we'll provide free, expert advice.

We divided up the list of writers and editors at key publications and mailed the first release. Each editor and each writer then received a follow-up call from one of our senior executives, working from a tightly written script, within 24 to 72 hours of mail receipt, to explain and enhance the story idea. Our goal was to build personal relationships. We mailed one release a week and followed up each by telephone.

Articles began to appear about two months after the initial release, and continued for six months. Every time we placed a story, we capitalized on our success: we advertised in that publication and mailed to its list (in many instances, their decision to place the editorial and our decision to place the advertising were mutually dependent).

Print ad and catalog copy carried the same theme, with an entire page of the catalog devoted to "value-add" definitions, background material, guidelines and advice. Every time the 800 number appeared, so did the phrase, "For free, expert advice . . . ."

The legitimacy and implied endorsement of the company name and offer appearing in news media gave response a tremendous lift. And in the final measurement, response traced back to publicity generated the highest average orders, and the greatest overall dollar sales.

Broadcast

Be careful of broadcast media. They're exciting and glamorous and they entertain. But often, your target market is only a small percentage of the viewers.

Home shopping networks and infomercials have grown at an astonishing rate. In this capacity, television has incredible reach. However, it is still very difficult to hone in on a specific market.

Two caveats:

1. Look at their estimates of viewing audience. Now look at your target market. How many viewers, in real numbers and percent, are not decision makers for you? Aptly, this concept is called "spill."

2. Can you impart enough information through broadcast to produce a qualified lead? A sale?

If you're using television for advertising or as a direct sales channel, be sure to leverage your television presence in your other media. Mailings should contain the same visual or copy theme. Telemarketing can ask if customers are familiar with the TV ads. This type of cross-referencing builds awareness across all media and helps you get the most for your money.

◆ Media Integration: An Example

One of the most successful integrations of media and message was the "gold box" television campaign created for the Columbia Record and Tape Club. Here, the celebrity emcee, Dick Clark, explained the benefits of joining the Club, and then told viewers about a gold box. "You'll find the gold box somewhere in the mailing that you will receive in a day or so. Just fill in the gold box with your additional selection of a free record or tape." The commercial produced enough response to pay for itself, but, more importantly, it gave a tremendous lift to direct mail response, proving the power of media and message integration.

One of the future aspects of advertising is the custom-made, the tailor-made. Instead of peddling mass-produced commodities, advertising is going to become a personal service to the individual.

Marshal McLuhan

Print

There are two major uses for direct response print advertising.

1.   To provide a very specific umbrella of awareness in support of direct mail and telemarketing. Concentrate your efforts in carefully selected vertical publications and remember: Awareness is not enough. Each ad must generate some degree of qualified response. How do you know which publications your audience prefers? Ask some of the following questions when conducting your IDM depth research with your targeted decision makers:

- What publications do you regularly read for information about (this subject)?
- In which of these publications should we advertise (this product)? Why?
- What information should the advertisements contain?
- What visuals would you want to see?

2.   To demonstrate commitment to the marketplace. During depth research for an AT&T business-to-business program, we asked executives if they looked to periodicals to gain information about new technologies and application solutions and if AT&T should be advertising. They told us in no uncertain terms, that they wanted to see AT&T's ads in selected vertical publications as a demonstration of AT&T's commitment and dedication to their market segment. They told us, "If we see AT&T's ads in these publications, we know they're dedicated, and will stay committed."

Direct Mail

It's important that we take a customer-based view of this medium—a direct communication from you to a decision maker via the mail. A communication of value and importance from one individual to another.

Lester Wunderman said it succinctly:

> We are living through the second great power shift of the 20th century. …The 1960s introduced two fundamental structural changes. The first was cultural. The post-war baby boom generation rebelled against massification. They were and are the "I am me" generation which demanded attention to their unique differences rather than their similarities.

At the same time, the development of the computer made it possible to identify, differentiate and separate individuals from the mass.

Our industry has developed a host of metrics and phrases, such as bulk, third class and cost per thousand, that blur the vision of the individual. Don't take your eye off the decision maker. An individual will receive your letter, and an individual will make the decision to respond or not to respond.

◆ Three Ways to Increase the Effectiveness of Your Direct Mail

Idea #1: Personalize the message.

We are not talking about either peppering a letter with the name of a celebrity who is holding millions of dollars for you, or seeing how many times we can use your last name in bold, 24 point type in body copy.

We are talking about directly addressing the unique needs and requirements of the individual. Each individual must find in your message value, satisfaction and identity—the sense that you understand and view them as an individual, that they are, or can be, a part of the solution you offer.

Idea #2: Personalize the communication.

Treat each decision maker with respect—through the direct addressing of the outer envelope, correctly using the decision maker's name in the salutation of the letter and on the reply device. Test it yourself; we've found it lifts qualified response by 10 percent to 15 percent.

Also, test first class mail versus third class. The additional cost is usually more than offset by the increased results, especially when mailing to current customers or highly qualified prospects.

Idea #3: Use direct mail as a springboard for telemarketing.

Direct mail provides a powerful call to action through the combination of mail, fax and telephone 800-number response. Where direct mail can fall short is in generating the sense of immediacy needed to compel the recipient to action. By adding outbound telemarketing to the mix, you can translate positive interest generated by mail into action.

Both message integration and timing can serve as the springboard.

- Carefully integrate your message between mail and telemarketing. IDM depth research will help identify the information required and "buying triggers" of your market. Direct mail can "touch all the bases," with telemarketing providing additional detail, as well as the opportunity to ask questions or challenge benefits. For instance, if you are mailing an invitation to an event, the direct mail can give an overview of the event, the topics, and speakers. Copy may say that, for additional information, use our toll-free 800 number, or one of our representatives will be calling you within the next day or two— please accept the call.
- Carefully integrate the timing of your mailings, looking to release mail in smaller "waves." According to the concept of response compression, which will be discussed later, outbound telemarketing follows receipt

of direct mail by 24 to 72 hours. Our mail release pattern must match telemarketing's capacity to attempt and complete those calls.

To test the effectiveness of IDM, Citicorp measured results and costs for three levels of media integration: (1) mail with an 800 number, (2) mail with an 800 number followed up by a telemarketing call to inquiries, and (3) mail with an 800 number followed up by a telemarketing call to inquiries and supported by print advertising. All three were measured against a control of mail only. The test clearly showed that, as additional media are strategically integrated into the mix, the response rates increase and the cost per sale decreases (see Exhibit 3-1).

The Double-Edged Sword of Telemarketing

The results of IDM depth research studies regarding media preference among business and consumer decision makers indicate that decision makers have a strong bias against one of the most powerful and most often misused mediums—telemarketing.

Let's take a quick look at the history of telemarketing and see what accounts for telemarketing's "bad rap." Through the '70s and '80s, telemarketing came on like gangbusters, with more and more companies using it as a powerful, personal way to contact prospects and customers directly with a persuasive message. By the early '80s, telemarketing was the hottest item in the media mix. Technology added sophisticated tools—databases, automatic dialers, computer-based scripts, ACDs, least-cost call routing, and so on. Clients and agencies started looking at ways to improve the efficiency and reduce talk-time. The focus shifted to "manufacturing" phone calls—make more calls, make more sales.

But, in spite of the success, some disturbing trends were cropping up in telemarketing during the '80s and '90s. Many of the best and the brightest companies were turning to the telephone as a "quick fix" for direct marketing programs that weren't working. Worse yet, the telephone began to be used as a mass selling tool—"broadcasting" the same message without adequate concern for whether the message had relevance or value to the person on the other end of the line. And, while still extremely effective, these calls "strip mined" the market and created a general resistance to unsolicited sales or marketing over the telephone.

There is, of course, another side of the telemarketing story—the "good" telemarketing. The use of 800 numbers is growing astronomically due to increasing acceptance among business people and consumers alike. People are calling 800 numbers for everything from information to service to outright purchases. The careful integration of an 800 number in your mailing can increase response rate by 50 percent to 100 percent. This requires thorough training, scripting, quality monitoring, and detailed results analysis – not just "dropping in" an 800 number.

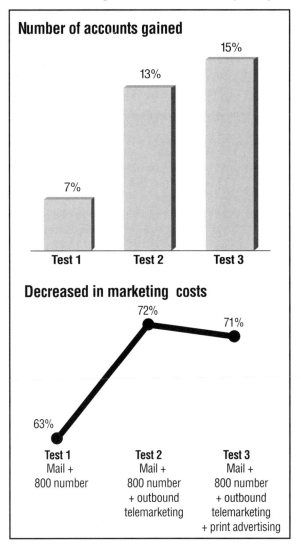

Media integration, the Citicorp way

Number of accounts gained

Test 1: 7%
Test 2: 13%
Test 3: 15%

Decreased in marketing costs

Test 1: 63%
Test 2: 72%
Test 3: 71%

Test 1
Mail +
800 number

Test 2
Mail +
800 number
+ outbound
telemarketing

Test 3
Mail +
800 number
+ outbound
telemarketing
+ print advertising

EXHIBIT 3-1.

Why is inbound seen as a welcome convenience and outbound an annoying intrusion? The answer is intuitively clear and has to do with choice and the personal, one-to-one nature of telephone communications. With both mail and 800, customers choose when to respond and how to respond. Furthermore, since the customer initiates the call to do something that he or she wants, it has intrinsic value. An outbound telemarketing call

IDM Media Contribution

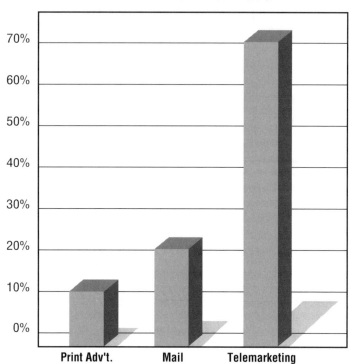

Exhibit 3-2. An effective IDM campaign generates double-digit response rates because of the synergy achieved through precision integration and strategic use of media: print advertising contributes 10 percent to overall response, direct mail another 20 percent, with 70 percent of the response generated by telemarketing.

that arrives "cold," however, has little perceived value, and may, in fact, violate the recipient's sense of privacy.

So what's the solution? Do we simply wait until customers respond to us? And let our message get cold in the meantime? Of course not. The solution is to plan both the content and the timing of the outbound telemarketing call (discussed later in this chapter) so that it is meaningful to the customer and productive to your organization. When properly integrated, telemarketing is readily perceived by the customers as a service—one that allows for a discussion and provides immediate answers to questions.

In addition to the 50 percent to 100 percent increase in response from an 800 number, the skillful integration of an outbound telemarketing effort can add another 100 percent to 700 percent lift in response over the base mail response. Suddenly, our initial 2 percent response has increased by a factor of 800 percent by adding interactive media to the "business as usual" mailing. And the good news is that the increase in response is usually so great that it results in a decrease in cost per sale!

Improving Reponse Rates
Through Integrated Media

	Typical Response Rate
Direct Mail	2%
Add 800 number to package	+1% to 2%
Add carefully timed follow-up phone call	+2 to 14%
Total reponse rate	*5% to 18%*

Exhibit 3-3. Here's a simple example of media integration, integrating just mail and telemarketing. When a mailing, which might generate a 2 percent response on its own, is supplemented by a toll-free 800 number, we see response rise by 50 percent to 100 percent.

The multiple messages delivered via different channels work together to create heightened awareness. The multiple communications leverage this awareness into action. The existing investment in mail becomes more productive. And the investment in telemarketing is far more profitable than if used by itself, because it employs the mail as a springboard for building awareness and response.

The integration of telemarketing into an IDM program must be value-based, requiring total quality control, scripting, training, strict communicator monitoring, and detailed results tracking. And based on what we've seen, most of these quality controls aren't operational in most companies!

Luck is when opportunity meets preparation.

Maury Wills
Legendary base-stealer of the LA Dodgers

Scripted vs. Nonscripted. There are two schools of thought about scripted telemarketing calls. One says that scripting the call creates a stilted, one-way, feature-dump. Customers are "steam-rolled" and have to forcefully interrupt to say that the message is not relevant. The other says that a tested, structured presentation will maximize both results and customer satisfaction.

Our research supports the latter view. We've found that interactive, customer-oriented, tightly structured scripts with extensive training and appropriate exit points for the customer will generate greater response than unscripted calls.

Within IDM, we believe that the first draft of the telemarketing script is "best guess." Each script must be tested and refined. Traditionally, we use the best communicators to test the script. They place some live calls, which are carefully monitored and form the basis for a follow-up Communicator Feedback Session. During this session, supervisors, the client and communicators discuss how to make the script more conversational and effective. Then, additional test calls are made until the group feels ready to begin increasing call volume.

Thus, the best thinking of the client and the real-life experience of the best communicators is combined in the script. With verbatim script adherence, all communicators are armed with the best possible, most consistent approach to the marketplace. And, because all communicators should now perform on a more level track, results are higher and more projectable and customer satisfaction is enhanced.

◆ Let's take a look at two case studies for customers' reactions to highly structured telemarketing.

In the first example, Citibank used telemarketing as part of a direct mail credit card solicitation. In a survey of 400 customers who had received Citibank's highly structured, carefully scripted telemarketing calls and 300 customers who had not received the bank's telemarketing calls, we saw some interesting trends. The customers who had not received the telemarketing call expressed negative comments about telemarketing in general. The customers who had received Citibank's scripted calls reported that the call was welcome and informative.

When we divided the 400 customers who received the telemarketing calls into groups of non-buyers (those who had not accepted the offer) and buyers (those who had), we saw an even more interesting result. Fully two-thirds of the customers who had no interest in the product and did not accept the offer reported a positive response to the telemarketing.

Clearly, the script had a lot to do with the response. But scripting is only part of IDM's Total Quality Control (TQC) telemarketing processes, which include in-depth training, structured, qualitative monitoring, and hourly and daily productivity metrics.

The second example concerns a national telecommunications provider of toll-free inbound service. The target market was small businesses and home offices.

Objectives of the program were to reverse both a steadily decreasing sales rate and rapidly increasing "do not call" (dnc) requests.

IDM strategies were as follows:

- Deploy IDM Interactive Scripting and verbatim script adherence. Up to this point, communicators were working off loosely structured call guides. The thought was that scripts discouraged the communicators' ability to listen and respond freely to decision makers' questions.

  Structured call monitoring and in-depth results analysis showed a wide disparity in the productivity of communicators and their ability to present the service and successfully address stated questions and objections.

  Tightly structured, interactive scripts developed with communicator's input as well as verbatim script adherence were tested against the loose call guides in an A/B test. The improvements in sales and cost of sale and the decrease in "do not calls" were so dramatic that verbatim scripting was rolled out to the entire program within two weeks.

- Segment the target market by need and prioritize the deployment of outbound telemarketing.

  Outbound had been deployed in the context of "the more calls we manufacture, the more sales we make." Declining sales and rising "do not calls" were proof that this was not working.

  Analysis of the database revealed high potential segments as well as segments that showed virtually no response, and a high percentage of "do not calls."

  High potential segments were prioritized, and low potential segments removed from the calling queue. Further analysis and research led to the development of specialized offers for some of these segments (e.g., seasonal offers were developed for seasonal businesses, such as ski resorts).

- Per the principles of response compression, mail release and telemarketing were timed so outbound calls reached the decision maker within 24 to 72 hours of mail receipt.

The results:

- Sixty-seven percent increase in sales rate with a 43 percent reduction in cost of sale. The combined results of prioritizing the deployment of outbound, IDM Interactive Scripting and verbatim script adherence and precision call timing cut waste and made every call more effective.

- Enhanced customer satisfaction as measured by a 50 percent reduction in "do not call" requests. Telemarketing was deployed based on the relevance of the offer. The structure of the script provided early exits for customers who were "not interested now" and effective responses and rebuttals to questions and objections.

Integrating Voice Mail

Some businesses see telemarketing as limited by the increasing proliferation of voice mail systems, which are often used to screen calls. But we've found that honesty goes a long way in obtaining response—even on voice mail. If the script is written so that the telemarketer can leave a clear, concise message about the purpose of the call and the nature of the offer, voice mail is no more of a challenge than any other type of screen.

Building on the Success of Inbound 800

The phenomenal increase in 800 usage clearly demonstrates that customers relish instant, informed, reliable contact with a company. It also demonstrates that they appreciate the control that an 800 number gives them to call at their convenience. Managing the inbound successfully is an important part of your entire IDM strategy.

Greg Lakin, Consultant and former Director of Direct Marketing at Bell Atlantic makes the inbound call center a precision selling tool. "We've learned over time that a response can be categorized based on the response vehicle. Thus, we can identify in the inbound call queue which is a business reply card response and which is a customer that has bought before. The calls can be handled according to the level of interest and the potential for business that each represents."

THE PRINCIPLE OF RESPONSE COMPRESSION

Compressing the time between receipt of the direct mail and the deployment of outbound telemarketing can dramatically lift both the quality and quantity of response. We call it response compression, and it can increase your aggregate response by 200 to 700 percent (see Exhibit 3-4).

Response Compression

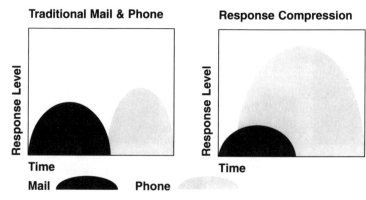

Exhibit 3-4.

Direct mail is frequently a separate department and separate budget item. Thus, marketers want to gain the greatest return on their investment, and traditionally wait until mail response drops before deploying outbound telemarketing. The concern is not to "cannibalize" lower-cost direct mail response with higher cost outbound telemarketing.

IDM focuses on the aggregate response. Said differently, why let 98 names get cold while waiting for two mail responders?

The IDM process deploys the outbound call as mail response is peaking, when awareness is likely to be the highest. IDM capitalizes on this heightened awareness and engages the decision maker in an interactive conversation to clarify benefits and respond to questions and objections.

Research and testing have proven that, for optimal results, the outbound call should reach the decision maker 24 to 72 hours after mail receipt. Recognition of previous media, the direct mail, advertising, and publicity is highest, as is recall of the basic marketing message and its benefits.

The results speak for themselves:

- 200 percent to 700 percent increase in aggregate response
- Improved dialog with decision makers, leading to higher qualification
- Greater list penetration achieved in less attempts, for improved cost efficiency

INITIAL AND ONGOING COMMUNICATIONS

The IDM process is structured to achieve a continuum of communication, encompassing initial and ongoing communications. Most companies engage in "event" or "B-52 blitz" marketing. As we said in Chapter 1, many companies are looking for the quick hit, the quick sale. IDM is structured to serve as an interactive, value-added communications strategy throughout a customer's life cycle. From the initial "hello" to ongoing communications designed to increase response, customer revenue, and lifetime value, the goal is to convert the highest number of prospects into qualified leads and sales (see Exhibit 3-5).

Initial communications begin with advertising. This may be broadcast media or carefully selected consumer or vertical business publications, as validated by your target market through Depth Research and actual results. Advertising is important for two reasons: to create an umbrella of awareness in support of direct mail and telemarketing, and to generate some quantity of leads.

However briefly, advertising must contain the critical benefits and buying triggers. It must be compelling, not entertaining. Copy and layout should drive response to the interactive 800 channel, so that decision makers can receive the additional information and make a qualified, informed decision.

Within one week, the first direct mailing arrives.

Media Integration Flow Chart

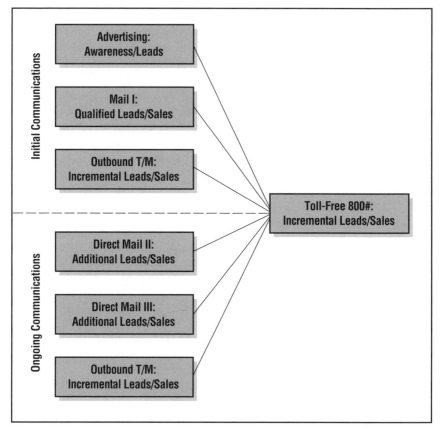

Exhibit 3-5.

Direct mail increases the level of awareness by providing more specific information. For instance, if the advertisement announced an upcoming seminar, the direct mailing can give details of the Agenda that are specific to your needs. The mail also serves as a springboard for outbound tele-marketing. Mention of the upcoming outbound call may be positioned within the direct mail copy (e.g., "Seating is limited; our representative will call you in the next day or two to answer any questions you may have and help with your registration.")

Direct mail must also build upon the sense of immediacy and urgency, and generate highly qualified response, leads, and sales. Again, the inbound 800-number channel should be emphasized, because of its interactive abilities in response qualification. Of course, include a business reply card (BRC) and fax response options.

Then, per response compression, the outbound call arrives within 24 to 72 hours of mail receipt. It is carefully integrated into the media mix through message as well as timing. Its objectives:

- Generate incremental leads or sales. The additional cost of outbound is more than offset by the increase in response, leads, and sales. Also important is the deeper prequalification achieved.
- Generate qualitative data, such as future needs, areas of importance, and reasons for "Not Interested Now."
- Reinforce BRC, fax, or 800-number response.

A good outbound call also creates a measurable "halo" effect. You can see 10 percent to 12 percent of telephone "Not Interesteds" subsequently respond via BRC, fax, or inbound, if the call has been courteous and professional.

At this point, information generated during the initial communications is used to shape the personalized Ongoing Communication process. For example:

- Depth research has given us an idea of the customers' unique set of needs and requirements—the issues they are struggling with, and how our product or service may be able to help. Through interactive telemarketing we've had the chance to refine our understanding and pinpoint specific areas of interest and need. We can now supply the decision maker with additional, increasingly specific information to satisfy those needs. For instance, this information might be a case history or a testimonial.
- We have been able to clarify the decision makers' buying triggers and hot buttons, and can again offer more specific information. For instance, we might communicate information on available technical support, or lease and rental plans.
- And, we have a better understanding of the timing of the decision maker's buying cycle—what involvement or engagement is appropriate and when. If their needs are immediate, perhaps field engagement is required. If they are in a "product search" stage, we must supply details on our product or service that accomplish competitive differentiation while matching their list of needs.

Ongoing communication then alternates between very personalized direct mail, telemarketing, and field sales, as appropriate. Its objective is to move a customer or prospect through the stages of the buying cycle, providing additional value in each communication, while gathering increasingly specific marketing information.

The IDM methodology uses personalized direct marketing communications to generate highly qualified leads, which are routed to the field only at the appropriate point in the qualification process.

To close this communications loop, customer and prospect information is supplied by the field based on their sales visits. This information is fed back into the system and drives Ongoing Communications to move the customer or prospect along the buying cycle until they are ready for the next field contact.

Clearly, the integrated database is essential to this level of ongoing precision marketing.

Ongoing Communications is the next frontier in marketing. And it's a very rich area for exploration. Very few companies have attempted it, and fewer have succeeded. Yet, it presents one of the best answers to businesses' need to reduce the cost of sale, while increasing value to its customers. Value-added communications allow each customer to self-select the avenue of distribution best suited to his or her needs.

This is proactive management of lifetime value.

KEY POINTS

- The integration and deployment of media must be driven by customer needs and requirements.
- Depth research is your key to determining customer needs, media preferences, and ongoing communication requirements.
- Integrating media as part of a total IDM program can reduce costs while increasing both quantity and quality of response.
- Each medium has strengths and weaknesses. Use them only when they are market-justified and cost-justified.
- Telemarketing is a powerful tool but must be used carefully to ensure customer response and satisfaction. Misused, it can erode your credibility and undermine the effectiveness of other efforts.
- Be prepared for organizational and cultural blocks since, by it's very nature, IDM cuts across "turf" and integrates functions that are used to running their own show.
- Measure total response, not just response by individual medium.

POSTSCRIPT

Some Thoughts on Media
Greg Lakin
Consultant and former Director of Direct Marketing
Bell Atlantic

When I was a lad my father was fond of taking me to the secret fishing place where the "big" fish lived. We always took along the secret bait that was guaranteed to catch the "big" fish. We would fish in the secret place until we caught our limit or we would change bait or we would conclude the fish had moved elsewhere and so would we. Funny where you find your career preparation.

In Direct Marketing, we use a variety of "bait" in our pursuit of the "big" fish. A typical collection of lures might include:

- News stories (PR)
- TV (spot and direct response)
- Infomercials
- Radio
- Print (newspapers and periodicals)
- Bill inserts
- Direct Mail
- Inbound response telemarketing
- Outbound telemarketing

Each of these lures—or what we will call media elements—and its role in the Direct Marketing process constitute the heart of the DM media plan.

News stories (Publicity/Public Relations)

New (or newsworthy) products are an excellent opportunity for exposure and brand building. Good marketers will generate releases or "media feeds" (to network and local news) with messages supported by advertising to gain market access. News feeds might list a corporate 800 number as an information source. At least two key customer benefits should always be woven into a story to reinforce media coverage and supplement advertising.

Remember, you can always issue a press release, but the news media will determine its worthiness. Don't pre-judge the outcome. Consider the positive brand impact Johnson & Johnson engineered through the Tylenol recall. Similarly, GM/Saturn took the quality concept of allowing any assembly line worker to "stop" the line to correct a flaw and turned it into a news-making innovation. Subsequently, the story was included in mass media advertising to reinforce Saturn's commitment to product quality.

The launch of Sprint into competition with AT&T and MCI as a long-distance supplier carried the challenge of product differentiation. Sprint chose to promote the use of digital technology as a superior feature. The news stories discussed the "noiseless" comparison to the competition and the digital technology that made it work. The mass media built on the idea that you could "Hear a Pin Drop." The PR message complemented the advertising and marketing message.

Television

The power of television is enormous both in terms of impact and cost. The wise direct marketing strategist needs to be aware of the many pricing options for broadcast advertising and must also be thoughtful as to how television advertising is to be used.

Spot TV

Typically, 15-, 30- or 60-second chunks of time, purchased within a narrow "run time" where exposure and market coverage can be predetermined, will dictate price. Spot television is the most expensive purchase, but it is precise in that markets can be timed and audiences targeted.

DRTV

Direct Response Television is a much lower cost option, usually purchased in 30- and 60-second time slots. The low cost comes from networks selling excess time at deep discounts. Therefore, the purchased spots do not have a precise "run time" but instead will be slotted in as time becomes available—typically during four-hour windows. The network also has the right to pre-empt the spots. The challenge, from a direct marketer's perspective, is in scheduling to handle response peak at the call center. Added frustration, and cost, can result if the DRTV spot is pre-empted.

Mural/Indirect/Bulletin Board

Cable television now allows multiple low-cost mass media paths for the direct response advertiser. Bulletin boards are available for five- to ten-second messages. Some have audio track capabilities. All have a high frequency repetition that is ideal for low-cost, regional lead generation.

Increasingly, indirect advertising, while not specifically response generating, is playing a powerful role especially in sporting events. One agency recently reported that every time a certain golfer on the Master's Tour was able to get a five-second hat shot with the logo in full view, the golfer was paid $500.

Sports arenas are now filled with signs, murals, and billboards positioned for maximum TV coverage during sports events. The happy result is mass media coverage for billboard rates.

Infomercials

Infomercials are broadly defined as "full length" programs where a product is promoted. The infomercial of the 1990s covers everything from special products only available via the commercial to general trade products packaged for promotion. All have a direct response component.

TV Retail

The growth of Home Shopping Network, QVC and others should be seen as an excellent channel to supplement other direct activities. New shopping channels and new ways of enabling people to cruise the "electronic mall" are adding to the power of this medium.

Radio

To the direct marketing strategist, radio represents an interesting challenge. The best target slot is "drive time" because of the number of people who are listening to their car radios during peak commuting hours. But how valuable is a DR radio spot delivered to drivers in cars?

The most effective radio direct response comes from the use of 800 numbers with easy-to-remember names. A frequent spot in Washington, D.C., is for Warner Plumbing—800 4 HOT WATER. It works. And it works even better now that so many drivers have car phones.

The caution about the use of 0, o, 1, L and I as high risk letters because of dialing transpositions holds particularly true for radio ads where customer memory translation is required.

Print

The role of print media will be strongly influenced by two factors: geography and target market. Cost as a function of audience observations are going to be higher for this medium than others, but the advantages may outweigh the costs.

Newspapers

Because of the local nature of this medium, you can be assured of specific geographic targeting. Test markets, locally marketed products, product trials, etc., are ideal for this medium. If a response component is included, make certain the availability of the call center operation coincides with the schedules for the print insertions.

I recently called several 800 numbers for brokerage houses that had ads in the Sunday Washington Post. The majority of the calls went unanswered after 10 - 20 rings, several were poorly handled, and only one went to a properly prepared call center.

Magazine

Magazines provide general geographic coverage similar to newspapers; however, the footprint is more flexible and often covers a substantially larger geographic area.

The direct marketer can most efficiently use subscription and reader profiles of the magazine to augment targeting done through other media. An added benefit of magazines is the use of inserts (free standing or perforated) that can be used as response reply forms.

For niche products such as computer software, janitorial supplies, surgical instruments, ethical drugs, etc., special audience magazines are—after direct mail and telemarketing—the most effective targeting vehicle available.

Bill Inserts

Marketers rendering recurring bills like credit cards, supplies, utilities and oil companies have long used bill inserts as the lowest-cost way to send messages to customers. A typical bill insert will likely cost less than 10 cents to produce and deliver.

The oil companies, credit card companies, and a few retailers have long used the "bang tail" envelope as a means of delivering a low cost message. The customer simply removes the flap with the promotional message and response card before sealing the envelope containing payment.

Many companies are now offering space in their mailings for promotional materials. If the target is in an undifferentiated mass market, this could be a good supplemental low-cost vehicle.

Beware, however, if you are marketing bill inserts, that the added bill insert weights do not throw your mailer into the next postage class.

Direct Mail

Ideally, direct mail can be the most targeted, focused, and precise medium. Carefully crafted with size and packaging considerations in mind, direct mail will always be a highly productive and profitable tool. When used with first class postage, the impact will be strengthened.

Inbound Telemarketing

The call center role is to support and supplement the media stimulation. It is how the sale is closed and fulfilled. Therefore, centers must be scheduled and staffed to meet the expected volume of calls from all media stimulation. Hours of operation should conform to the behavior of the market being stimulated. If TV is running during the 10 PM news, the call center must be staffed and ready.

Often, agencies and contractors are used for call center and fulfillment work. Treat the contractor's employees as if they were your staff. Don't presume the contractor has unlimited resources and capacity to handle unscheduled volume.

Outbound Telemarketing

Outbound telemarketing is most effective when prior media messages have produced aided awareness in the market. Outbound is a supplement to mail, bill inserts, or TV and, as such, is considerably more effective than cold calling.

Outbound tends to be a very high-cost medium and is potentially very erosive to the customer base. Therefore, outbound without the stimulation of other media is not especially effective. One possible exception is fund raising. Fund raising tends to use volunteers or professional contractors who can often use the fund's name recognition as a substitute for collaborative media.

Selecting the Right Media Mix

The first step is to begin with a well-defined, well-understood shared vision of the program's objectives. Attach the cost and profitability objectives. Then begin the process of allocating costs and coverage to each potential medium. This will help you select the combination of elements to generate maximum impact.

Normally a mass marketer will use TV, mail, and, if possible, bill inserts, the direct response call center, and sometimes outbound follow-up. The skilled practitioner will use the techniques of IDM to maximize impact, effectiveness, and yield.

But most important:

Test, measure, and evaluate. Build response curves. Stay in touch with your history. Experiment. Start in contained markets with sample programs.

Keep the variables around media testing small so that reactions from the market can be measured precisely.

Spend wisely. Spend as much time planning the measurement and analysis as you do planning the messages. And spend more time on planning the measurement and evaluation than you think you can afford. The payoff is exponential.

A good fisherman knows when it's time to change the bait. Or to move to another spot.

The IDM Creative Process:
Customer-Driven, Market-Justified

As it enters the ear, does it come in like broken glass or does it come in like honey?

Eddie Condon, on listening to jazz

Like good jazz, creating an IDM program is a fine mix of individual talents and overall structure. And, like jazz, how well you've succeeded is determined by your audience.

No matter which channels or media are part of your IDM strategy for a specific market, the content of the IDM creative message must be clear, focused, connected and appropriate to each channel or medium. Your objective is to leverage the message across multiple media to maximize the total impact on the individual.

As we discussed in Chapter 3, an IDM campaign uses traditional media—television, radio, advertising, publicity, direct mail, telemarketing, and field sales—in nontraditional ways. Each medium establishes contact with the customer in a unique way and carries it's own message. IDM success is based on the aggregate effect of the media working together. Each point of contact (and each medium) needs to build on previous contacts as well as to lay the groundwork for the next contact.

IDM creative must be developed with a recognition of the overall message that needs to be conveyed and how it will be communicated across different media. The right message to the right person at the right time in the right media creates the same harmonious effect as good jazz. The whole message is more powerful than the sum of the parts.

CREATING THE IDM CAMPAIGN

To create an effective IDM campaign, you need to consider three critical areas:

1. Integration of multiple functions
2. Knowledge of the customer
3. Precise timing of implementation

1. Integration of Multiple Functions

Creating a program that has value for the customer or prospect means contributions from multiple functions within the company. Throughout preparation, planning, and implementation, integrating multiple functions will pay off in a better program.

The cross-functional team is the brain of the IDM development process. This team evaluates research, forms strategies, implements decisions, deploys communications, analyzes results, and fine-tunes creative. The team usually consists of representatives from the following functional areas:

- Sales management and field reps
- Product management
- Marketing
- Research
- Publicity/public relations
- Advertising
- Direct mail
- Telemarketing
- Fulfillment

Functioning without turf or walls, the team can focus on identifying and communicating value to customers.

Since the IDM team includes people from sales, marketing and creative specialties, remember that, in many cases, these people have never been in the same meetings together. Your IDM planning session is often a first. Roles and responsibilities need to be clearly defined and ideas encouraged. Make sure that communication among team members is frequent and open.

Since the depth research is so vitally important as the basis for the creative, make sure that the creative team is part of the telephone research. Avoid the all too common tendency to isolate the "creatives" and bring them into the process only after the research has been digested and the creative direction set.

Find out what the writer needs to know about the customer to draft the right message. See what questions the designer wants answered to produce an effective mailing package. Ask the sales force what the problems are in reaching the audience. Ask the fulfillment department how to pace the advertising and mailing for optimum fulfillment turnaround. Include the whole team in the depth research planning. Put them on the phone to hear the customer's answers directly. If you're creating the ad, there's a big difference between hearing the customer talk about needs and having the marketing director tell you what those needs are.

Ongoing Communications and the Team.   As your IDM plan evolves, keep all members of the team actively involved. To make sure that the leads are qualified leads, include qualifying questions (as determined by sales) in the telemarketing script. If technical support is a part of the customer contact, talk to that group and find out what they need to know about the customer to provide better service. Include the creative team in feedback sessions so that they are aware of the issues. Use the knowledge you gain during the process to refine and tailor the ongoing communications to better address customer and prospect needs.

2. Knowledge of the Customer

Integrating media and messages may seem like a complex juggling act at first, but in reality it simply requires paying close attention to what you know (and can find out) about your customer—then using this as the basis of the creative plan. Information about the customers provides a clear picture of their needs, preferences, buying cycle, and decision-making process.

Where do you get the needed information? Databases are one source; input from the sales force is another; asking the customer or prospect is a third. If you have established some form of integrated database, information from all three of these sources will be coordinated in the system. In all cases, you'll want to verify accuracy and test concepts by conducting IDM depth research interviews with a sample of your target market.

IDM Depth Research: the Basis of Creative Development.   IDM depth research means going to the source and asking the customers to tell you what they need and how to communicate with them. As we discussed in Chapter 2, depth research forms the basis of the IDM plan. Not a word goes on paper, not a graphic is designed, not a photograph shot or a line of script drafted that cannot be logically linked to customer needs, wants, or preferences as determined by interviewing a small sample of the customer or prospect group.

♦   The following examples are from an IBM depth research interview guide and demonstrate how questions uncovered specific information that was identified as important to the cross-functional team. The depth research was conducted to obtain information for the IBM case study focusing on medical practices, which begins later in this chapter.

- Sales force needs and database development required information about the current installed base, use of service bureaus, and competitive presence. For example:
  "Is your practice currently automated?" (If no: "How do you process claims now?" "Why aren't you automated?")
  "What combination of hardware and software is currently installed? When was the system installed?"
  "What applications are in use?"
  "What is your level of satisfaction with the system?"
- Marketing and creative needed to know who makes the decisions and what the decision-making process is. For example:
  "Would you please describe the stages your practice went through in evaluating and purchasing your hardware and software solution?" What were the key milestones?"
  "Who was involved in the process?"
  "What is the role of the physician? The practice manager?"
  "Did your search concentrate on software or did it include hardware?"
  "What did you look for in a software solution?" "What did you look for in a software provider?"
  "What did you look for in a hardware solution?" "What did you look for in a hardware provider?"
- Sales management was interested in determining the perceived value of the IBM Representative and IBM Business Partners. For example: "Within your search, did you meet the IBM Representative, the Agent or the IBM Industry Remarketer?" "What is your perception of the role/value of each of these representatives presale?" "Postsale?"
  "Have they lived up to your expectations?"
- Marketing was interested in overall perception of IBM:
  "What attributes or values do you think of when IBM is mentioned?" If price is mentioned as first or second, probe for perception of value: "Did you pay a premium for IBM?"
- Marketing also needed to know what events, offers, and media had value:
  "During your decision, did you attend any value-added events, such as management briefings or audio teleconferences?"
  "If IBM were to develop information-sharing events, what do you think the content should be?" "What issues should be addressed?"
  "Who should the speakers be?" "What topics should be addressed?"
  "If such events had been held when you were evaluating computer systems, would you have attended?"

> "Aside from specific events, IBM is evaluating the following offers. Would you please give us your reaction: consultative needs analysis, profitability analysis, software search."
> "Are there any periodicals or other published media that you read regularly for information about technology?"
> "How many telemarketing calls do you receive in a week?" "What's your reaction?"
>
> The IBM depth research interviews consisted of more than 50 carefully constructed questions.

Learning More as the Process Continues.   Of course, you don't stop learning about the customer once the depth research is over or the plan is rolled out. IDM continues to be a two-way dialogue in which you obtain more information with every contact. Therefore, your creative approach will continue to evolve as you obtain more information about the customer. The creative process is a series of contacts in a continuing process of ever-closer engagement with the customer.

The IDM creative approach must view each contact not as an isolated sale or event but as a part of a process of establishing the value of your company, product, or service to the customer over time. This means looking at a number of factors beyond the content of separate creative pieces, including:

- What is the value of each contact—value as determined by the customer or prospect?
- How does each contact support the next?
- How will the media inter-relate?
- How does the offer or event support the overall strategy?
- What information can be obtained at each contact point that will help build the ongoing relationship?
- How will each contact move the customer or prospect to a closer engagement with your company, product, or service and closer to a buying decision or a repeat buy?

Good IDM, like good jazz, keeps the audience coming back for more.

3. Precise Timing of Implementation

Timing of the creative development and production is critical to the success of any IDM campaign. Carefully plan and monitor each part of the process to assure on-time delivery and roll-out of each component. TV ads must hit as planned; mail needs to go out while awareness is high, and telemarketing calls must be made no more than 72 hours after the customer has received the mailing. Response compression (as described in Chapter

3) is one of the key principles of IDM telephone follow-up. By timing the telephone call to follow the mail or other communication closely, you can substantially increase response. The call arrives when the offer is fresh in the prospect's mind and when good answers to the questions can bring the "fence sitters" into the fold.

A suggested timeline for the development and production of your creative materials is included in Appendix A.

THE CREATIVE PROCESS AT WORK: IBM AND USAA

To illustrate IDM's creative side, let's go behind the scenes of two successful campaigns to see how multiple contacts are used to meet two very different business objectives.

EXAMPLE 1: IBM'S LEAD GENERATION PROGRAM

The medical industry is an important market for IBM. The objective of the IDM campaign was to penetrate private medical practices ranging in size from three to forty-nine physicians—a segment that the sales force had characterized as "hard to see the decision-maker." Even though IBM had a large installed base, the activity in this market segment was below projections.

Understanding the Market Through Depth Research

As a first step, IBM wanted a clear picture of the current perceptions about IBM within the targeted market. Why was the decision maker "hard to see?" What did decision makers know about IBM? What did they want to know? What was the perception of the competition? What was the best way to communicate with the decision maker? Who, in fact, was the decision maker?

The carefully scripted and planned depth research interviews asked these and other highly detailed questions of selected customers and prospects. The answers provided valuable information and insight into the needs, wants and perceptions of medical practices—detailed information that was not available through any other means. Listening, *really* listening, to the customer is the foundation of the IDM creative process.

Developing the Strategy based on Accurate Customer Information

The depth research interviews supplied important information which could then be used to develop a plan and a creative strategy. For example:

- Contrary to previous assumptions, the physician was not the decision maker. The office/practice manager was. Physicians chose not to be directly involved in the search for information technology, preferring to concentrate on the practice of medicine.

  The impact of this information on the strategy is obvious: IBM needed to focus sales and marketing efforts on the office/practice manager.

- Practices that saw software as more important to running the business than hardware (80 percent of the target market) viewed IBM as a commodity vendor. They made their hardware decisions based on price, corporate stability, service and support, and trouble-free operation—in that order.

  The 20 percent of the market that focused on hardware viewed IBM as an important partner. These practices based their buying decisions on corporate stability, service and support, and quality. These practices put price last.

  How did that information influence the strategy? It showed that IBM needed to leverage its strengths in corporate stability, service and support, and quality to reinforce the value to the 20 percent who were aware of the benefits of IBM, and demonstrate the value to the 80 percent of the market that saw IBM as a commodity.

- The responses to the depth research interviews also showed that, even though customers did not expect IBM to be an expert in the medical marketplace, they did expect them to be visibly committed to the market. "Be an expert in hardware. Do what you do well."

- The responses showed that there was confusion about the separate roles of IBM representatives and IBM's third-party sales agents. Typical comments included: "I don't know who all these people are or what their roles are, but I do know I'm paying their salary. No value." "Too confusing. Too many layers. The division of responsibility isn't clear and doesn't satisfy my needs."

  Customers expressed a clear preference for IBM to manage pre- and post-sales activity to cut through the confusion. "Flatten the organization—get closer, increase your knowledge of the marketplace." "Manage your business partners better; more closely."

- Customers expressed interest in receiving practical information with IBM taking the leading role. "Develop a multi-vendor type of trade show with every medical solution that runs on IBM equipment." "Extract information to help business/management make decisions." "Help us know what to look for in the hardware."

  Customers reacted positively to offers of consultative needs analysis if it focused on automating business and medical management practices; negatively to financial, profitability, or regulatory matters.

- When we asked about the media and how IBM should communicate, customers provided clear direction on what would have value to them. "Don't make it look like junk mail." "If you want to invite me to something, do a classy, rich looking invitation—like an invitation to a party or a wedding." "Most effective is a direct business letter. I read them."

And when we asked about telemarketing, customers reported receiving between one and ten outbound telemarketing calls a week, "I screen out most with voice mail. If I know what it's about, I'll call back." The clear preference was for calls that had value. "Say that you're following up. Announce the call in the invitation. Be helpful." "Make sure that you're inviting, not selling." "Set up a time to discuss the issues."

The above examples point out the essential truth about IDM creative: let the customer determine the content of your program. After all, they know their needs. They know their media preferences. And they are quite willing to tell you about them. An IDM campaign is not a creative guessing game.

Setting the Objectives

Ramona Anton, IBM's Health Segment Manager, headed up the IBM sales team. "The main issue from our point of view was: How do we get the customer to understand that we have a knowledgeable, experienced team in place with responsibility for the customer's well-being? We wanted to clear up a lot of misunderstandings and send a clear message that we were committed to the medical marketplace. In the process, we would create a happier customer and, not insignificantly, more sales."

The IDM program objectives that came out of the research were:

- to position IBM and business partners as the value-added information resource for medical practices of three to forty-nine physicians
- to generate a significant increase in quality and quantity of leads

The strategy to carry out these objectives was based on introducing the "IBM Medical Management Team." The Team personalized IBM and demonstrated that IBM and IBM's business partners are a cohesive, value-added resource for the office/practice manager facing the challenges of managing information flow within the practice.

Business partner technical and industry strengths could be applied to actionable solutions under IBM's umbrella of corporate strength and stability. The Medical Management Team could provide total information management solutions—not just discrete hardware and software elements.

Since the task of migrating from commodity vendor to value-added partner is a formidable one, the strategy was implemented as a two-phase program (see Exhibit 4-1):

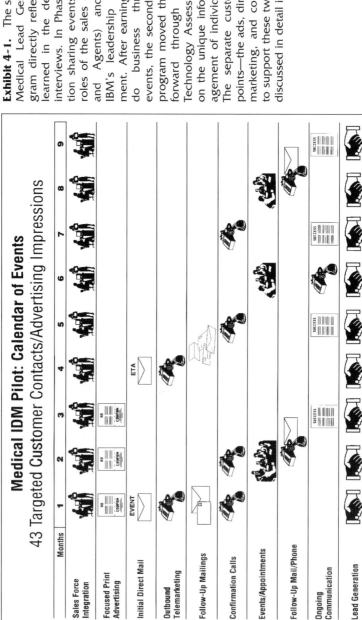

Medical IDM Pilot: Calendar of Events

43 Targeted Customer Contacts/Advertising Impressions

Months	1	2	3	4	5	6	7	8	9
Sales Force Integration									
Focused Print Advertising									
Initial Direct Mail									
Outbound Telemarketing									
Follow-Up Mailings									
Confirmation Calls									
Events/Appointments									
Follow-Up Mail/Phone									
Ongoing Communication									
Lead Generation									

Exhibit 4-1. The structure of the Medical Lead Generation Program directly reflects what was learned in the depth research interviews. In Phase 1, information sharing events clarified the roles of the sales contacts (IBM and Agents) and established IBM's leadership and commitment. After earning the right to do business through these events, the second phase of the program moved the relationship forward through an Evolving Technology Assessment focused on the unique information management of individual practices. The separate customer contact points—the ads, direct mail, telemarketing, and communications to support these two events—are discussed in detail in this chapter.

- The first phase aimed to establish the IBM Medical Management Team as a valuable resource by sponsoring a series of information-sharing events.
- The second phase sought to build relationships through needs analysis and consultative advice. This would provide useful information about the customer's specific applications and would position the IBM representative as a trusted source of information systems knowledge.

The Content of the Program

Phase I: Executive Forums.   Customers, through research, advised IBM to take a leadership role and visibly demonstrate commitment to the market. To respond to that need, IBM instituted Medical Management Executive Forums as Phase 1 of the program. Sponsored by IBM, the forums were held in various cities and focused on information that customers needed (again based on the research). By aligning itself with medical industry experts, IBM could begin to establish commitment to the market and the credibility of the Medical Management Team.

It's important to stress that the content of the forums was developed based not on what IBM wanted to sell but rather on what the office/practice managers wanted to know.

Advertising.   Ads in medical management journals announced the information-oriented events and invited the reader to the forums. Copy was straightforward, laying out the value to be gained by attending: ". . . you will get an inside view of healthcare reform, examine changing technology needs and discuss critical issues that face medical practices in the '90s." Specific details in the ad were drawn directly from what customers told us they needed: how to process billings and payments more quickly, improve collections, and streamline operations.

The IBM Medical Management Team was introduced in the headline and explained in the text: "IBM and IBM's Business Partners, who understand your business needs, will be there to demonstrate their medical management application solution for you."

The opportunity to network with peers was an added value to attendance at the seminar: ". . . you'll also have the opportunity to share valuable insights with colleagues."

And as in all good direct-response ads, the reader was asked to respond by registering or asking for more information.

Even the media placements were driven by the depth research interviews. During the research, office/practice managers were asked which magazines were read. As a result, the media buy could be greatly reduced in quantity but upgraded in quality. Because of this and other efficiencies in production, the advertising budget was one fourth of the previous year's budget yet generated an increase in qualified leads (see Exhibit 4-2).

A special invitation to medical practice executives from the IBM Medical Management Team.

The IBM Medical Management Team invites you to participate in the Medical Practice Executive Forum. At this special event, you will get an inside view of healthcare reform, examine changing technology needs and discuss critical issues that face medical practices in the 90s.

This important seminar will show you how to process billings and payments more quickly, improve collections and streamline operations. IBM and IBM's Business Partners, who understand your business needs, will be there to demonstrate their medical management application solutions for you. And you'll also have a chance to share valuable insights with colleagues.

It's an opportunity no medical practice executive should miss.

Attendance is limited, and there is no cost to you. Call 1-800-775-4426 today to reserve your place or complete the registration card below.

THE MEDICAL PRACTICE EXECUTIVE FORUM

Scheduled Executive Forums:
Detroit, MI (5/12), Cincinnati, OH (5/19), Columbus, OH (5/26), Erie, PA (6/2), Cleveland, OH (6/9)

Medical Practice Executive Forum Registration Card

(Cut along dotted line)

Name _____ Title _____

Practice Name _____

Address _____ Phone _____

City _____ State _____ Zip _____

Send or fax to:
IBM Medical Practice
Executive Forum
Bond Court Bldg.
1300 East Ninth St.
Cleveland, OH 44144
fax 1-800-944-1248

City and date I will be attending: ☐ Detroit, MI (5/12) ☐ Cincinnati, OH (5/19) ☐ Columbus, OH (5/26) ☐ Erie, PA (6/2) ☐ Cleveland, OH (6/9)
I would like to bring the following colleague(s):
Name(s) _____ Title _____ Phone _____
I have immediate needs. Please have a member of the IBM Medical Management Team contact me regarding: _____

Call 1-800-775-4426 to reserve your place, today.

Exhibit 4-2. Information-based ads stressed the value of IBM's Medical Practice Executive Forums with copy points that were directly linked to what customers and prospects said in the depth research interviews.

Direct Mail. Phase 1 direct mail consisted of a personal invitation to the Forums, a letter from IBM's Health Segment Manager, Ramona Anton, an agenda, a registration card, and Anton's business card.

By having the creative team involved in the depth research interview process, the copy and content of the invitation flowed directly from the needs expressed. Everything in the communication to the customer addressed some aspect of the needs, preferences, and wants of the target audience.

For example, IBM had been avoiding the use of the logo on previous mailings, believing that the logo might not mean much to this particular audience. However, when we tested various creative approaches as part of depth interviews, the response was quite the opposite. In fact, the office/practice manager wanted to know what IBM had to say about their business. The IBM logo, in fact, would differentiate the invitation from "junk mail." Comments such as "Use the IBM logo. I would read it. I rarely get anything from IBM" led to a design that featured the IBM logo on the envelope and throughout the package.

The look was consistent with a formal invitation—quality paper, clear and formal tone, no hard sell, just helpful information. Again, this approach came straight out of the depth research interviews.

Since the research showed that customers wanted commitment from IBM, the letters were straightforward, personal and with a clear focus on providing value to medical practices. The letters introduced the Medical Management Team by name, explained the value of attending the Forums, and stressed a personal tone—"You are invited . . ." "My name is . . ." "We brought all this together for you . . ." "The Medical Management Team, dedicated to responding personally to medical executives like you . . ." "We want you to have our names and phone numbers . . ." "Let me introduce the team . . ."

The topics that the Forums covered were the ones identified as important through the depth research interviews. The letter emphasized the relevance of the topics by stating that, "At the Forum, leading experts will speak with you about healthcare reform, changing technology and other critical issues" and, "You'll also have the opportunity to participate in breakout sessions to discuss important topics such as: coding changes, managed care, how to process billing and payments more quickly, improve collections . . ." and other clearly identified topics.

The link between Business Partner expertise was also clearly established: ". . . many of IBM's Business Partners, including . . . will demonstrate their medical application solutions from 9 AM to 5 PM" (see Exhibits 4-5 and 4-7).

Telephone Follow-Up. Twenty-four to seventy-two hours after the receipt of the letter, the office/practice manager received a telephone call from the IBM telemarketing sales representative. The purpose of the call was to answer questions and encourage attendance at the forums. The telephone script was carefully constructed to include qualifying questions as determined by the field. Remember, since the field is following up on the leads, it's important to get their input on what is a qualified lead.

Exhibits 4-3 and 4-4. The logo on the envelope (top) and an R.S.V.P. sent the message that this was an event with potential value to their business. The invitation (bottom) began the "personalization" of the message.

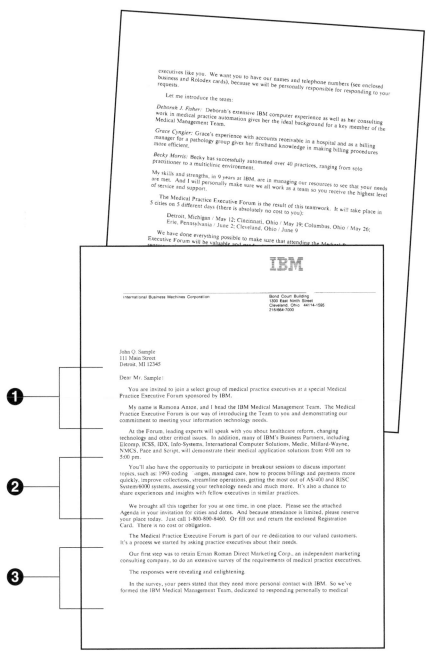

Exhibits 4-5, 4-6, 4-7, 4-8. The business card provided a way for customers to communicate with IBM and demonstrated IBM's dedication to the market. An agenda provided precise information on how the Forum would be useful. The registration card provided a convenient way to respond. The invitation package was designed to provide detailed information and build on the awareness generated by the ad.

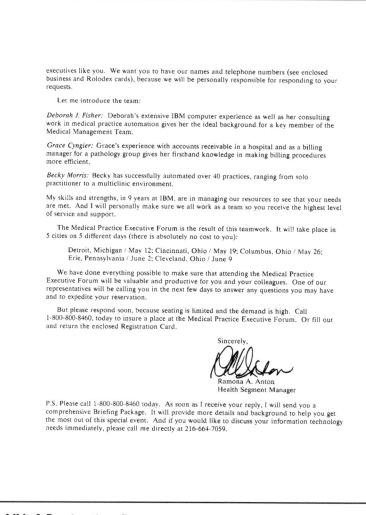

executives like you. We want you to have our names and telephone numbers (see enclosed business and Rolodex cards), because we will be personally responsible for responding to your requests.

Let me introduce the team:

Deborah J. Fisher: Deborah's extensive IBM computer experience as well as her consulting work in medical practice automation gives her the ideal background for a key member of the Medical Management Team.

Grace Cyngier: Grace's experience with accounts receivable in a hospital and as a billing manager for a pathology group gives her firsthand knowledge in making billing procedures more efficient.

Becky Morris: Becky has successfully automated over 40 practices, ranging from solo practitioner to a multiclinic environment.

My skills and strengths, in 9 years at IBM, are in managing our resources to see that your needs are met. And I will personally make sure we all work as a team so you receive the highest level of service and support.

The Medical Practice Executive Forum is the result of this teamwork. It will take place in 5 cities on 5 different days (there is absolutely no cost to you):

> Detroit, Michigan / May 12; Cincinnati, Ohio / May 19; Columbus, Ohio / May 26; Erie, Pennsylvania / June 2; Cleveland, Ohio / June 9

We have done everything possible to make sure that attending the Medical Practice Executive Forum will be valuable and productive for you and your colleagues. One of our representatives will be calling you in the next few days to answer any questions you may have and to expedite your reservation.

But please respond soon, because seating is limited and the demand is high. Call 1-800-800-8460, today to insure a place at the Medical Practice Executive Forum. Or fill out and return the enclosed Registration Card.

Sincerely,

Ramona A. Anton
Health Segment Manager

P.S. Please call 1-800-800-8460 today. As soon as I receive your reply, I will send you a comprehensive Briefing Package. It will provide more details and background to help you get the most out of this special event. And if you would like to discuss your information technology needs immediately, please call me directly at 216-664-7059.

Exhibit 4-5.   *(continued)*

Exhibit 4-6.

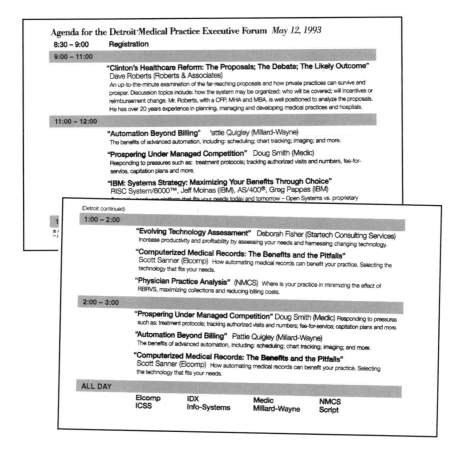

Exhibit 4-7.

The Medical Practice Executive Forum *Registration Card*

THE MEDICAL
PRACTICE
EXECUTIVE
FORUM

John Q. Sample
President
111 Main Street
Detroit, MI 12345

I will be attending the Forum at the following city and date:
☐ Detroit, MI (5/12) ☐ Cincinnati, OH (5/19) ☐ Columbus, OH (5/26)
☐ Erie, PA (6/2) ☐ Cleveland, OH (6/9)

I would like to bring the following colleagues:

Name	Title	Phone
Name	Title	Phone
Name	Title	Phone

Send or fax to:
IBM
Medical Practice
Executive Forum
Bond Court Building
1300 East Ninth Street
Cleveland, OH
44114-9564

fax 1-800-477-8370

I would like to discuss my information technology needs immediately. Please have a member of the Medical Management Team contact me regarding:

IBM

Call 1-800-800-8460 today to reserve your place.

Exhibit 4-8.

The telemarketing script was written to avoid any hint of hard sell. Telemarketers were trained to be polite, professional and well-informed about the event. Following is an excerpt of the script:

Intended Contact Introduction

02. Good morning/afternoon. This is _____. I'm calling to invite you to the IBM Medical Practice Executive Forum on May 12, in Detroit. You may have received your invitation in the mail. This is an important event for medical practice managers, billing and support staff and interested physicians.

May I help by taking your reservation now? (Pause - if no response, go to Q & A #1)

1.	Yes	To reservation script
2.	No - not interested	To 03
3.	Have questions	To Q & A
4.	Already made a reservation	To reservation script
5.	Did not receive the invitation	To 10
Z.	End call	To End

05. The Forum will introduce you and your colleagues to new technologies to show you how to process billings and payments more quickly, improve collections and streamline operations. Many of IBM's Business Partners will be there to demonstrate their medical management solutions for you. I believe you could benefit from attending.

If it's more convenient, there are other dates and locations you could attend.

Detroit, May 12
Cincinnati, May 19
Columbus, May 26
Erie, June 2
Cleveland, June 9

Would you like me to make a reservation for you?

If the conversation took place with an assistant, the telemarketer had specific text to cover that situation.

Switchboard Introduction

01. Good morning/afternoon. This is _____ calling. I would like to speak to _____ please.

If needed: What is this in regards to?
             I'm calling to invite _____ to the upcoming Medical Management Executive Forum.

The IBM Medical Management Team has assembled leading experts to speak about healthcare reform, changing technologies and other critical issues. In addition, many of IBM's Business Partners will demonstrate their medical application solutions. Those attending will have the opportunity to participate in breakout sessions to discuss a variety of topics.

May I speak with _____?

If needed: Who are you?
             My name is _____. I'm calling on behalf of the Medical Management Team.

If the invitation had not been received, we needed to know if there was a problem in the mailing list. The script requested information to verify key recipient information that was then forwarded to the database for updating.

10. I'm sorry; let me verify your mailing address.

If correct: You should be receiving your invitation today or tomorrow. May I briefly describe the Forum to you and explain how your practice can benefit by you attending?

If incorrect: (Capture the correct address) May I describe the Forum to you and explain how your practice can benefit by you attending?

If requesting a fax:
        (fax only 2-3 days prior to event)

If the prospect was not interested, a second level of the offer provided more detailed information.

07. Could your practice benefit from examining new medical management application solutions designed to process billings and payments more quickly, improve collections and streamline operations? If so, I'd be happy to make a reservation for you.

    1. Have question   To Q & A
    2. Yes - want a reservation   To reservation script
    3. No - not attending   To close script
    4. Not certain if attending   To 11

    Z. End call   To End

08. There are several dates and locations to choose from, such as:
        Detroit, May 12
        Cincinnati, May 19
        Columbus, May 26
        Erie, June 2
        Cleveland, June 9

Can I make you a reservation at one of these events?

    1. Have question   To Q & A
    2. Yes - want a reservation   To reservation script
    3. No - not attending   To close script
    4. Not certain if attending   To 11

    Z. End call   To End

A separate section of the script addressed specific qualifying questions that were developed by working closely with the field. The questions were asked of both nonregistrants and registrants, and always with the customer/prospects' permission.

<u>Attendees</u>

01. I would like to provide IBM with basic information regarding your requirements so they can address your needs at the Forum. What is the major issue facing your practice as you evaluate new technology?

<u>Non-Attendees:</u>

01. I would like to ask you a few questions to provide IBM with some basic background on your practice. What is the major issue facing your practice as you evaluate new technology?

1.	Billing and collections	To 03
2.	Patient scheduling	To 03
3.	Chart tracking	To 03
4.	On-line interface to hospital systems	To 03
5.	Computerized medical records	To 03
6.	Record imaging	To 03
7.	Other	To 02
Y.	Unknown/refused	To 03
Z.	End call	To End

02. Describe other   To 03

_____

_____

03. Is your practice computerized?

1.	Yes	To 04
2.	No	To 08
Y.	Unknown/refused	To 09
Z.	End call	To End

04. What is the primary software package you use for your office
applications, such as accounts receivable and scheduling?
                                                            To 05

_____

05. TSR if Service Bureau: When was the contract signed?
    TSR if Software: When was this software installed?

1.	5 years ago or more	To 06
2.	4 years ago	To 06
3.	3 years ago	To 06
4.	Within the last 3 years	To 06
Y.	Unknown/refused	To 06
Z.	End call	To End

06. When was your hardware installed, was it at the same time?

1.	5 years ago or more	To 07
2.	4 years ago	To 07
3.	3 years ago	To 07
4.	Within the last 3 years	To 07
Y.	Unknown/refused	To 07
Z.	End call	To End

07. How satisfied are you with this solution?

1.	Very dissatisfied	To 08
2.	Dissatisfied	To 08
3.	Satisfied	To 08
4.	Very satisfied	To 08
Y.	Unknown/refused	To 08
Z.	End call	To End

08. Is your practice considering new automation?
    1. Yes   To 09
    2. No   To 12
    Y. Unknown/refused   To 09
    Z. End call   To End

09. Why is your practice considering new automation?
    1. Practice is outgrowing the system/current methods   To 11
    2. Want to automate/automate other applications   To 11
    3. Service/reliability problems   To 11
    4. Other   To 10
    Y. Unknown/refused   To 11
    Z. End call   To End

10. Describe other
    _____ To 05

11. We'd like to understand where you are in the decision-making process. Would you say you are:
    1. Actively looking for a system now   To 12
    2. Gathering information on available software
       applications   To 12
    3. Beginning stages of information gathering   To 12
    4. Beginning stages/not yet started looking for
       information   To 12
    Y. Unknown/refused   To 12
    Z. End call   To End

12. Would you like to have IBM perform an evolving technology assessment to help you plan for increased productivity and profitability by taking advantage of new and proven technology?
    1. Yes   To 13
    2. No   To 13
    Y. Unknown/refused   To 13
    Z. End call   To End

13. Would you like an IBM Marketing Representative to visit you at your practice?
    1. Yes - within 10 days   Return to script
    2. Yes - within 4-8 weeks   Return to script
    3. Yes - in 3 months or more   Return to script
    4. Not ready to meet with rep   Return to script
    5. Not interested   Return to script
    Y. Unknown/refused   Return to script
    Z. End call   To End

Confirmation Card. Within 48 hours of the call, all attendees were sent a confirmation card to confirm information and reinforce the decision (see Exhibit 4-9). Again, the card followed the tone and look of the campaign.

This type of personalized response leveraged the previous efforts by continuing to demonstrate an awareness of and dedication to the needs of the prospect. Each step showed that IBM was paying attention to the medical market.

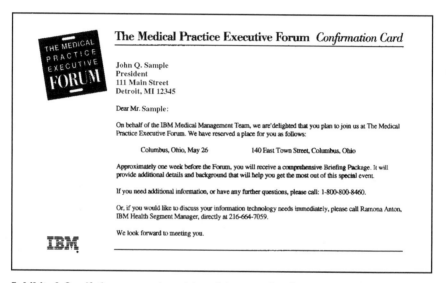

The Medical Practice Executive Forum *Confirmation Card*

John Q. Sample
President
111 Main Street
Detroit, MI 12345

Dear Mr. Sample:

On behalf of the IBM Medical Management Team, we are'delighted that you plan to join us at The Medical Practice Executive Forum. We have reserved a place for you as follows:

Columbus, Ohio, May 26   140 East Town Street, Columbus, Ohio

Approximately one week before the Forum, you will receive a comprehensive Briefing Package. It will provide additional details and background that will help you get the most out of this special event.

If you need additional information, or have any further questions, please call: 1-800-800-8460.

Or, if you would like to discuss your information technology needs immediately, please call Ramona Anton, IBM Health Segment Manager, directly at 216-664-7059.

We look forward to meeting you.

IBM

Exhibit 4-9. If the prospect registered to attend a forum, a confirmation card arrived soon after the telemarketing call. The quick response signaled IBM's interest and confirmed the prospect's decision.

Attendee Briefing Package. All attendees received a package of materials within a few days of the confirmation card. Each briefing package was personalized to the attendee, with a letter from the IBM Health Segment Manager.

The letter reconfirmed attendance and provided additional useful information and reinforced the value of the event. To keep an open path of communication, the letter included not only an 800 number for general event-oriented questions, but a direct telephone number for the Health Segment Manager which could be used to address practice-related information technology issues (see Exhibit 4-10).

Pre-Event Confirmation Calls. One week prior to the Forum, attendees received a confirmation call to make sure that the briefing package had been received, to answer any questions, and to reconfirm attendance. Then, a few days prior to the Forum, attendees received a second confirmation call to verify attendance or handle any last-minute concerns.

Exhibit 4-10. The briefing package included a personalized "welcome" letter (from the IBM manager), a full agenda for the specific forum that the prospect was attending, directions to the forum, biographies of the IBM Medical Management Team, descriptions of the main speech and the breakout session, speaker biographies, IBM business partner biographies and questions to consider to get more out of the forums. All the materials were developed to maximize the value of attending the Forums.

All contacts were designed to build and enhance previous and future contacts. Timing them closely maximized the impact, and making sure that the message had relevance meant that the contact was perceived as valuable to the customer.

In addition, each communication was designed to obtain more information about the customer's needs and interests. This information became part of the database and was used to refine the message in subsequent mailings as well as provide valuable information to the sales force.

Phase 2.   Phase 2 introduced the Evolving Technology Assessment. This was a personalized process to help the office/practice manager analyze the business needs of the practice and evaluate the options.

The sequence of events was similar to Phase 1 and consisted of precisely timed direct mail, outbound telemarketing, follow-up mailings, and confirmation calls.

The direct mail consisted of a personal letter from the IBM Manager (Exhibit 4-11) and a brochure to introduce the Evolving Technology Assessment (Exhibit 4-12). The copy stressed the value of the technology assessment. The headline: "Is your office's business practice as good as its medical practice? We can help you ensure the answer is yes."

Outbound Telemarketing.   The mailing was followed up within 24 to 72 hours with a telephone call to provide additional information, answer any questions, and set up appointments to complete the Evolving Technology Assessment. The assessment would then serve as a basis for a recommendation addressing the most pressing business concerns of the practice. The recommendation would draw from the full expertise of the Medical Management Team—IBM and business partners.

Confirmation calls were made a few days prior to the scheduled meeting to handle any last-minute concerns and reconfirm participation.

Customer Satisfaction Survey.   Testing reactions and obtaining information was an important principle of the IDM program. The Evolving Technology Assessment was followed up with a "thank you" letter and a customer satisfaction survey.

The letter stressed the relationship and the importance of the customer's comments in helping IBM better serve the medical market. Again, the letter stressed the value of the Medical Management Team and the accessibility of the team to provide "advice and counsel." Remember that the goal here is partnership and relationship building, not a single sale or a "one-shot" meeting (see Exhibit 4-13).

The customer satisfaction survey (Exhibit 4-14) had a clean, professional look that was easy to follow and fill out. Personalization at the top sent the message that "Your opinion counts," again, strengthening the idea that IBM is committed to providing value to the medical practice market.

The creative strategy of personalized engagement had significantly improved the office/practice manager's perception of IBM—and the perception of value of the IBM team. Similarly, the message and the delivery medium for the message were ranked high in meeting the customer's needs.

Our first step in developing this process was to ask medical practice executives like yourself about their needs via an extensive research project. Many told us that they needed more
personal contact with IBM, which led to the formation of the IBM Medical Management Team.

In addition to myself, the team consists of Deborah J. Fisher, Grace Cyngier and Becky
Morris. All of us have extensive experience with implementing and upgrading medical
applications and information technology.

You may recall our second step: we sent you an invitation to a special Medical Practice
Executive Forum sponsored by IBM. The Forum featured presentations on healthcare reform,
changing technology and other critical issues. It was scheduled for five cities in May and June:
Detroit, Michigan, Cincinnati, Columbus and Cleveland, Ohio, and Erie, Pennsylvania.

Attendance for the sessions has been outstanding. We've received positive comments from
medical Practice Managers and doctors.

The next logical step: the Evolving Technology Assessment.

Whether your needs are for better billing procedures to handle insurance payments, better
scheduling of patients, better control of cash flow - or other possible business requirements -
the Evolving Technology Assessment process can help you define solutions.

We're placing our broad range of medical practice business resources at your command.
In exchange, we are asking that you take time from your busy sched...
your needs. If your practice is looking for m...
you will find it to h...

understand
tly, we think

ient time
he enclosed

peak with

IBM

International Business Machines Corporation   Bond Court Building
                                                   1300 East Ninth Street
                                                   Cleveland, Ohio 44114-1595
                                                   216/664-7000

John Q. Sample
ERDM
111 Main Street
Detroit, MI 12345

Dear Mr. Sample:

g
s who

> As part of our rededication to serving the needs of medical practices, we have recently
> completed research with practices in your area regarding their critical business requirements.
> Practice Managers have identified these key areas:
>
> • Billing/information exchange between practices,
>   patients and insurers
> • Scheduling
> • Planning for future growth
> • Patient care
>
> If any of these issues is important to you, I'd like to ask you to make an investment
> towards handling each of these key areas more effectively. It's not an investment of money.
>
> Instead, I'm asking that you make an appointment to spend one hour or less completing
> the enclosed Practice Profile with our IBM Medical Management Team representative.
>
> This Practice Profile is our first step in working with you to complete an Evolving
> Technology Assessment specifically for your practice.

We've created the Evolving Technology Assessment process based on research regarding
the requirements of Practice Managers for value-added information about the business side
of the practice. The Evolving Technology Assessment is a three-phased process designed to
identify how new and proven information technology can support you in better addressing
critical concerns such as billing, scheduling and patient care:

Phase One: Together, we complete the enclosed Practice Profile identifying
your critical business concerns.

Phase Two: Our IBM Medical Management Team analyzes your Practice Profile
and provides a list of possible application solutions to satisfy your requirements.

Phase Three: You choose the solutions that are best for your practice, when and
if you need them.

This Evolving Technology Assessment process is the result of our commitment to better
serving the needs of medical practices.

(over, please)

Exhibit 4-11. The letter accompanying the brochure was anything but hard sell.
It made it clear that the choice of systems was in the hands of the customer, but
that the IBM team was there to help.

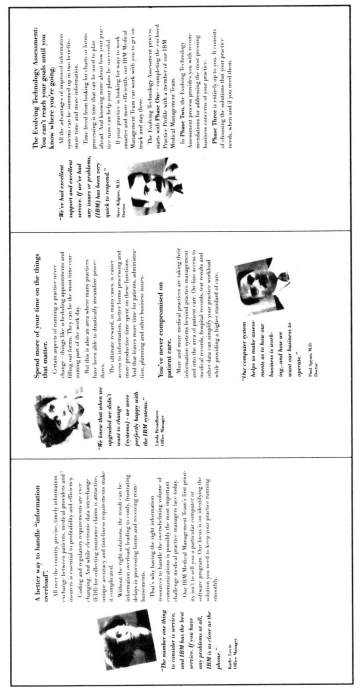

A better way to handle "information overload".

All over the country, precise, timely information exchange between patients, medical providers and insurers is essential to profitability and efficiency.

Coding and regulatory requirements are ever changing. And while electronic data interchange (EDI) for collecting insurance claims is attractive, unique accuracy and timeliness requirements make it complicated.

Without the right solutions, the result can be information overload, leading to costly, frustrating delays in processing forms and receiving reimbursements.

That's why having the right information resources to handle the overwhelming volume of communications is possibly the most important challenge medical practice managers face today.

Our IBM Medical Management Team's first priority isn't to sell you a particular computer or software program. Our focus is on identifying the solution you need to keep your practice running smoothly.

"The number one thing to consider is service, and IBM has the best service. If you have any problems at all, IBM is as close as the phone."

Kathy Lavin
Office Manager

Spend more of your time on the things that matter.

Certain aspects of running a practice never change - things like scheduling appointments and filling out forms. They can be the most time-consuming part of the work day.

But this is also an area where many practices have been able to drastically streamline procedures.

The ultimate reward, in many cases, is easier access to information, better forms processing and more productive time spent on these functions. And that leaves more time for patients, administration, planning and other business issues.

"We knew that when we upgraded we didn't want to change (systems) - we were perfectly happy with the IBM systems."

Linda Broadhurst
Office Manager

You've never compromised on patient care.

More and more medical practices are taking their information systems beyond practice management and into the area of patient care. On-line access to medical records, hospital records, test results and other data can simplify your practice workload while providing a higher standard of care.

"Our computer system helps us make assessments as to how our business is working—and how we want our business to operate."

Paul Apyan, M.D.
Doctor

The Evolving Technology Assessment: You can't reach your goals until you know where you're going.

All the advantages of improved information systems can be summed up in two benefits: more time and more information.

Time freed from looking for charts or forms processing is time that can be used to plan ahead. And knowing more about how your practice runs can help your plans be successful.

If your practice is looking for ways to work smarter and more efficiently, our IBM Medical Management Team can work with you to get on track and stay there.

The Evolving Technology Assessment process starts with **Phase One** - completing the enclosed Practice Profile with a member of our IBM Medical Management Team.

In **Phase Two**, the Evolving Technology Assessment process provides you with recommendations for addressing the most pressing business concerns of your practice.

Phase Three is entirely up to you. It consists of choosing the solutions that your practice needs, when and if you need them.

"We've had excellent support and excellent service. If we've had any issues or problems, (IBM) has been very quick to respond."

Steve Kilgore, M.D.
Doctor

Exhibit 4-12. Testimonials from people in the same business (with names and pictures to make it even more real) provided credibility. Photos of the Medical Management team put a human face to IBM and reinforced the idea of "We're here to help."

97

IBM

International Business Machines Corporation   1300 East Ninth Street
                                                              Cleveland, Ohio 44114-1595

John Q. Sample
John Sample Direct Marketing
111 Main Street
Detroit, MI 12345

Dear Mr. Sample:

Thank you!

For us, the hallmark of 1993 has been IBM's rededication to medical practices and the
formation of the IBM Medical Management Team.

The IBM Medical Management Executive Forums, which took place during May and
June, and the Evolving Technology Assessment, which was offered to you during July and
August, were developed based on research conducted with your peers. The response from
the medical community has been gratifying.

We'd like to hear from you. We'd like to know what you thought of these programs and
what your opinions are regarding IBM and the Medical Management Team.

To help us continue to improve the service we offer you, would you please complete the
enclosed Customer Satisfaction Survey and return it to us in the postage paid envelope
provided. The survey is part of our ongoing commitment to providing you with
unparalleled assistance regarding information technology. I assure you, your voice
will be heard.

On behalf of the Medical Management Team - thank you in advance. And thanks also for
the warm response to the Forums and Evolving Technology Assessment efforts. We look
forward to receiving your survey, and to working with you in the future as we implement
additional programs for medical practices in 1994.

Sincerely,

Ramona A. Anton

Ramona A. Anton
Health Segment Manager

P.S. Of course, if you have information technology needs which are immediate, please call
me directly at 216 664-7059.

Exhibit 4-13.

Precise Implementation of a Carefully Developed Creative Strategy

"IDM brought a very important quality control element to the process,"
according to Ramona Anton. "It's more than the cookbook approach of 'you
talk to your customers, evaluate what they say, develop your direct mail and

---

Customer Satisfaction Survey

Ernan Roman
Ernan Roman Direct Marketing
3 Melrose Lane
Douglas Manor, NY 11363

Please correct your name and address, as appropriate.

I. Events and Promotions

Please give your evaluation of the importance of, and your satisfaction with, the following attributes of IBM's events and promotions. Your suggestions for improvement would be greatly appreciated.

Evolving Technology Assessment

Did you take part in IBM's Evolving Technology Assessment?

	Importance	Satisfaction

If not, why not? (Your comments and suggestions for improvement would be greatly appreciated)

Importance	Satisfaction
□⁵ Extremely Important	□⁵ Very Satisfied
□⁴ Important	□⁴ Satisfied
□³ Somewhat Important	□³ Neutral
□² Marginally Important	□² Dissatisfied
□¹ Not Important At All	□¹ Very Dissatisfied
□⁰ No Opinion/Don't Know	□⁰ No Opinion/Don't Know

Relevancy to you and your practice's needs.

Importance	Satisfaction
□⁵ Extremely Important	□⁵ Very Satisfied
□⁴ Important	□⁴ Satisfied
□³ Somewhat Important	□³ Neutral
□² Marginally Important	□² Dissatisfied
□¹ Not Important At All	□¹ Very Dissatisfied
□⁰ No Opinion/Don't Know	□⁰ No Opinion/Don't Know

Provided meaningful information, counsel and advice.

Importance	Satisfaction
□⁵ Extremely Important	□⁵ Very Satisfied
□⁴ Important	□⁴ Satisfied
□³ Somewhat Important	□³ Neutral
□² Marginally Important	□² Dissatisfied
□¹ Not Important At All	□¹ Very Dissatisfied
□⁰ No Opinion/Don't Know	□⁰ No Opinion/Don't Know

Medical Management Executive Forums

Did you attend?

If not, why not? (Your comments and suggestions for improvement would be greatly appreciated)

Importance	Satisfaction
□⁵ Extremely Important	□⁵ Very Satisfied
□⁴ Important	□⁴ Satisfied
□³ Somewhat Important	□³ Neutral
□² Marginally Important	□² Dissatisfied
□¹ Not Important At All	□¹ Very Dissatisfied
□⁰ No Opinion/Don't Know	□⁰ No Opinion/Don't Know

Relevancy to you and your practice's needs.

Importance	Satisfaction
□⁵ Extremely Important	□⁵ Very Satisfied
□⁴ Important	□⁴ Satisfied
□³ Somewhat Important	□³ Neutral
□² Marginally Important	□² Dissatisfied
□¹ Not Important At All	□¹ Very Dissatisfied
□⁰ No Opinion/Don't Know	□⁰ No Opinion/Don't Know

1

Exhibit 4-14.

follow-up with a call.' Those are the repeatable steps that can be used with any industry, any campaign. But the quality control, the upfront research, the involvement of a truly cross-functional team and the ability to engage the customer across multiple media is uniquely IDM. It's the tight quality control over every customer contact point that sets the IDM creative process apart."

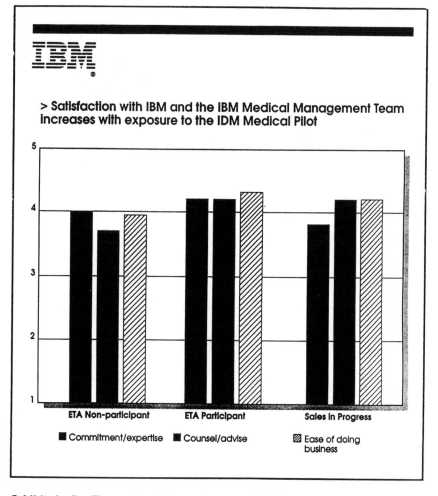

Exhibit 4-15. The results of the customer satisfaction survey showed a significant improvement from the attitudes expressed at the beginning of the program.

"The key to the IDM creative strategy was the structure of increasingly relevant messages. Every contact moved the relationship forward. This is what moved the customer from indifferent to interested to engaged," according to Curt Gillespie, IBM Business Unit Executive.

"The results attest to the success of the approach," adds Gillespie. "For the first phase—the Medical Management Executive Forums—we saw an 841 percent improvement in response over previous programs. We received more qualified inquiries for this initial phase than we had projected for the entire pilot with an increase in leads of more than 442 percent.

"The second phase showed equally satisfying results. The Evolving Technology Assessment had a response rate 127 percent greater than our very aggressive forecast. As a result of these activities, IBM is in qualified presale activity with 16 percent of the marketplace."

Summary

IBM approached its marketing challenge from a truly cross-functional perspective. Because sales and the third-party distribution channels were involved in the initial planning, the campaign was appropriately designed to strengthen their image with customers and, consequently, add value to the sales contact. In addition, the preliminary depth research clarified the role of doctor and office manager in the decision-making process and reshaped the entire focus of the communication effort to reach the *real* decision maker. By asking decision makers (the office/practice manager) what their interests were (rather than assuming interests), IBM was better able to provide real value—and create greater customer satisfaction.

EXAMPLE 2: USAA COMMUNICATES TO A CLOSED MARKET

A provider of financial services (investments, insurance, loans, credit cards, banking, etc.) to military officers and relatives of military officers, USAA is seen by many as a leader in managing customer relationships for the long-term—for life, in fact.

The creative principle linking all of USAA's communications is "life events." Dan Gibbens, Assistant VP of USAA Federal Savings Bank, puts it this way: "We've been around since 1922. But in the late '80s, we did an in-depth analysis of our membership. We found that our members went through certain lifecycle events that indicated needs for financial products."

USAA then built lifecycle plans focusing on the events that occurred in members' lives, not the products that USAA offered. "The philosophy is outlined in our guide to services," explains Gibbens (Exhibit 4-16). "It's pub-

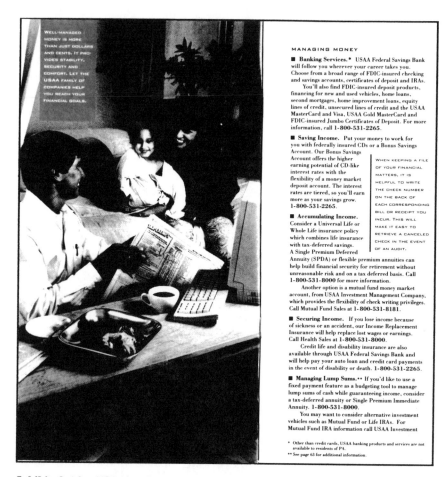

Exhibit 4-16. USAA's catalog provides an overview of the services but focuses on life events that signal a need for those services—a truly customer-focused approach.

lished every two years and focuses on life events—buying a home, getting married, educating kids, retirement—and how USAA can help. Our focus is not on any single account transaction but on the need that our members are experiencing. We try to deliver a comprehensive set of financial services and quality of life-related products that meet that need. More than 80 percent of our membership put the guide away like a telephone book and keep it for future reference."

The Member's Point of View

Two examples of how USAA orchestrates creative by focusing on life events are car ownership and home ownership.

Buying a Car. USAA uses bill inserts to describe available auto services. One example is a bang tail envelope with information about Auto Pricing Plus . . . "comprehensive pricing information which includes dealer invoice and manufacturer's suggested retail prices, vehicle specifications, dimensions, safety equipment lists and comparably priced vehicles." In addition, if the member requests information about automobile loans, insurance, or leasing, or if database information shows that the timing is right for a new car (e.g., a lease is up), the member will receive a listing of all the services USAA provides to "help you with your new vehicle." In all communications the emphasis is not on selling but on the value of the service to the member: "Let us take the typical dealership hassle out of acquiring a new car and make it fun again." An 800 number is prominently displayed to encourage response. However, response is up to the customer. USAA follows the principle that the member must initiate the sale.

As an additional service, before mailing out a requested Auto Pricing Plus kit, the respondent's credit is checked and, if the respondent is eligible, a pre-approved sight draft for an auto loan is included in the package.

Buying a Home. Research by USAA showed that 90 percent of mortgages were influenced by the realtor. So, the need was to communicate to the real estate agent who would then recommend USAA mortgages to eligible homebuyers.

The creative strategy was to partner with a relocation agent and begin communication with the member six months ahead of the move. The Mover's Advantage Program was developed to ease the transition from one home to another. The creative treatment positions the real-estate agent as a trusted partner, enhances the agent's credibility and encourages the agent to supply USAA mortgage information to the member.

Exhibit 4-17.

The program has been extremely successful, significantly growing USAA's share of mortgages within the first year.

MULTI-MEDIA IS THE MESSAGE

The creative key to IDM is synchronizing the contacts with the customer to maximize the communication. This does not mean bombarding the customer with repetitive messages. It does mean being aware of what message you are sending via which medium. As we discussed in Chapter 3, each medium has a specific role. Use the medium for what it does best and synchronize the media to laser-focus a cohesive message to the right customer at the right time.

Summary

USAA is an excellent example of the basic principles of IDM in action:

- Integrating the customer into the creative process
  The customer is not the target for USAA communications but is rather an integral part of the development process. As we've mentioned earlier, the process starts with precise questions to find out needs, preferences, and attitudes from the customer. Hearing customers voice their concerns can provide more creative direction than hundreds of pages of industry research.
- Integrating the message across multiple media
  USAA creative links the message from one medium to the next. Since the response is not discrete, but cumulative across all the media that are used, the developers of content for one medium need to know and communicate with the developers of content for other media. Each communication needs to build on the previous one and create a springboard for the next. This requires a strategy and a well thought-out plan before the first word goes on paper or the first photograph is taken.
- Precision control of implementation
  Since timing when prospects see which message is an integral part of a successful IDM strategy, deadlines and production time must be carefully monitored. Slippage in one area is bound to affect the overall impact.
- Integrating different functions into one team
  The creative team often includes different people with different specialties. Managing the team requires clear objectives up front and clear communication of those objectives across the entire creative team. In IDM, as in jazz, no matter what the improvisations are, the group has to be playing from the same score.

KEY POINTS

- The IDM creative process calls for the precision deployment of messages and multiple media to communicate a focused message tailored to customer needs.
- Depth research is the starting point for creative development.
- Include sales, marketing, and creative people in the development process. Let them hear customer's needs during depth research.
- Timing is critical. A suggested timeline for development of creative is included in Appendix A.
- Drawing on multiple functions strengthens the creative approach but requires careful management of "turf" issues.

POSTSCRIPT

Media Integration
Dan Majkowski
Americas Customer Marketing Manager
Hewlett-Packard

Media integration has been part of our marketing for years. One of the challenges we faced was that standard marketing theory focused on commodity products without factoring in the direct sales force. So we quickly ran into the problem of sales force integration—probably right after media integration.

Now, H-P is not a dictatorial company that says "thou shalt go and do this thing." Good ideas work through in their own time and, if they work, they survive. So it was with sales force integration. We started with cross-functional work teams called marketing councils that included top level sales managers, their direct reports and the marketing group. The team worked together to determine what had value to the sales force. We're not going to spend resources developing programs if the field sees no value in them. At the same time, the teams let the marketing group educate sales force management about the value of marketing tools—media integration, program vs. event, etc. The marketing council became a forum.

As we started to move into the national level of marketing, we started seeing some very strategic issues coming to the table. What role does the division—the product-generating entity—have in marketing? And how do we work together with manufacturing, engineering, field sales, and marketing?

We have always been a very technology-oriented company and proud of our world-class manufacturing. The divisions needed to take a very strong role in marketing their products, even though the technical marketer looks at marketing a little differently than a marketing specialist.

So that was another level of challenge: integrating the divisions and their field sales people into the marketing process. What we're doing is consistently and deliberately moving away from the traditional vertical orientation to one that's more horizontal. My firm belief is that marketing must work as one single platform across the company. Our challenge at H-P—as a technologically oriented company—is to integrate the highly competent and powerful operational and technology people into the marketing process.

The sales force really serves as our conduit to the market, providing information on customer needs and wants that then drives product design, engineering, and marketing. We've formalized this process by setting up sales-customer council meetings—essentially cross-functional teams with the customers—to discuss what customers expect from H-P. It has really been a breakthrough for us.

I think there's a two-part transition that accompanies any marketing change process that you want to implement:

1. Show people where you are going. That's the vision part. Articulate it as well as you can. But remember that people have to learn to live with shades of gray and frameworks, not perfectly completed structures—it's not black and white.
2. Know what your risks are. What happens if you do not change? This is often a fiscal scenario—profit margins, expense functions and the like.

Both parts are essential to encouraging people to move in the desired direction—one to show the advantages of the new; the other to show the consequences of staying status quo.

The major thing we've learned from the IDM process is that you have to be very focused on your objectives. Don't do things just because they feel good or you've always done them. We've achieved increased response rates and more leads. Why? Because IDM has taught us to set clear objectives, to deploy media and messages with precision, and to stringently measure results against the objectives. That's true integrated direct marketing. That's how you know whether you're succeeding.

POSTSCRIPT

The Role of Direct Media

Mitchell A. Orfuss
President, JWT Direct

For all the talk about the wisdom of "media integration," it remains the exception. For all sorts of organizational reasons revolving around power, turf, inertia, and fear of change, the integration of media is harder to achieve than it should be, and more necessary than ever. Integration is not equivalent to multi-media. The notion of multi-media has been with us for twenty years now, arguably for fifty. Integration is something newer: multi-media with strategic purpose, the product of zero-based, process-driven, target-driven, data-driven marketing.

What are "media" to the direct marketer? Media are markets where "value" is exchanged for (other) "value" through response. Media are points of sale—the same as shelf space and distribution in general marketing. Media persuade customers and prospects to talk back to companies that advertise, which helps them believe that large companies want them to be heard. Media hold out twin—and seemingly contradictory—promises of volume (reach many targeted consumers) and precision (with little or no waste). This is the art of the direct-response media professional. Media have environmental context that provides the content that advertisers slide through them. What kind of context? For example, we think of public relations as trustworthy, impartial, and informative, even before we are exposed to it. Good PR feels like reportage, so we tend to believe it. Television portrays "brand-ness"—the personality of a product, its long-term promise. Radio stands for local-ness, accessibility, and intimacy. Print aims to be informative and stimulating—halfway between the drama of television and the factualness of public relations. Direct mail has a different role: it precedes (and sometimes substitutes for) face-to-face selling, attempting to involve us for several minutes at a time and, through that involvement, elicit a direct response. Think of inbound telemarketing as a live, courteous, helpful, flexible, service-oriented ear—where the buck stops instantly; customers and prospects who call in seek satisfaction now—want it (whatever "it" is) handled during that call, by the person on the other end. Outbound telemarketing follows up. It goes where it's earned the privilege of going—by virtue of a relationship already established some other way, or a prior attempt to start a relationship. Outbound steps forward in the best light when a known customer needs to be cared for, or to follow up direct mail.

Horizontal and shallow a generation ago, media today are increasingly vertical and deep.

CHAPTER 5

Getting to Know You:
Customer Contact Management

*The more messages,
the more confused the customer gets.
Businesses spend a lot of money to create
dissatisfaction.*

Al Ries
Chairman, Trout & Ries

In previous chapters, we discussed how to integrate media and message. But we looked at it from the marketer's point of view. Let's now take a step back to look at your marketing efforts from the customer's point of view.

Put yourself in the customer's shoes for a few minutes: Imagine that you've just tried to increase your bank credit card limit and received a no. In the next mail, there's an offer for a home equity loan (directed to their most "valued" customers). In the same mail, there's also an offer (looking completely different than the home equity offer) for a credit card. That evening you get a call from the bank's telemarketing promoting a special Pay-by-Phone service. Are you likely to listen? To sign up?

Or, let's say you've just switched to a new long distance company. As a follow-up, you receive a "welcome" call to discuss additional services. Then a few days later, another person (from the same company) calls to welcome you (again) and offer additional services (again). How receptive do you think you'd be?

Or, imagine you've just bought an expensive car that's had a mechanical problem that the dealer hasn't been able to fix. While the dealer is diagnosing the problem (for the second time), you receive a customer satisfaction call from the manufacturer. When you raise the issue of the

109

mechanical problem, you're told that the telemarketer has no place on their screen to record a complaint like that. What's your satisfaction level at this point?

These are real examples. You've probably experienced something similar.

The problem lies not with the individual communications, but rather encompasses all the points of contact with the customer: ads, public relations, sales, etc. Al Ries, Chairman of Trout & Ries, a major advertising agency, describes the situation this way:

> Any time you send a message that diverges from your core message, you create confusion. Not only doesn't it help you, it can hurt you. Too many people in communications believe the more the merrier. The more you say, the more messages you have, the more programs you run, the more money you spend, the more successful you'll be. The truth is quite the contrary. I'm a real believer in the need to focus the message. One of the advantages of integrated direct marketing is that it keeps you from floating all these messages that are counterproductive.

Chapter 2 emphasized the importance of a dynamic, integrated database. But even though you can target the messages precisely, it's still important to look at the big picture and manage the impact of those messages on the receiver. How much are you really sending out to the customer? Are other products or departments within your own company competing for the customer's attention? Which are actually addressing needs and which are simply fishing expeditions? Consider what happens in the customers' minds when all your messages reach their target. Is there value that the customers can see in each of the contacts?

Even the best marketers can find themselves with a customer contact management problem. *The New York Times* (May 16, 1994) described the *Reader's Digest* database as "the largest private consumer database in the world. Seven days a week, 24 hours a day, the files . . . are updated with information about people who subscribe to *Reader's Digest* magazines, books, compact discs, cassettes and videos. . . . The database is its lifeblood."

Reader's Digest's database is the source for information to communicate with customers regularly and with precision—based on buying patterns, interests, etc. But, according to *The New York Times* article:

> A couple of years ago, the stream of special offers of various company products began to flow out of control because of a lack of coordination among the company's divisions.
>
> A *Reader's Digest* subscriber with an interest in travel, for instance, might receive offers for travel books, for a video about England and for a subscription to *Travel Holiday,* a company magazine.
>
> But the offers came too fast and many people found themselves with unwanted books, compact disks or videos because they had failed to return cards to the company indicating they did not want them.

(As a result), sales in the book and entertainment divisions began to slip, and word of the problems began to spread in the financial community. The company's stock, which traded as high as $56 a share in December 1992, fell to $38.875 by September 1993. The company said in May of 1993 that it would reduce promotional activity in the books and home entertainment businesses and make its mailings more selective.

The lesson here is that even integrated database marketing can develop into myopia. To succeed, you need to manage the contacts with customers and prospects from a much broader context—and from the customer's point of view.

CUSTOMER CONTACT MANAGEMENT: A DEFINITION

Customer Contact Management is a customer-driven coordination of communications to customers and prospects that can encourage immediate response and sales, as well as building long-term relationships and customer satisfaction. It means taking the longer-term view—investing in a relationship rather than trolling for an immediate sale.

Customer Contact Management builds from the same key question that forms the base of any IDM strategy: What are the customer's needs? These needs are then mapped against the different brands, the different lines of business, the different geographies, the different sales channels (direct and indirect), and the different media that touch the customer. The goal is to eliminate the B-52 "bomb 'em into submission" approach to the marketplace and instead take a high-level view to prioritize, sequence, and ration contacts so that the customer is not overwhelmed into inaction.

Consider, also, the unplanned contacts such as employees, signs on buildings, stores and delivery vehicles, wrapping, and even litter. These are also areas where you "touch" the customer. Consider the impact of these unplanned touches when preparing the "planned" contacts.

THE IMPACT ON PROFITABILITY

As depth research consistently demonstrates, the average person is bombarded with brochures, mailings, reports, and telephone calls. Messages from the same company are often fighting for the customer's time. The result—everyone loses. Messages blur. Customers shut out any and all communication. It becomes too much trouble to sort through the messages to see what has value and what doesn't. But it's not the customer's job to sort out the messages. If customers have to sort it out, chances are they throw it out. Call it option overload. Call it simple confusion. But it's a reaction that can cut into your profitability. And (here's the hard part) it's a reaction that marketers within all companies are spending money to create.

Managing customer contact across all communications that reach your customer eliminates the confusion and results in:

- Greater cost efficiency. Mailings and communications can be pared down so that you're sending the right message at the right time and eliminating wasted messages to people who are not potential buyers or who are receiving related messages from another part of your company.
- Greater customer satisfaction. Prospects and customers don't feel bombarded with contradictory messages and perceive your company as being more responsive to their needs.
- Improved message impact. Simplifying the communications points can clarify customer's understanding of what you can do for them. Multiple, conflicting messages can only muddy the waters.

According to Al Ries, "The biggest complaint customers have is the confusion factor. And that's directly linked to the multiplicity of messages people are receiving. Major corporations spend millions for mass communications. Yet you ask the typical customer, 'what's the company trying to sell you?' and most will say, 'I haven't the vaguest idea.' When you stand for everything, you stand for nothing."

GETTING THE MOST FOR YOUR MARKETING DOLLAR

The basic principles of contact management build on a process that catalog marketers have used for a long time to determine who are the best prospects to receive their catalog:

- Recency: How recently did the customer buy?
- Frequency: How frequently did the customer buy over a set period of time?
- Monetary value: What was the dollar value of the last purchase?

Customer Contact Management expands on that process. Use your research to determine:

- What has this customer bought in the past?
- What are customer's current needs, and how do these affect their buying behavior?
- What is the value of the customer to your organization?
- How can you coordinate your messages to enhance initial and ongoing profitability?

Once you have this information, you can orchestrate the communications so that the customers receive only those that have value to them. Customers and prospects see how you can meet their unique set of needs and requirements. They can see that you understand their business. And they have a positive impression of the company. By eliminating the messages that don't meet customer needs (i.e., timing, sequence, or content, which are not appropriate), you save yourself time and money and save the customer confusion and unnecessary overload.

RELATIONSHIPS INSTEAD OF "FISHING"

The customer contact management process is logical and designed to help you navigate the complex, interactive, and dynamic relationships that businesses have with their customers through:

- Respect for the customer's time, needs, and preferences
- Flexibility in communications to respond to evolving needs
- Trust built by providing value over the long term

The goal of customer contact management is to become more knowledgeable about your customer's and prospect's needs and to create a "virtual" closed market, concentrating on those businesses that present the best opportunities. The fishing expedition is a thing of the past. It wastes too many resources by sending out messages that get lost in the flurry of communications. And it rarely pays off enough to make it worth the expense.

As Mike Paterson, the recently retired Senior Vice President, USAA Marketing/Sales and Service, says about USAA, "We exist solely for the purpose of servicing our USAA members. This reflects the first axiom of relationship marketing—you can't have a meaningful relationship with everyone. So, as we say down in Texas, 'Pick your partner for the dance and stay with her for the whole affair.'" (See the USAA example later in this chapter.)

If the customer or prospect is not interested at this time, find out why. And then determine how to modify the process, the message, or the offer to improve it in order to better meet the customer's needs. If this prospect has extremely little likelihood of becoming a partner, you may want to say thanks for the dance, and turn your attention to more promising prospects.

APPLYING CUSTOMER CONTACT MANAGEMENT PRINCIPLES AT IBM

IBM has incorporated the principles of customer contact management as part of an IDM campaign to reposition itself with manufacturing businesses in one of the regions served by IBM sales reps, IBM business partners, and remarketers.

Yvonne Brandon, IBM Consulting Campaign Strategist, headed the IDM implementation team. According to Yvonne, "The core principles of IDM provided a structure to research the market. It meant letting customers tell us what they like and don't like. What gets their attention and what turns them off. What their environment is like, what their issues are and what messages encourage them to invest their company's money. We made the effort to focus on customers as people and not as checkbooks and contracts."

The problem, as determined through depth research, was that the manufacturing business contacts had been receiving multiple messages—some from IBM, some from the business partners, some from the remarketers. The result? A fragmented approach with much confusion about IBM's role and commitment to the marketplace. This created inaction and dissatisfaction in a market segment with great potential. Customer statements such as "Demonstrate that IBM has a team of resources rather than a very fragmented, subdivided company. The team must include real world business, industry-specific expertise," were typical. "Stay in front of me—I have time-sensitive needs. Too often I don't know what IBM has available and the window passes."

"Part of the problem," said Brandon, "was rooted in the fact that we had multiple databases that did not give us the information we needed. We knew we had to get beyond the 'glass house' and into the executive suite. And we needed to do it with a coordinated, 'one-company' approach."

Depth research provided the direction for developing a year-long plan to reach the market and establish a basis for continuing communication. Each contact with the customer was managed as part of an overall strategy of establishing IBM's credibility as a business resource—one that could see beyond the hardware and software to the business issues that kept these executives awake at night (see Exhibit 5-1).

The Business and Production Planning Program consisted of carefully orchestrated mailings and phone calls to provide information and encourage attendance at IBM-sponsored workshops. The workshops were structured to provide the expert information that research determined was important to customers.

According to Brandon:

> Having the customer tell us what gets their attention and which messages have an impact allowed us to communicate in a meaningful way with a population of decision-makers with whom we did not have any previous meaningful contact. This not only improved our response rates but allowed us to get the message to these people that we were more than a supplier of hardware.
>
> The results of the program have been extremely gratifying. Not only have we measurably improved customer satisfaction and favorably affected the impression of IBM as a valued partner to these industries, but we also wrote 1.4 million dollars of business in the first 90 days of the program with the accounts that responded. I don't want to imply that all that revenue was a direct result of the campaign, but it does tell us something important: We were in contact with the right audience. And we were in contact with them in the right way.

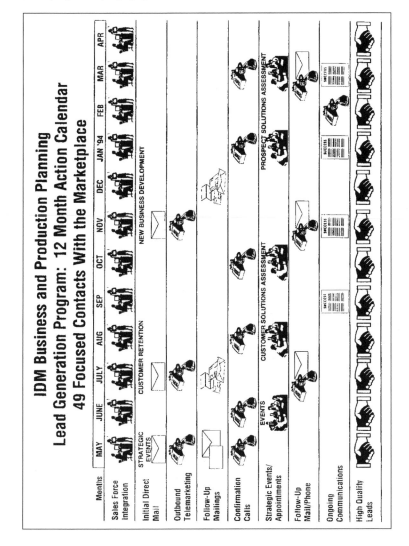

Exhibit 5-1. The sales force played a critical role in providing information about the audience and ensuring that personal follow-up calls were made to leads. Since these were high-level contacts, the commitment of the sales force during the events and during ongoing communications was key to success.

115

The Workshop begins at 10:00 am and runs to 4:00 pm. From 4:00 to 5:00 pm the presenters will gather at a Q&A Roundtable to field your questions and concerns. The enclosed brochure will tell you more about the day.

Please call 1 800 800-8460 now to reserve your place as our guest at this important event. If you prefer, please return, or fax (216 664-7995), the completed business reply card.

The concept of the Agile Organization involves all departments. Therefore, to gain the greatest benefit, cross-functional executive attendance is encouraged.

As soon as we receive your registration, we will send you a confirmation. And about a week before the Workshop, you will receive a comprehensive Briefing Package which will contain additional information designed to help you get the most from this special event.

We believe the sharing of key information and best practi-... relationships where all parties grou... colleagues and ...

IBM

International Business Machines Corporation	P.O. Box 3300
	Pittsburgh, Pennsylvania 15230
	412/237-7700

Ernan Roman
Ernan Roman Direct Marketing
3 Melrose Lane
Douglas Manor, NY 11363

Dear Mr. Roman:

The Agile Organization. It's a vision based on meeting the challenges of domestic and international competition. And it's a vision that applies to large, medium and small manufacturers.

Agile Organizations compete based on their ability to react to opportunities, to customize or produce a wide variety of product families, to develop and introduce new products to meet the market-driven requirements for ever higher quality, speed and customer satisfaction.

Agile Organizations must be totally integrated, with information flowing seamlessly among all departments, as well as between manufacturers, suppliers and customers.

Please accept my invitation to be our guest at an Information Sharing Workshop: The Agile Organization, to be held on successive Tuesdays: October 5 in Pittsburgh, October 12 in Charleston and October 19 in Cleveland. This Workshop is sponsored by IBM.

Following an overview of the Agile Organization by some of its originators and active proponents, Terry Schmoyer and selected representatives of the Agile Manufacturing Enterprise Forum at the Iacocca Institute, Lehigh University, we'll examine real world implementation, as told by hands-on management, and the proven processes that are available today.

Bob Kanode, North American Mobile Computing Manager for IBM's Personal Computer Company's Thinkpad® manufacturing facility will present a case study of IBM's successes – and problems – in implementing the Agile imperatives.

Breakout session topics will focus on what's working now in helping to meet rising quality standards, shorten lead-times, increase profitability and achieve aggressive customer satisfaction goals.

Breakout session topics will include: Sales Force Mobilization, the ISO 9000 International Quality Standards, Manufacturing Logistics, Continuous Flow Manufacturing, and more.

Exhibit 5-2. The introductory mailing was written to focus on the needs that customers said were most important: staying ahead of technology and trends, forming and managing networks, and benchmarking with similar industries.

Exhibit 5-2. *(continued)*

Summary

Through IDM, IBM leveraged customer contact to provide one message and to manage the communication of that message to provide value to the customer. The letters, brochures, telemarketing call, the event, and all subsequent communications were built around the needs that customers described in depth research interviews. Instead of multiple messages from IBM and separate communications from third-party sales channels, IDM created a coordinated campaign.

THE POWER OF SHARED INFORMATION

Customer Contact Management, logical as it is, is often difficult to implement.

When you begin to peel the onion of customer contact, you quickly see that it requires a sharing of information, strategies, and tactics. This sharing is blocked by organizational structures in many enterprises, in which departments are separate profit centers, measured independently and competing for corporate dollars and attention.

According to Dave Garwood, an acknowledged expert in manufacturing reengineering:

> As business grew, the volume of tasks to be done expanded and we erected functional or departmental silos, divided the duties and assigned individual responsibilities. The engineering department became a silo with the VP of engineering at the top and the newest engineering intern at the bottom. Corresponding silos were erected for sales, manufacturing, purchasing, finance, etc., for administrative convenience. Performance measurements were created to evaluate the effectiveness of each silo. Everyone's eyes became focused vertically, up and down their silo. Unfortunately, we often lost sight of what was important to the customer and, thus, to the business.

That rigid vertical approach works against the freedom to move flexibly across the company. IBM's efforts are gradually introducing more flexibility into the marketing and sales process. According to Curt Gillespie, IBM Business Unit Executive, "Using the database as the crown jewel of the system, we'll be able to keep track of our relationships with our customers, be more responsive and give them more of the personal touch. But it is a lot of work to link other organizations within IBM to make sure that everything is smoothly coordinated."

"Contact management will be enhanced as the result of more effective data sharing by the local resource with responsibility for the particular customer," according to Mike Lawrie, IBM US Vice President and Area General Manager. For example, the IBM person on the Chrysler account will have an understanding of all IBM contacts with Chrysler. This will help us manage our overall communication plan more efficiently."

Peter Andino, IBM's Director of Market Management, General Business Market Development, comments on the process of implementing the reengineering of marketing and sales at IBM:

> We learned a number of things while we were doing this:
>
> 1. Bottoms-up dedication and execution is the only way this works. The best thing that happened to us was getting a lot of field reps and managers together in a room to say, "What do we really want?"
> 2. Never underestimate the strength of cultural resistance. Whatever you think it is, it's two to three times that hard. Management systems, job description, career paths, sales plans, everything needs to change to show that this is a fundamental change in the way we go to market and not a "program du jour."
> 3. Have top level support to show that the company is truly serious about changing. Provide executive direction at every step of the process. But be careful not to step on the toes of the grassroots doers. You have to meet somewhere in the middle.
>
> The whole sales to marketing transformation requires a lot of emphasis on the communications internally at IBM to really explain every step of the way—what we're doing, why we're doing it, how we're doing it. I look to the IDM process to help us link marketing strategies to precise, cost effective go-to-market tactics.

USAA: CUSTOMER CONTACT MANAGEMENT IN ACTION

Customer Contact Management can be very effective as a process that focuses your marketing on meeting the needs of customers with the greatest potential. In many ways this is a process of concentrating your markets rather than diluting your message across the entire target population. Let's look at an example of a closed market and see what advantages and lessons it holds for the rest of us.

In Chapter 4, one of the examples we looked at for developing relationship-oriented creative material was USAA. The creative materials are simply one aspect of a total relationship-building strategy. The other part is managing the contact with the customer in a closed market. "It took a paradigm shift to take our eyes off of product. We had to realize that our business wasn't products, it was serving members. We were not there to support products. We were there to support our member's needs," according to Mike Paterson, Senior Vice President, USAA Marketing/Sales and Service, recently retired.

> USAA is an organization of over 2.5 million people [and includes] 95 percent of all United States active-duty military officers. There are some 14,000 USAA employees to serve this membership. USAA is the fourth largest

homeowners insurance provider and the fifth largest auto insurer in the United States. USAA ranks 21st in the Fortune Service 500 rankings based on assets managed. Their Federal Savings Back is fourth in sales volume among standard MasterCard issuers and the life insurance company has over $53 billion worth of life insurance in force. USAA is in the top ten of all no-load and low-load mutual fund providers in the United States and in the top 10 percent of all mutual fund companies for assets under management. Given all this diversity under one umbrella, USAA has no sales force. All the interactions are mail or phone. This means that USAA is the largest mail order company in the United States and the fourth largest internationally. In addition to the daily mail, the company processes 12 million computer transactions and well over 300,000 voice calls every day.

All this is by way of background on a very unique closed-market situation. Paterson continues:

> There were so many USAA companies under the mantle of USAA, which our members perceive as one company, that we had to realize we had a shared, finite, incredibly valuable market with a consistent focus on the member, instead of the various lines of business. So we came together by using the model of the members life cycle and the major human and economic events embedded in that life cycle. Our lifetime relationship with them and the marketing process of serving that relationship became a conscious, shared strategy.

For more about how this strategy is implemented through the creative materials, see Chapter 4.

Based on USAA's experience, relationship marketing takes work, and it may not be for everyone. "The first reality of relationship marketing is that your corporate culture must be customer oriented," adds Paterson. "If the primary focus of a given company is its bottom line, relationship marketing probably won't fit. Your employees won't believe it, your customers won't believe it, and it's a waste of money and your attempt will fail. But, more importantly, the shift may not be appropriate."

Dan Gibbens, VP Marketing for USAA adds:

> In an open market arena you're very product oriented. You spend a lot of time developing a product that you think has a certain purpose or meets a certain need and then you go out and find markets for your products. You're really tied into the product itself and all your development processes are tied into making the best widget possible. And then you go out and find a market for that widget. In a closed market, you can't afford to be that way, because you might design products that are great but solve no need for your closed market. So you have to be customer oriented. Most companies talk about being customer-focused. The truth is they're product-focused and become customer-focused only after they've developed their product.

USAA's successful relationship marketing partnership is nurtured and developed over a long period of time. Often, it lasts the lifetime of the client. The statistics on customer retention in various areas were compared to industry standards. They show that USAA must be doing something right:

- Property and casualty retention—USAA 96.4%; Industry 85%
- Life insurance retention—USAA 96.8%; Industry 89%
- Credit card retention—USAA 98% (voluntary and involuntary); Industry 86%
- Mutual funds retention—USAA 41% of members switching to another fund; Industry 52%.

Gibbens explains USAA's strategy in the following way:

We are constantly working to keep our products as competitive as possible. We continually scan our competition to ensure that we are close to the lead on pricing and features. But as a product moves to a commodity where everybody has the same widget, then the differentiating factor is the service which you give or the steps you take to deliver whatever promises are in the contract. If your product is unique, you can spend all your time and energy marketing products. But as your product approaches a commodity stage, you better have a relationship in place, because your customers will pick whoever they do have a relationship with.

"Getting serious about relationship marketing means getting below the buzz phrase and recognizing that you have to go back through any marketing opportunity and look at it through your customer's eyes," adds Paterson.

One of the keys to member perception of USAA as an organization with which they have a lifetime relationship is to get in early in the process of serving the event (for example, home buying or car ownership) and to stay with the member seamlessly. As an end result, the member emerges with a reaffirmed feeling of comfort and trust. All of the product transactions that went into the process are secondary to the value of the relationship bonding that occurs by completing this process effectively in the eyes of the member.

What does it take to build these relationships? According to USAA, it takes a lot of computer synchronization. It takes a lot of time. It takes a lot of training and education of employees. And, as a given, the product has to be good.

Working within a closed market requires first-rate service, as well. Patterson explains:

In a closed market, there also has to be superior service, based on operational excellence and/or customer intimacy. If the product is not right, not only does the product lose face, but, more importantly, the company behind it suffers as well. In a closed market, you have to work to empower your customers and understand that to educate and inform, to make your service or product meaningful to their lives, is much more important than the razzle-dazzle of an ad. Razzle-dazzle wears thin. In the open market, you can bombard them with message; in the closed market, you have to be careful not to overdo it. This is where you have to depend on your database to be robust enough, and tailored enough, and customer-oriented enough that you can talk to the specific awareness or interests of the individual member or client.

At USAA, database infrastructure is central to the relationship-building process, merging selected data from all the separate USAA companies but taking it far beyond product data. "We see each member contact as an opportunity to validate or update database information," explains Paterson. "Each year 20 percent of our members receive a printout of the key data in our files about them. Our request for validation is explained as a means of saving the member's time and avoiding the irritation of inappropriate or boring mail. We've worked the better part of a decade now on getting a database robust enough and accurate enough to allow our telephone reps to talk confidently to any family member and offer substantive advice, based on an integrated knowledge of our entire relationship within that member's family."

"We are the largest single-site inbound WATS in the world," explains Gibbens, "handling about 88 million calls a year, and 350,000 calls per day. This is customers calling us with orders or questions, as well as our reps calling customers to follow up. We take pains to maintain extremely high service levels, answering 95 percent of the calls within two rings. When you have a closed market, you have to be absolutely compulsive about providing top-of-the-line service with every customer contact. You can't just move on to another market."

To enhance the communication with the customer, USAA uses an imaging system to enter all letters from the customer into the database. Telephone reps are able to have all the customers records, transactions and communications at their fingertips whenever the customer calls. "This is no mean feat for a company with as many different services and companies under the USAA umbrella as we have," adds Gibbens. "But it's absolutely essential that we manage all the customer's business smoothly and retain the perception of 'one company for all their financial needs.'"

MAKING IT HAPPEN

To implement effective customer contact management at your organizations, you need to look at a number of strategic issues.

- What do customers think of you?
  Based on research from the field sales force, from the media, and from past history, put together as much information as you can about

how customers see you before you start your program. Then during the program, be sure to include questions at each contact point (telemarketing, sales calls, events) that allow you to obtain additional information about what customers want from your company—what they like and what they don't like.

- What is the customer seeing from your company?
  Internally and across all functions, examine and evaluate the communications that are reaching the customer: What impressions do they create? Analyze what has value and what hasn't. It's a good idea to set up a cross-functional creative and strategy review board to evaluate relevance, appropriateness, and timing of all promotions.

- Include the field sales force at every step of the process.
  We've said this before and we'll say it again. The field sales force needs to take an active role in all stages—providing information, interacting with customers, setting qualifying standards, and updating information. The whole point of this is to provide qualified leads so that they will generate ongoing business.
  Terry Cook, IBM's Marketing/Opportunity Manager, has been working with the IDM process and understands some of the problems faced by organizations when bringing sales into the marketing process: "It's difficult for them to change gears and think 'marketing and long-term partnership' if the compensation and measurement systems are still saying 'sales and volume.' Having a compensation plan that emphasizes quality instead of quantity is essential."

- Make sure your database is working for you.
  As *Reader's Digest* discovered, the database can't do it on its own. Technology provides the input but people make the decisions. Even though the database is your critical link, remember that you're marketing to people, not to data.

- Develop "one organization" thinking.
  The organization must take ultimate responsibility for the customer relationship. This means that high-level support is needed to cut through turf issues and broaden any narrowly focused pockets of communication within the organization.

On the tactical level, contact management follows some clearly defined steps:

1. Determine what customers need to know and when they need to know it. This will be driven by your depth research and input from the field including information about:

- The decision-making process, roles and responsibilities of decision makers and influencer, the buying cycle, decision steps, buying triggers, and media preference

2. Continually update the database.

Make sure that the information in the database is accurate and actionable. Contact management provides the opportunity to develop and test both a consensual database (customers and prospects who have expressed a desire to be contacted) and a predictive database (communicating based on the potential for future business).

3. Sequence the communications across the corporation.

It goes without saying that top-level management needs to have ownership for a corporate-wide effort such as this. However, in order to work effectively, all plans and calendars of events should be reviewed in a company-wide context.

We suggest a three-step process to implement a truly centralized review of all strategies and creative:

- Step One: Each profit center publishes its calendar of events by market.
- Step Two: A team reviews all information, negotiates as needed, and reaches agreement to a "master plan."
- Step Three: A combined, company-wide calendar is created and distributed to all functions.

4. Maintain the centralized focus with ongoing communications.

As you deploy increasingly specific, increasingly targeted communications, it's important to avoid conflicts and confusion. Your goal is to maintain a useful dialogue with customers, not simply keep your name in front of them.

5. Standardize measurements and establish useful common baselines.

All departments must be measured uniformly and all metrics must have a common definition. Establish a pre-contact management baseline to measure your results against. Standardized measurements and comparisons to baseline are critically important as you fine tune your program and build long-term relationships.

IDM measurement is treated in detail in the next chapter.

"As You Sow, So Shall You Reap"

According to Scott Hornstein:

> The bottom line of customer contact management is that customers will judge you based on all the contacts that they have with your company. Just controlling your department's message won't accomplish much if the other communications and contacts from your company are sending conflicting, confusing, or contradictory messages. Even if all messages are effective on their own, in the aggregate, you may be causing customer inaction through sheer overload.

Look at your company as a customer would. What is arriving through the mail with your company name on it (brochures, invoices, invitations, announcements, etc.)? What other points of contact do you have with the customer (packaging, signs, buildings and grounds, employees, etc.)? How can you best manage all those contacts to maximize the potential for trusted, long-term relationships? Because, make no mistake **about it**, the future of marketing lies in those long-term relationships. Con**fuse the** customers or overwhelm them and they'll go elsewhere.

KEY POINTS

- Customer Contact Management looks at all the points of contact that your division and your company has with a specific customer or prospect.
- The process coordinates and orchestrates those contacts from the customer's point of view. Ask yourself—about every contact, "What message does this send to the customer?"
- Determine the role of the contact in the longer-term goal of lifetime customer retention. How does the communication interact with previous contacts and how does it affect future contacts?
- Weed out or modify conflicting messages. They will confuse the customer and tend to cancel each other out. The response to confusing/conflicting messages is generally no response.
- Measurement and objectives need to be broadened to include a broader perspective. "Silo" thinking can hurt customer retention for the long term and, eventually, profitability of all areas of the company.
- A shared database is critical.

The Proof Is in the Numbers:

Measuring the Success of IDM

The true test of a brilliant theory is what first is thought to be wrong is later shown to be obvious.

Asar Lindbeck,
Nobel Prize Committee for Economics

What IDM is really all about is accomplishing more—more response, more leads, more sales, more customer satisfaction—with the same resources. In many cases, IDM may even lower your costs. The bedrock principles of IDM are productivity and cost-efficiency.

The secret to achieving these goals lies in the measurement of success. Only through accurate measurement of *integrated* results will you see how best to leverage people, resources, and media to:

- Reduce the volume but increase the impact. In Chapter 2, Judie Neiger talked about Hewlett-Packard's decrease in average mailing size from 70,000 pieces to 10,000 pieces—with greater quality and quantity of leads and greater conversion to sales.
- Redeploy existing budgets for greater results. In the Adept case study, which is in this chapter, you'll see how the budget for traditional business ads and trade shows was redirected to mail and telemarketing. This doubled qualified response, reduced cost per lead, and increased lead conversion as well as the bottom line.
- Research the market to improve message and media effectiveness. Through intensive research and sales force involvement at every step of the process, as in the medical case study in Chapter 4, IBM was

able to generate an 841 percent improvement in response and a 442 percent improvement in leads over baseline from a market that had previously been difficult to penetrate by the sales force.

- Time media deployment for maximum quality and quantity of response. Throughout, you've read about the benefits of precision timing so that direct mail follows print by no more than a week and the outbound telemarketing reaches the decision maker within 24 to 72 hours of receiving the direct mail. This response compression lifts response by building on the impact of each medium to create a powerful cumulative effect.
- Sequence contacts for long-term relationships. IBM's Business and Production Planning Program (Chapter 5) used IDM to send increasingly tailored messages at each point of contact with the customer and thus build a relationship—not simply generate leads or single sales.

MEASURING TO BUILD LONG-TERM RELATIONSHIPS

One very important qualitative measurement looks at "what does the customer want, and what does the customer need?" This is the key to building customer relationships. And customer relationships are the key to building long-term business.

This specific qualitative measurement has an important near-term lesson: how to view the business and deploy resources now to set the stage for enhanced future profitability.

AT&T found out long ago that it's five times more expensive to sell to a new customer than to an existing customer—a powerful metric as you consider budgets and media allocations. What is the percentage of your time, your resources, your marketing budget that is devoted to the 20 percent of your market that generates 80 percent of your revenue?

Moreover, the cost of prospecting has become so high that, in many cases, the return on investment is declining. Of course, no one can afford to stop prospecting: New customers will always be important. But recognize that it is an uphill struggle in which you're "fishing" for either:

- Someone else's discontented customers
- Someone else's loyal customers
- Price or "best offer" shoppers

In many businesses, it is time to start thinking of your customer base as a closed market. Your customers have proven their value to you. Now, what can you do to anticipate and satisfy more of their needs?

♦ The proliferation of telecommunications advertising, direct mail, and telemarketing is all going after new customers or trying to bring ex-customers back in the fold. This has resulted in a large number of tele-com shoppers who switch based on the latest, best promotion. The next marketing step for any of the "big three"—MCI, AT&T and Sprint—is to cut through the clutter with simple, concrete offers that build customer satisfaction so that customers continue to buy from the current supplier rather than shopping for a better "deal."

♦

IDM QUALITY AND PERFORMANCE METRICS

In order to know whether the program is meeting your objectives, you must have an effective, precise, and comprehensive way to measure your results. Otherwise, you will not be able to make the adjustments down the road to do more of what works well for you—or less of what didn't work so well.

IDM includes a comprehensive set of quality and performance metrics that have been used by large and small businesses to monitor and continuously improve the IDM process. IDM metrics provide a process for obtaining information about the program in real time—early enough so that you can make "on-line" modifications. This type of productivity data is essential to both initial and long-term success.

The nature of an IDM program demands that the metrics carefully measure the impact and contribution of each medium and provide the basis for an in-depth analysis of the overall results. In order to implement and benefit fully from the measurements, you will need to establish:

- Accurate baselines: What results have you achieved in like programs and what was the cost?
- Goals: Given all the variables, such as seasonality, market conditions, and competition, what can reasonably be expected?
- Benchmarks: What have other "best in class" companies in your industry or related industries achieved?

It's important to continuously monitor all your media for the duration of the program and through ongoing communications to leverage results. Things change. And your metrics are your best early warning system.

Appendix E contains key IDM quality and performance metrics.

Measuring Telemarketing

Let's focus on telemarketing as an illustration, since the bulk of your qualified response generally comes through telephone contact—either outbound telemarketing or inbound response to your 800 number. The telephone is the most immediate medium and also the one that requires the most immediate measurement.

Before the start of your campaign, make sure you have established your baseline, as well as goals or projections based on a realistic assessment of the potential of the target market. Define the universe and then measure response, qualified inquiries, leads, and sales against the appropriate universe.

At the start of a telemarketing campaign, analyze both quality and productivity every hour, for the first day or so, and daily thereafter. Because no matter how carefully you have planned your message and targeted your audience, you can find "surprises" once people get on the phone. An early detection and correction can prevent serious damage to your customer base and improve your response. Have someone assigned to monitoring calls with a specific set of criteria and the ability to raise a red flag if the message is not being delivered or received as expected. The beauty of telemarketing is the ability to make changes quickly and effectively.

The types of metrics that provide accurate information about and insight into the productivity of telemarketing include:

- On inbound calls
  - Blockage, abandons, and rings to answer: Are the customers who want to reach you able to get through?
  - Number and type of misdirect: Is our message relevant to the marketplace, do they see value? Are there customer satisfaction issues that need to be addressed?
- On outbound calls:
  - Disconnected, out of business, wrong numbers, not qualified: Is the database a help or impediment to productivity? Can list segments be suppressed, others prioritized?
  - Dials per hour, contacts per hour, completed calls per hour: How productive is telemarketing? Are we reaching goals?
  - Talk time: Is the message being delivered efficiently? Should there be "early outs" for not-interesteds to shorten talk time and increase productivity?
- Overall
  - Training and monitoring results: Do the telemarketers understand the program? Are they following the script, providing the right information, and using the correct telephone skills?
  - Customer satisfaction rating: Do customers see the value?
    Reasons for not-interested: What do we need to tell other customers to generate interest? How can questions and objections be answered more effectively?
  - "Do not mail" and "do not call" requests: Are we satisfying the customers or annoying them?

Direct Mail

For direct mail, the metrics are not as immediate but just as critical. The phone calls can also help you measure feedback on the mail, including relevance of the copy/offer, impact of the design, and, because you will likely be releasing your mail in "waves," some adjustments (such as copy revisions to the letter or suppression of low-responding segments) can be made to leverage response in real time. Plus, analysis of net returns can provide direction on database segments with the greatest potential for future communications.

Often, there is a temptation to base measurement on the number of gross registrations of executives who agree to attend an event or the number of people requesting additional information. But the true measure of the effectiveness is net attendance at events (not just registrations). This identifies decision makers who are interested enough to devote time to see for themselves what you are offering.

Advertising

The goals of print advertising are both awareness and response.

While measurements exist to quantify the abstract concept of awareness, our suggestion is that you focus on measuring response—the direct contribution of the medium to results.

Some key metrics regarding the effectiveness of print advertising include:

- Percent response
  - The actual response divided by the circulation
- Response by medium
  - What percent came in by BRC, fax and inbound
    1. Look deeper into the inbound response to determine the level of productive response.
    2. Inbound may include "misdirect" response, or calls that are inappropriate (e.g., "How's the weather where you are? I have a billing problem. Can you have a service technician come out?").
    3. The percentage of misdirect will indicate how productive the inbound channel has been.
- Contribution to overall response
  - Generally, advertising's contribution to overall response should approximate its percentage of budget. If 10 percent of the budget is directed to print, it should generate approximately 10 percent of overall response.
- Conversion to lead, conversion to sale
  - Response from print is generally softer, or less ready to buy than response from direct mail or telemarketing. These individuals have

less information to go on. However, the response from print must convert to lead and eventually to sale, or the targeting of the publication is called into question.

PLANNING TO MEASURE

How you'll measure the results is as important to the planning process as how you'll get those results. When planning measurement of IDM, you must be careful to standardize the definitions. All departments, all profit centers, all media must share common definitions, such as "What is a lead?" As in any quantitative process, how you define the elements of your formula has a large impact on the consistency and accuracy of your results. This is especially important to a cross-functional, multiple-media approach such as IDM.

The following are terms that are often defined differently depending on who you're talking to:

1. Universe. What is the true opportunity existing in the market you're trying to reach? Not every company on a list is a prospect; not every name is a decision maker. Depth research, list enhancements, telemarketing list scrubs, and common sense will give you a better idea of actual, actionable size of the markets you are reaching. Before locking on the universe, look at your offer, product, or service and assess the number of decision makers, influencers, or decision-making units who represent realistic opportunities.

2. Response. A response is simply positive action taken by a customer or prospect to an offer (e.g., free literature). Qualified response is positive action taken that requires some commitment to action (attend an event, for example) or disclosure of qualifying information. Which is relevant to your marketing effort?

   Be sure to carefully differentiate between response, registration, and attendees before using these figures to calculate costs. The number of people who say they are going to attend a particular event is an indicator of interest. Net attendance is a declaration of interest. Leveraging that conversion rate is one of IDM's key challenges.

   Remember that responses are not leads until Field Sales says they are. Your sales force is the final arbiter of what is and is not a qualified lead.

3. Qualified inquiry (and cost per qualified inquiry). This is where input from the sales force is critical. In many companies, there is a credibility chasm between marketing and the field. The field doesn't trust the quality of leads and marketing believes that sales doesn't follow up soon enough to turn leads into customers. To begin to bridge that gap, to find middle ground, the term "qualified inquiry" was coined.

The definition of a qualified inquiry is:
- a response that meets the sales force definition of a qualified opportunity
- categorized according to field criteria, for example, AA, A, B, C, etc. Remember that an inquiry is not considered a lead until the sales force has inspected and qualified it.

4. Lead (and cost per lead). To repeat, there's only one vote that counts: the field. It's only a lead when they say it is. But there are a number of steps that are critical to measurement and analysis:
- Per field criteria, what category was the qualified inquiry?
- Per field follow-up within 24 hours, what happened during the first conversation (e.g., is this a lead, and if so, what category)?
- What happened after the first visit?
- Does the lead make it to sales forecast, for what product/service, to close in what timeframe, at what estimated dollar volume?
- What did it cost to get that lead?

Many marketers focus on the cost per *lead*. All marketers should be focusing on cost per *sale*.

5. Sale. There are a number of key steps within the sales process that are critical to measurement and analysis. Clear understanding of this will provide a clearer definition of what exactly is meant by a "sale":
- How long did the sale take to close, from initial lead follow-up to contract?
- Who was involved in the final decision-making process?
- What was the dollar volume of the sale?
- What products or services were involved in the sale?
- What is the potential for add-on sales (e.g., post-warranty maintenance, supplies, etc.)?

Closed Loop Lead Management is a process that follows the lead from marketing into sales and provides qualitative and quantitative feedback whether or not a sale is made. It is essential to understand this process to obtain accurate measurement of a marketing program and enable continuous improvement. Yet, because of the traditional distance between sales and marketing, most companies fail to follow through on this. Hewlett-Packard has succeeded. Here's how:

Judie Neiger, Marketing Communications Specialist at Hewlett-Packard, implemented a Closed Loop Lead Management Process to increase the quality of leads and marketing programs.

> We developed the Closed Loop Lead Management process to monitor, measure and provide management support for sales follow-up activity on leads. This lead-tracking system can support and enhance the relationship between buyers and sales people and give the sales team a competitive edge.

Closed Loop Lead Management is a system that tracks leads over a period of time, until a sale is consummated or the lead is discarded. Closed Loop Lead Management also maximizes selling opportunities created by marketing programs. Simplicity is key to the system, for both success and management support.

H-P plans to refine, expand and automate the process, review enhancements with the sales team and continue to make the systems easy to use. Sales reps and district managers will continue to follow up on leads and give managers monthly status reports.

H-P has seen the following benefits from the Closed Loop Lead Management process:

- Measures the increase in the conversion of qualified leads to orders.
- Offers district managers and sales reps the opportunity to increase face-to-face selling time.
- Provides a systematic approach for district managers and sales reps to manage leads.
- Improves management of longer-term leads (for example, sales opportunities that will mature in greater than 12 months) by the marketing organization which will provide assistance through direct mail and telephone follow-up.
- Provides convenient and consistent methods to provide feedback on the quality of leads generated from marketing programs.
- Continuously improves the quality of marketing and sales productivity, enabling H-P to increase its overall competitiveness in the marketplace.

6. Lifetime value. This is a tricky area and one which most companies are just beginning to understand. What exactly is the long-term relationship with the customer worth to the business? There are complex formulas to calculate this (see Appendix B). Whether you use a formula or have your own metrics, lifetime value must be included in the equation when you measure the results of your IDM effort because it is one of the consistent objectives of the program.

Here's a simplified way to establish a baseline for lifetime value of a customer. First, group your customers by logical commonality, e.g. industry, by product. Then, estimate the life expectancy of the product. During that life expectancy, what purchases would you expect that customer to make and what is the value of those purchases?

◆ Calculating Lifetime Value—An Example.

A technology company wants to estimate lifetime value. They segment their customer base first by industry and then by product.

Within manufacturing they find customers with a range of products. In looking at older products, they find an average three-year life expectancy. During that time, the customer bought the hardware and operating software. The cost of peripherals, such as terminals and printers, is added. Application software is added. Post-warranty maintenance and software services are added, as are regular memory upgrades and supplies.

If we average all the purchases, we find the mean lifetime value of that customer segment.

Through individual analysis we find ways to leverage lifetime value—greater penetration of peripherals, maintenance, services and supplies. Additionally, technological expertise can be channeled into consultative services that will increase lifetime value and assist the customers in using the technology to become more successful.

7. Customer satisfaction. Related to lifetime value, this is an equally difficult area to quantify. Yet it is a key element in maintaining customer relationships and building new ones. Therefore, set up a consistent process to sample your customers' satisfaction with your company, your products, and your communications. While more formal, quantitative processes may be preferable, depth research is also an excellent tool to take the temperature of your market, with questions such as "Is Company X easy to do business with?" "Are their invoices clear and understandable?" "Is the service prompt and effective?"

Consider "do not call" and "do not mail" requests as important indicators of customer dissatisfaction. These are customers who have turned their back on your contact with them. It's important to find out why and, even if you can't improve the situation with that customer, you can make sure it doesn't continue to infect other customers.

8. E:R (Expense to Revenue). The value of this basic measurement is only as good as the numbers you put into the equation. To get the true picture, be careful to include all expense items including:

   • External costs such as production, placement, list rentals, data processing, copy, design, postage, etc.
   • Internal costs such as management time, marketing support, cost of sales, internal resources (word processing, mailing, coordination, etc.).

From our experience with a wide range of companies, we've established some benchmark E:Rs based on the type of program:

   • Pilot/market introduction: 15 percent to 25 percent
   • Value-added event: 10 percent to 20 percent
   • Aftermarket: 5 percent to 10 percent.

This section has provided the basic "building blocks" of your measurement system—both qualitative and quantitative metrics form the picture of what's working and what needs to be modified. Consistent, regular measurement is your window on your IDM program and tells you what to maximize and leverage, what to minimize and what to eliminate.

BUDGETING FOR IDM

When budgeting for IDM, first rethink where you spend your money. As we said earlier, apportion your budget between customers and prospects. It may be better spent serving existing customers, especially the key 20 percent of revenue generators, than in fishing for new ones. Refer to Chapter 5 for a full discussion of the benefits of customer retention and ongoing communications.

Budgeting for an IDM program is based on the objectives of your plan, input from the sales force, database analysis and what your customers told you in the depth research interviews and the IDM media guidelines.

Before we discuss the guidelines and considerations, let's first look at Adept Technology, Inc. for an example of what can be accomplished by reallocating your budget.

Adept Technology is a growth company that designs, manufactures and sells industrial robots for assembly processes. The company was founded in 1983 and has grown rapidly to $50 million in annual sales. Adept was twice named as one of the top ten companies in the Inc. 500.

Adept is the market leader in the United States and is tied for number one in Europe. However, maintaining that share against foreign competition was presenting a growing challenge to sales and marketing. Adept turned to IDM for help building leads and maintaining existing customer relationships without increasing marketing or sales budgets.

According to Bryan St. Amant, former Market Programs Manager at Adept, "Part of our success where other similar businesses had failed is our strategy of careful cash management. This also means that we need to grow the business and continue to launch new products with extremely lean marketing budgets."

"Our biggest challenge is not necessarily selling against competition; it's selling against the status quo. In many cases, prospects see robots as something that they may need—someday," says St. Amant. "If we sit around and wait for that 'someday', we'll wait forever. So our marketing and sales is centered on educating customers to the dollars and cents advantages of changing their assembly process to utilize our robots."

The problem that Adept faced was that a long, "educational" sales cycle could easily eat away at profitability.

Trade shows were a favored route of promoting the business. In terms of time, resources, and contacts, the trade shows established presence and name recognition but little else. Years of advertising had created a quality image, but at a high cost. "When we looked at what our leads were costing us, we found that we had average costs of $150 per raw lead. And a virtually negligible conversion rate," adds St. Amant.

To generate more leads at lower cost, St. Amant began to introduce some of the principles of IDM. The first step was an integrated advertising/direct mail campaign. Adept's marketing had been focused on image advertising and trade show participation. This high-cost method had achieved good name recognition. The new strategy substituted lower-cost, targeted print advertising supported with direct mail to leverage that name recognition. This first step reduced the cost per lead from $150 to $200 to $15 to $30 with no loss in quality.

"We now had more leads, but we were still not getting sales force follow-up. I realized that marketing alone could not do it. I had to involve the sales force if the lead-generation program was going to be effective."

The integration of telemarketing into the mix more than doubled the response rate from 4.5 percent to 12 percent with the additional bonus of weeding out non-qualified prospects. The process improved the quality of

Typical Program Response Rate

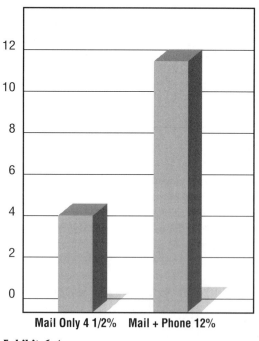

Exhibit 6-1.

Integrated Direct Marketing Calendar

Months: Jul | Aug | Sept | Oct | Nov | Dec | Jan | Feb | Mar | Apr | May | Jun

New Suspects
- 👉 First-Time Buyer's Program
- ✍ ⊠ ☎ 👉 Low-End Assy/Hdlg Robots (Sept)
- ✍ ⊠ ☎ 👉 Vision Inspection End-Users (Sept)
- ✍ ⊠ ☎ 👉 Robot Controls Retrofit (Oct)
- ✍ ⊠ ☎ 👉 Motion Control OEMs (Oct)
- ✍ ⊠ ☎ 👉 Assy/Hdlg Robots TBD (Dec–Jan)
- ✍ ⊠ ☎ 👉 Low-End Assy/Hdlg Robots (Feb–Mar)
- ✍ ⊠ ☎ 👉 Food Pkg End-Users (Feb–Mar)
- ✍ ⊠ ☎ 👉 Iceberg OEM Launch (Mar)
- ✍ ⊠ ☎ 👉 TBD (May)

Known Prospects
- ✍ ⊠ 👉 Integrator Coop Open House Program
- ✍ ⊠ 👉 Integrator Coop Mail Program
- ☎ 👉 Telemarketing Re-Contact Program (Jan–Feb)

Existing Customers
- ✍ ⊠ 👉 On-going Service Contract/Training Sign-on Program
- ✍ ⊠ 👉 Quarterly Service/Upgrade Mailing

✍ Write Offer/Generate List   ⊠ Send Mailing   ☎ Outbound Telemarketing   👉 Leads to Field Sales

Exhibit 6-2.

Integrated Direct Marketing Calendar

Installed Base

	Jul	Aug	Sept	Oct	Nov	Dec	Jan	Feb	Mar	Apr	May	Jun
Target Market	✍ ⊠ ☎ ☞ Service Contract/SparesRenewal Program (Ongoing)											
		✍ ⊠ ☎ ☞ OuterLInk										
Existing Customers		✍ ⊠ ☎ ☞ Customer Training Sign-up Mailing (Ongoing)										
			✍ ⊠ ☎ ☞ ServiceExpert Mailing									
			✍ ⊠ ☞ Automation News									
				✍ ⊠ ☎ ☞ Options/Upgrade Mailing								
					✍ ⊠ "Thank You" Cards							
							✍ ⊠ ☎ ☞ OuterLInk					
								✍ ⊠ ☎ ☞ Service Program Mailing TBD				
									✍ ⊠ ☞ Automation News			
											☎ ☞ TM Survey	
											✍ ⊠ ☎ ☞ TBD	

✍ Write Offer/Generate List　⊠ Send Mailing　☎ Outbound Telemarketing　☞ Leads to Field Sales

Exhibit 6-3.

138

Reengineering the Sales/Marketing Process

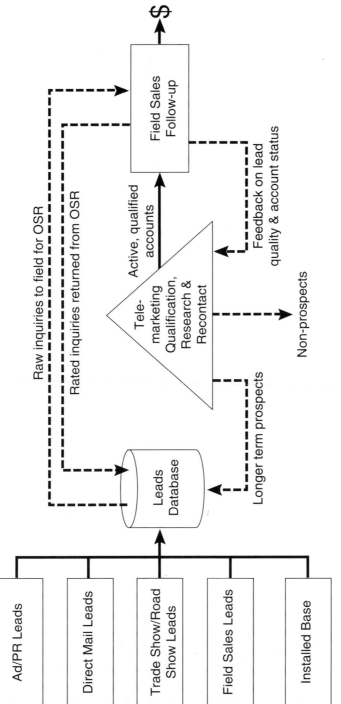

Exhibit 6-4. An important component of Adept's IDM program is telemarketing qualification, research, and recontact. This process assures qualified leads for the sales force as well as supplying information on prospect potential for future business. All information on prospects and existing customers is entered into the dynamic database.

the leads so that fully two thirds of those leads were now followed up—double the previous lead follow-up.

In addition to prospecting, Adept initiated an IDM program to offer value-added services to their installed customer base. "Our existing customers are our most valuable asset. We wanted to not only maintain contact with them but upsell them to services that would make sense for them, given their needs," according to St. Amant.

"It's really a lot more than integrating your marketing mix," adds St. Amant. "It's integrating the whole sales process with the marketing process. The IDM process has been so effective that I'm adding an inside salesperson to handle the telemarketing leads. I anticipate that this alone will help us generate an additional $1 million in sales."

Results to Date: Adept Technology

	Pre-IDM	Post-IDM	Percent Change
Response rate	4.5%	12%	+167%
Cost per lead	$150	$30	– 80%
Lead follow-up	30%	60%	+100%

Since 1988, Adept has launched new products and grown its market base with no addition to the marketing budget. As part of the process of maintaining ongoing communication with customers, Adept created an interactive customer database. The sales force is able to access the customer database from laptop computers and add to it based on sales calls and information. This on-line capability ensures accurate, timely "intelligence" about customers.

"It's a straightforward and logical process. You might encounter some resistance from marketing and sales because these functions are not used to working as a team," cautions St. Amant. "But once they see the results, it's clear that this is a superior way to approach the market. The bottom line is that sales have grown by 20 percent in the United States and the marketing budget has not grown at all. Is all this attributable to IDM? I can't say for sure, but I'm certainly going to continue along this route."

BUDGETING GUIDELINES BY MEDIUM

IDM is based on allocating money to areas where it will have the most impact—gaining the greatest return for every marketing dollar spent. Although every company has a different budgeting structure and different media allocations, following are guidelines for you to consider when reallocating your own resources.

Advertising

Results from IDM programs indicate that no more than ten percent of the overall budget should be devoted to print advertising, and then only in highly targeted vertical publications.

This may be different than you're used to, but it is sufficient in an IDM program where direct mail and telemarketing will be shouldering the brunt of the response-generation work. Since the ads must create awareness and generate response, in the best of all worlds, repeat each ad three times. Based upon published discounts, consider greater frequency of insertion but only if it makes sense in terms of the timing and synchronization of the entire plan. On the plus side, greater frequency may provide greater coverage and a longer period of awareness to support the direct mail and telemarketing follow-up.

Direct Mail

Allocate the remaining 90 percent of your budget to the workhorse team of direct mail and telemarketing, with approximately 20 to 25 percent to direct mail.

Here are three rules that can help keep your direct mail costs on track:

1. Identify each of the required resources and how much they'll cost. Don't forget the costs for internal resources. Key expense steps in the process include:
   - Copy and design
   - List rental
   - Merge/purge
   - Printing
   - Data processing
   - Lettershop
   - Postage
   And don't forget to budget for the important "extras" such as proof-reading (few things can spoil a professional impression as quickly as a typo), quality photography or illustration, and retouching to create the finished look you want.
2. Research the best resources for what you want to accomplish. These may not be the cheapest but, if the value of what you're trying to accomplish is high, the best resources will pay off in the long run by providing the type of quality work you need. And what you really need is partnership and value-add, experts who will go out of their way to share their expertise and insights and make you successful.

3. Obtain estimates in writing based on specifications in writing. That way there are no misunderstandings later on or surprises when the bills come in. Each supplier or resource should develop and commit to its own estimate and timeframe for deliverables, in writing.

> It seems that everybody has a relative who's a writer or a designer—so you can always get it done cheaper. What you can't always get is quality work. That costs money. The folks who are the great communicators, who have real talent and a track record of success, charge. Investments here pay off in multiples.

List Rental

Be prepared to pay for quality. Highly qualified lists may run as high as $100 to $200 per thousand names for one-time usage, and usage is defined as one direct mailing or one telemarketing call. (Many lists don't permit telemarketing so check before committing resources.) Usually, your minimum order, no matter how few names you really want, is 5000.

There are additional charges above the base rental cost for extras or "sorts." This includes specifying that you only want certain SICs, titles, zip codes, and so forth.

Be clear about your usage requirements because cost of the list is based on how it's used. If you are buying the list to supplement one that you already have in house, you may be able to negotiate a lower rate since the information will be used as an enhancement not as the primary source of names.

Also, if you do plan to deploy both direct mail and telemarketing, you may not necessarily have to pay double. Negotiations for double usage, or unlimited usage over a period of time, may prove productive.

Production and printing. The costs of producing and printing brochures, newsletters, direct mail letters, and other print communications vary widely based on the specifications of the finished piece. Quality and complexity have a cost. So design becomes a marketing and creative decision—what's necessary to communicate (based on experience and Depth Research results) and what is cost-justified.

In this age of fast turnarounds, desktop publishing is often being used to create everything from direct mail letters to color brochures. It has the aura of being a quick, inexpensive way to produce communications materials. However, experience and expertise make a large difference in the quality of the product and have a direct bearing on your results.

In terms of printing, again, you get what you pay for. Experience counts, and you'll get a better deal and a better finished product if you rely on an expert. Saving a few dollars to go with a less experienced vendor may actually result in mistakes that will cost far more to rectify than going to a slightly more expensive printer in the first place. Select a printer who has a proven track record, get references on new printers or brokers or rely on your direct response agency.

When putting together your budget, keep in mind that there are both fixed and variable costs. Copy, design, data processing and printing and lettershop set-up are fixed costs. No matter how many or how few pieces you print, these costs are the same and, in smaller runs, are usually greater than the variable costs. Fixed costs must be amortized over the total number of pieces produced. The variable costs—ink, paper, press time—will increase or decrease according to quantity. Thus, the more pieces you print, the lower the cost per piece.

Postage.   Postage costs are affected by size, weight, quantity and class of mailing. The extra costs for first class will, in most cases, pay off in increased response. We've tested this theory time and again and have found consistently higher results from first class. Think of your own reaction. Which are you more likely to open and read—a letter with a first class stamp or a "bulk rate" indicia?

◆   As a rule of thumb, here are two examples to illustrate what it might cost to produce and mail a communication piece:

- 2-color, #10 personalized envelope, personalized 1-page letter, 4-panel brochure, separate business reply card, first class mailing, 1-ounce weight, 10,000 to 15,000 quantity:

  $1.50 to $2.50 per mailed piece.

- 4-color, 6" x 9" personalized envelope, 2-page personalized letter, 6-panel brochure, business reply card, first class mailing, 2-ounce weight, 10,000 to 15,000 quantity:

  $3.50 to $5.00 per mailed piece.

Contingency
Add a 10 percent contingency to all budgets to cover miscellaneous expenses (tax, messengers, freight, etc.) and last-minute changes or corrections. No matter how carefully you plan, something unexpected always seems to happen just as you are about to go to press.

◆

Telemarketing

Service bureaus can handle both inbound and outbound calling for a fee of $30 to $60 per hour. Fixed costs, such as set-up, programming, training and scripting are extra and will vary based on the level of involvement your campaign requires.

♦ A basic three-step formula for estimating outbound telemarketing costs:

1. Universe × 80% (estimated list penetration) = estimated number of completed calls
2. Completed calls divided by estimated completed calls per hour = total hours
3. Total hours × hourly rate + fixed costs = total budget.

Experience has shown the following range of completed calls per hour for a business-to-business program:

- Telemarketing list scrub: 10 to 12 completed calls/hour
- Response/registration generation: 5 to 7 completed calls/hour
- Response generation plus survey (5 questions average): 2 to 4 completed calls per hour.

Always add a 10 percent contingency to your estimates.

♦

"We don't have that kind of money."

One of the benefits of looking at all your costs is that it lets you realistically decide whether you can afford to do the type of campaign you envision. If you can, great! Full speed ahead. If you can't, you'll need to look to areas where you can cut costs without sacrificing your objectives.

Where you cut depends on what's most important to your market and your business. Ask yourself these questions:

- Why are we advertising? What is the expected return and the projected cost per response? What will the ads contribute to the overall response?
- Are there low priority or anticipated low-response segments of the target market that could wait?
- How important is four-color or even two-color printing for the brochure, direct mail, or ad?

Can outbound telemarketing be prioritized to save money? For example:

- Place most-likely-to-respond customers/prospects first, or eliminate those least likely to respond. This can be decided on-line during the first few days of the telemarketing effort through careful list segmentation and hourly/daily analysis of productivity data.
- Is there a segment that is experiencing more "do not call" requests than others? Consider giving this segment a rest.
- Are all business-to-business contacts with decision-making units? If not, can the ones that aren't decision-making units be eliminated? Is it possible to call one decision maker per enterprise rather than all decision makers and influencers in a single enterprise?

Per IDM results, following are average costs for highly qualified response, i.e., event, attendee, or lead (based on a target market of 7,500 to 10,000):

- Cost per response/registration: $50 to $125
- Cost per executive attendee/qualified lead: $200 to $350

BUILDING THE BUSINESS CASE

A business case is a "pilot" of your IDM program to verify assumptions about measurement, budgets, and results. The business case details all projected expenses and revenue and provides an expense to revenue ratio—and does it *before* marketing dollars are invested.

The business case must reach across company functions so that you can tap specific, specialized resources for information or estimates to plug into the case. Go to the source. Include key decision makers in the development process. Decisions will be made to spend, or not to spend, money based on the business case, so get their buy-in early. They will be better able to understand the work to be accomplished and have greater confidence in the accuracy of the figures if they have been included in the development process.

Define your target market carefully and establish projections for the business case that are absolutely defensible, based on past performance and industry standards. The following is a step-by-step guide to building a business case for your IDM program.

Step 1: Establish a Baseline

Look at the history. What happened as a result of previous communications? Responses, leads, and sales based on past experience with the same or similar markets can help you predict future responses, leads, and sales. Consider the following:

- What was the universe?
- What was the offer?
- What was the response rate?
- How many leads were generated, and does the field agree that these were leads?
- What was the lead conversion ratio?
- How many sales were made?
- What was the size of the average sale?
- How long did it take to make the sale?
- What were the total costs of this program?

Step 2: Calculate Projected Expenses

Develop the expense items, making sure you consider all expenses, including:

- Support personnel
- Event facilities and catering, as appropriate
- Sales representatives

Often, there's a tendency to sweep in-house costs under the rug or to assign them to a different budget. But it's virtually impossible to get a clear picture of your campaign's potential profitability unless you look at all the costs. Ultimately, the corporation must pay for all expense items.

Step 3: Estimate Responses and Revenue

Make your projections based on your baseline (see Step 1), industry benchmark, and consultative input as appropriate. Response projection should include:

- Percent response overall and by medium
- Percent of qualified inquiries from inbound and outbound telemarketing
- Percent attendance at events (as applicable)
- Percent leads forwarded to the field, per lead classification
- Expected close ratio, per field input
- Expected number of sales, per field input
- Expected average order, per field input
- Expected time to sale, per field input

Average order multiplied by projected number of sales will yield total projected revenue. Divide the expense by the projected revenue to calculate the expected E:R, which is expressed as a percentage.

♦ The following sample business case is based on an actual client case history that included a year-long promotion. The promotional calendar revolved around the introduction of a high-technology product. Two specific events were planned: first, an information-sharing event to be held regionally across the geography; and second, a workshop to be held at branch offices. Ongoing Communications strategies were deployed throughout the year.

- Target market: 10,000 decision-making units
- Baseline:
  - Expense: $535,000
    - Media: $100,000
    - In-house personnel and resources: $135,000
    - Cost of sales: $300,000
  - Revenue: $1,000,000

- Average sale: $40,000
- Number of sales: 25
- E:R: 53.5%
- Expense Projections: $750,000
  - Media: $400,000 (two waves of promotion)
    - Advertising = $40,000
    - Direct mail = $85,000
    - Telemarketing = $250,000
    - Cost of events = $25,000
  - In-house personnel and resources: $100,000
  - Cost of sales: $250,000
- Revenue Projections
  Wave #1 = Event
  - Leads from initial calling = 20
    - 80% of the market is reached
    - .25% leads
  - Leads from balance of universe = 128
    - 12% registration = 958 d.m.u.s
    - 67% attendance = 642 d.m.u.s
    - 20% AA, A, B leads = 128
  Wave #2 = Workshops
  - Leads from initial calling = 12
    - Universe is now reduced to 9951 d.m.u.s
    - 80% of the market is reached (7961)
    - .15% leads
  - Leads from balance of universe = 32
    - 12% registration = 954 d.m.u.s
    - 67% attendance = 639 d.m.u.s
    - 5% AA, A, B leads = 29
  Ongoing Communications
  - Leads = 74
    - universe is now 9907
    - 15% qualify for Ongoing Communications (1486)
    - 5% leads over the year
  - Total leads = 266
  - Lead Conversion
    - Benchmark = 25%
    - Estimate, per sales force = 45%
  - 120 sales projected
    - Sales force estimates $50,000 average sale

$6,000,000 projected in sales against $750,000 in expense = E:R 12.5%

- Recommend doing projections, and thus E:R comparisons per three scenarios

- Most Likely case: as above
- Conservative: decrease response, attendance, leads
  For this example
  - Decrease initial lead rate by .5
  - Decrease registration rate to 10%
  - Decrease attendance to 65%
  - Decrease lead rate by 5 percentage points
- Aggressive case: increase response, attendance, leads
  For this example
  - Increase initial lead rate by .5
  - Increase registration rate to 15%
  - Increase attendance to 70%
  - Increase lead rate by 5 percentage points

Testing the Plan

Always test your plan. Without a valid test, your projections are built on nothing but assumptions. With testing, you'll be able to proceed with a much higher level of confidence, based on the customers' reactions.

Only one thing is certain: The marketplace is always changing. Testing is one way of keeping abreast of the changes and continually sharpening your marketing approach. Every promotion should contain at least one test, and it's especially important to test against your assumptions (Is the control package still the control package?).

For large decisions, such as price increases, validate your results through ongoing testing prior to rollout. This will minimize the effects of seasonality and general economic factors. A sound strategy is to continue the test after rollout (called a back test) in order to monitor the results at previous pricing levels to maximize your information on other options, should unforeseen circumstances arise.

Building a Testing Matrix.   What are the variables you want to test? Each should be significant to the success of your program (e.g., price, offer, package, creative execution) and worthy of your investment in the test.

Set up a testing matrix, which will consist of cells. The first cell will be your control, which will mirror your current volume promotion. Each following cell will test one variable, and one variable only. Subsequent cells will test additional or incremental variables. Don't over-test, but make sure you do include enough cells to provide proper perspective, and to challenge widely held beliefs.

Populate each cell with randomly selected names from the same market segment (otherwise you've introduced another variable). For instance, let's say we want to test potential price increases to Market A. The testing matrix might look like:

Test Cell	Market	Variable
#1:	A	Control
#2:	A	Standard price + $X
#3:	A	Standard price + $Y

If we wanted to understand the effect of the potential pricing increase over markets A, B, and C, the testing matrix might look like:

Test Cell	Market	Variable
#1:	A	Control
#2:	A	Standard price + $X
#3:	A	Standard price + $Y
#4:	B	Control
#5:	B	Standard price + $X
#6:	B	Standard price + $Y
#7:	C	Control
#8:	C	Standard price + $X
#9:	C	Standard price + $Y

How Large a Test?   Logarithmic probability tables are available to help establish quantities for each test mailing. In order to achieve statistically significant results these tables are based on the target response rate, acceptable range of error and degree of confidence you need in the results.

Large companies mailing to consumers (Columbia House, Bell Atlantic) often test using quantities of 50,000 to 100,000. Based on your constraints, you can determine the size of your test cells based on your comfort level with the number of names per test cell and the actual number of responses. Will the percentage response rate swing with the addition or subtraction of one or two responses?

For instance, 2,500 to 5,000 names per cell may be adequate to give you the "seat of the pants" comfort you need. Let's say you select 2,500 names per cell and are projecting a 10 percent response rate:

9% = 225 responses
10% = 250 responses
11% = 275 responses

This "feels" comfortable, because we're working with a substantial number of responses to base our decisions on.

Interim analysis.   Following are sample reports that we've developed to monitor the pulse of a program. These reports include:

- Outbound Telemarketing Daily Productivity Report: Telemarketing Database Scrub
  - for productivity measurement concerning the IDM Telemarketing Database Scrub

- Inbound Telemarketing Daily Productivity Report: Response/Registration Generation
- Outbound Telemarketing Daily Productivity Report: Response/Registration Generation
- Central Response/Registration Log
  - a daily report of overall response or registration, detailing the contribution of each medium
- "Reasons for Not Interested" Report.

These reports should be read hourly for the first few days of the promotion and daily thereafter. (Full reports are included in Appendix C.)

QUANTIFYING CUSTOMER SATISFACTION

The last word on measurement belongs to Mike Lawrie, IBM US Vice President and General Manager.

The way we used to generate customer satisfaction information was to send surveys based on the type of system the customer had installed. But that skewed the results toward our mainframe customers because that's where we had the biggest installed base. Now we weight it by revenue and we get a different picture. Our mainframe revenue stream is only about 10 percent of our total revenue. We have found that over 50 percent of the Information Technology (IT) opportunity is not in the IT departments. It is either in smaller accounts, or in departments of larger accounts or professionals in specific areas.

When we do a hardware transaction with customers, we will ask them how satisfied they are with that transaction. When we do a consulting engagement, we will survey them based on that transaction. Did we live up to their expectation? Did we provide a solution? Did we deliver it on time? Was it within budget? We will also do third party surveys of satisfaction and feed all of the information into our database.

Through statistical analysis we can determine the greatest dissatisfiers among our customer base. By being able to quantify customer dissatisfaction, we are in a much better position to do something about it. We are able to statistically analyze and quantify what has long been a "touchy feely" area of customer service.

This is significant in a number of ways, not the least of which is the ability to compensate people based on customer satisfaction ratings. Profit sharing is directly linked to how well we have met the customer's needs. And it's true for every employee—sales, administration, managers, and vice presidents. Everyone is motivated to not only know what is making customers unhappy but to also do something about it.

With all this surveying going on, we need to be extremely cognizant of who we send customer satisfaction surveys to and why. Too many surveys to one person will obviously work against customer satisfaction.

The one thing we absolutely know, both qualitatively and intuitively, is that where we have a high customer satisfaction, we are engaged more frequently. We may not win them all, but at least we compete. And when we compete, our win ratios go up dramatically. That's what good customer satisfaction can do for you. The measurements give you a road map of what you need to do to improve.

POSTSCRIPT

Measuring an Actual Campaign Using a Traditional Media Allocation

The company, a large manufacturer of telecommunications equipment, was introducing a new product to new and existing business customers. The overall goal of the product launch was to retain market leadership and maximize revenue potential in an extremely competitive marketplace.

Strategically the new product was designed to:

- attract new system prospects
- upgrade existing customers to the new product
- satisfy current customers

Because of the strategic nature of the product, the company decided to launch it with extremely visible network television spots. National and local print advertising (Free Standing Inserts) and local radio were deployed. An 800-number was integrated into the mass media, with the message supporting the direct response media.

Mail was versioned by customer and prospect with both 800-number and BRC response options. A postcard followed the direct mail to reinforce the message. Telemarketing was selectively deployed to generate incremental leads and sales through response compression.

Mail and phone were synchronized per response compression to generate the highest response, prequalify all leads, and generate direct sales.

Customer service calls were timed two days and two weeks after installation of the product to continue the dialog with direct sale customers, assist with installation and troubleshooting, and generate information on customer satisfaction.

Results

- Response = 129% of forecast
- Leads = 116% of forecast
- Sales = 169% of forecast

This was good, but how could results be improved? The answers are in the IDM analysis.

Chart #1
Media Efficiency Analysis:

Media Mix	% of Total Cost	Inbound Misdirect
Television	41.2%	42%
Radio	6.0%	—
Print	13.1%	15%
Mail/telemarketing	39.5%	10%

Chart #2
Media Efficiency Analysis:

Media Mix	% of Total Cost	Leads	Sales of the New Product
Television	41.2%	5.4%	11.9%
Radio	6.0%	0.3%	0.6%
Print	13.1%	17.3%	11.2%
Mail/Telemarketing	39.5%	74.5%	67.6%

Results
The majority of leads and sales were generated by the combination of direct mail and telemarketing.

Television was inefficient in producing leads or sales. At 41.2% of the total budget, TV yielded:

- 42% of all misdirects*
- 5.4% of leads
- 11.9% of sales

The tightly linked combination of Radio and Free Standing Inserts was productive in generating leads and sales and gave assistance to the mail/phone messages.

Cost reduction achieved by mail and telemarketing:

- Leads—costs reduced 67% from projected
- Sales—costs reduced 33% from projected

Recommendations
Decrease general advertising because of a relatively small target market

- 600,000 decision-making units
- 50,000 decisions per month

* Inbound misdirects (inbound calls unrelated to the purpose of the 800 number) are seen as an indicator of media inefficiency: The investment in that response cannot be recouped, nor will it yield any benefit to the corporation.

Media expenditures should be 75 percent direct response/25 percent general awareness advertising to be much more effective in producing sales of the new product.

Customer service "welcome" calls, timed at critical intervals, reduced returns by 35 percent. The purpose of the call was to say "Thank you for the business," and "What assistance can we offer?"

Putting Together Your IDM Plan:
Worksheets and Guidelines

—————————————————— **Ultimately, integrated**

communications will surely prevail. ——————————

Bob Stone
Beyond 2000: The Future of Direct Marketing

A detailed, precisely sequenced marketing action plan is the core of any IDM program. Developing that plan and making it work requires strong leadership and vision. This chapter provides a framework to help you develop and implement an IDM program at your business that meets your own marketing and business objectives.

The step-by-step process that is explained here revisits the main issues covered in earlier chapters—now from a tactical perspective. It will help you organize your thinking, educate peers, managers, clients, and vendors, assign adequate time and resources, and manage the planning, development, and implementation phases.

As the IDM manager, keep in mind that a change like IDM, by its very nature, is threatening. It brings together functions that are not accustomed to working together. It asks people to put aside turf issues and internal politics. Budgets are reallocated; media is used in unique ways. Every member of the team needs to see the big picture rather than focusing on individual areas of specialization. IDM brings in big changes and new ways of doing things.

Pam Russell, Campaign Strategist Manager for IBM's Integrated Marketing Initiative, provides some insight into making the process work. "I realized early on that success for the program was inextricably linked with the ability of the leaders to envision a new reality and translate that into definable terms for the team.

"My approach was participative—a 'let's roll up our sleeves and get it done' approach.", continues Russell. "My team responded well to the creative and interactive methods; much better than a structured, top down 'how-to.'

"Communication became key. Since we were so geographically dispersed, we relied heavily on weekly team conference calls, fax transmission, and informal visits. Effective written and verbal skills became one of our key measurements. Engaging people's imagination in pursuit of the vision became a very real goal."

IDM is planning- and research-intensive. This means more upfront development time—something that the "let's have a campaign next week" factions may find hard to deal with. The old guard will jealously defend the old way of doing things. But the bottom line is that your IDM program will be as good as the leadership you provide. Leadership is key to keeping the IDM team focused and moving toward a common goal.

Dan Majkowski, Americas Customer Marketing Manager at Hewlett-Packard, comments on the process as it works at H-P:

"The key to managing the development of an IDM campaign is to remember—and remind people—that IDM does not mean relinquishing individual power but rather consolidating power for the common good. There aren't the usual divisions of labor and clear-cut lines of responsibility. A lot of areas of IDM development blend and merge with other areas."

FOUR PHASES OF IDM PLANNING

The IDM planning process consists of:

- Phase 1—Developing the Initial Marketing Action Plan
- Phase 2—Conducting IDM Depth Research and Developing the Final Marketing Action Plan
- Phase 3—Implementing the IDM Program
- Phase 4—Ongoing Communications

As we discuss these phases, we will walk through a sample timeline. The timeline is your main tool for accomplishing and managing the changes it entails (see Exhibit 7-1).

The timeline includes:

- 4 weeks for Phase 1
- 4 weeks for Phase 2
- 8 weeks for Phase 3

Phase 4, Ongoing Communications, will extend over time. The exact time period will be appropriate to your product or service and the decision-making cycle.

Integrated Direct Marketing: Program Implementation Process	1	2	3	4	5	6	7	8	9	10	11	12	13	14	15	16
Phase 1: **Initial Marketing Action Plan** – SWOT/GOAST – Initial Planning & Strategy Development – Field Integration – Database Development		▓	▓	▓												
Phase 2: **IDM Depth Research** – Development – Depth Research Interview Guide – Depth research – Final Marketing Action Plan – Strategy Validation					▓	▓	▓	▓	▓							
Phase 3: **Implementation** – Implementation of Strategies and Media Mix – Initial Generation of Response and Qualified Inquiries – Analysis of Interim Metrics for Continuous Improvement – Leads into Sales Process										▓	▓	▓	▓	▓	▓	▓
Phase 4: **Ongoing Communications**																

Exhibit 7-1.

A fully developed timeline, called the Working-Week Calendar for IDM Program Implementation, which assumes development and execution of a strategic event, is included in Appendix A.

Note that the timeline allots 16 weeks for development and implementation. Many decision makers have a hard time understanding why it takes that long. In reality, most corporations struggle to achieve the timeline, especially when conducting initial pilots.

This timeline has proven itself and can be a critical tool as you lead and manage the IDM process. We'd encourage you to use it as a template.

- When using the timeline for your own project, write the specific due dates next to the key events listed whenever possible. A general statement such as "week of . . ." is usually too loose, and your schedule will slip.
- Make reviewing the timeline the closing item of your first IDM team meeting. Fill in the dates and specific activities. Establish, with the group, the responsibility and exact due dates. That way, you create buy-in and ownership.
- Once Phase 1 is underway, issue the timeline weekly as a status report. This is an excellent tool that keeps the program moving, and gives management and team members regular status and an early alert when problems or delays crop up.

Copy it, make the changes necessary for your program, but use it as your road map. It will get you from start to finish every time. To help you with the planning and implementation process, let's now look at the timeline in more detail.

PHASE 1: DEVELOPING THE INITIAL MARKETING PLAN

IDM is a front-loaded process, devoting time to planning and research. And much of the success of your IDM program is determined in how thorough you are in the first phase—before any marketing dollars are spent.

The Importance of the IDM Manager

The events in Phase 1 are the responsibility of the IDM manager. The IDM manager plays a critical role throughout the process, but at this stage— while the team is being assembled and preliminary goals established—the IDM manager is the primary driver. Later in the process, the team provides critical input to create a program that represents shared goals and leverages individual expertise. But, throughout the program, you (or the designated manager) provide the vision and the leadership that drives the program and maintains focus.

According to Brian M. Gillespie, a former District Manager with AT&T, and the current Director, Worldwide Central Reservation Operations for ITT Sheraton Corporation, "IDM is not a new way of doing things; it is a new way of thinking about customers. Focusing on serving customers, targeting communications, and integrating resources will reshape sales and marketing organizations into a single cohesive unit. The new role of the IDM Manager is a strategic necessity."

Garry Dawson, Marcom Manager at Hewlett-Packard, has had extensive experience in bringing IDM campaigns to fruition. The experience has led Garry to formulate some "rules of the road." These include:

1. Identify and involve all decision makers and influencers in the planning process as you form the core program team—including sales.
2.. Establish your role as a consultant to the team (see "What's Expected of an IDM Manager").
3. Identify the budget and resources available.
4. Select a primary objective and poll the team. All team members, across all functions, should have multiple, complementary objectives such as:
   • Awareness
   • Lead generation

- Relationship building
- Closed business
5. Set the expectations and measures for success.

"Reward people for taking risks," recommends Pam Russell, IBM Campaign Strategist Manager. "Even if the change was not completely bump-free, I reward the people who have gone out on a limb and come up with a good plan. I have yet to reward anyone for doing something that they think is great but that simply maintains the status quo. I want all my people to think like change agents."

6. Make sure that expectations and measurements are quantifiable.
7. Prepare a timeline. This can be expanded or modified as the development process continues, but it provides a guide as you work through the process.
8. Describe the target audience/prospective buyers:
    - Select titles, departments, decision-making units, etc.
    - Review prior research and programs.
    - Learn what the competition is offering.
9. Clearly state the message and the value to the customer: What is your company's unique market position?
10. Determine the database(s) and check the actionability.
11. Include the sales force as early as possible.
12. Select the media and the communications vehicles; use the proven lead management systems already in place (see Chapter 6 for more detail); develop ongoing communications.
13. Integrate and manage vendors and internal resources.
14. Measure against performance objectives.
15. Modify for follow-up if needed.

♦ What's Expected of an IDM Manager?

- Learn and apply best practices. Turn knowing into doing.
- Don't repeat the past but learn from it.
- Think (and encourage) team, not individual, performance.
- Create cross-functional teams within the vertical organization.
- Incorporate individual objectives into team objectives.
- Keep internal customers informed.
- Reengineer marketing and sales to new roles in the process.
- Most importantly, provide clear direction and strong leadership for the rest of the team.

Assembling the Cross-Functional Team

Who should be part of the planning and implementation process? Here's a sample list of titles and functional areas:

- Executive sponsor/management
- Field sales management/representatives
- Product management
- Database resource
- Marketing
- Publicity/Public Relations
- Advertising
- Direct Mail
- Telemarketing
- Fulfillment
- Creative services

Not all the people will need to be involved in all phases of the project. However, be sure that sales is involved from day one.

The specifics of who is part of your IDM Cross-Functional Team will depend on the structure of your own business. List the decision makers, decision influencers, and experts who should be part of the IDM team.

Managing Expectations for Required Commitment

Putting together a team also means letting people know what's expected of them and what level of time commitment may be involved. Here are some examples of expected roles and "rule of thumb" time commitments. The estimates may err on the high side, but it's a practical error; it's always difficult to get more time when you need it. Use these as the basis for developing your own guidelines.

Executive Sponsor/Management is responsible for:

- "Big picture" focus
- Support
- Input to goals and objectives (what do we want to accomplish?)
- Resource allocation and apportionment
- Input to depth research (what do we need to find out and why?)
- Input to creative offer and development (what can we offer that has value?)
- Interim steps and program assessment

The time required? Approximately 10 percent of the executive's week.

Field Sales (or alternate channel)

- Input to goals and objectives (what do we want to accomplish, from the field perspective?)

- Insight into customer decision-making process, buying cycle, etc.
- Benchmark data
- Definition of a lead and criteria for lead categories (AA, A, B, etc.)
- Win/loss reporting
- Company strengths and weaknesses (as perceived by customer)
- Competitive issues
- Sales issues
- Selection of contacts for depth research
- Addition of questions for depth research interviews
- Input to database development
- Input to creative and offer development
- Development of a closed loop lead management system
- Interim and program assessment

The time required from field sales: approximately 25 percent of the salesperson's week, on the average. Sales will contribute more time during planning and development, and less during media deployment.

Product Management

- Input to goals and objectives
- Input to database development (who are the decision makers and who are the influencers? Which purchases create the opportunity for additional sales?)
- Contribute to creative development and review for accuracy
- Development of a closed loop lead management system (what can be found out from field/customer contact about product needs, satisfaction, competitive factors. etc?)
- Contribute to offer and event development and logistics
- Sales force communications (what are the advantages from the customer/field perspective?)
- Interim steps and program assessment
- Input to follow-up and ongoing communications (what products/ services make sense to customers?)

Time requirement? Approximately 15 percent of a product manager's week throughout the development and implementation process.

Database Resource

- Identify database and procure current customers and prospect database resources
- Obtain necessary suppression files ("Do not mail/Do not phone" requests)
- Incorporate internal and external databases
- Assist in the identification and procurement of outside list sources, enhancements, or overlays, as needed

- Take part in the development of a closed loop lead management system
- Meet database requirements for ongoing communications.

Time requirement? Approximately 30 percent of the database representative's week that can go as high as 60 percent during data-intensive events (merge/purge, updates, mailing list coordination, etc.).

Marketing

- Input to goals and objectives (what do we want to accomplish?)
- Input to database development (are we reaching the right people?)
- Input to creative content of communications and development of the offer (what do we want to say, how do we say it?)
- Input to telemarketing (what do we say over the phone, how do we train people, when do we call, how often?)
- Manage the creative development and production (who does what, when to create the ad, mail, script, etc.?)
- Manage the timing (when are the pieces completed, what is the schedule for communication with the customer?)
- Implement IDM quality and performance metrics (how did we do?)
- Implement ongoing communications
- Assist in development of a closed loop lead management system
- Interim and program assessment

Time requirement? Approximately 60 percent of the week for the duration of the program.

The time requirements for other functions will vary at different points in the program. For example, creative services may need to contribute 100 percent when brochures and ads are being produced, but may be only minimally involved during the database process.

As part of your role as IDM manager, make sure that all team members know what's expected of them and agree to the time requirements. In most cases, you or the team member will need to discuss his or her participation in, and time requirements for, this virtual enterprise with the team member's manager.

Every member of the team contributes. The development process involves everyone in every aspect of planning. This means that all team members have a clear picture of not only their role but of how the whole program fits together. The net results of that is greater understanding and commitment to the overall goals.

The First Team Meeting

The first team meeting is the kick-off for the program and is therefore critically important. Be sure to distribute basic information well ahead of the meeting along with an agenda to make sure key topics are covered.

Agenda for the First Meeting

- Initial view of target market
- Sales input, including win/loss reporting
- Baselining: overview of recent and current marketing efforts and results
- Benchmarking
- Situation analyses
  - Strengths and weaknesses
  - Opportunities and threats
- Initial View of:
  - Goals
  - Objectives
  - Audience
- Preliminary discussion of strategies and tactics
- Review of pro-forma timeline

The first action item on your agenda should be for the team to articulate, as precisely as possible, their initial view of the target market relative to the product or service to be promoted. It's important to get as clear a picture as possible of your potential customers first, before any other planning is done.

Following are some of the points that need to be considered when defining your target market:

- What is the profile of customers who have responded/bought in the past?
- Who else should be considered an opportunity?
- If possible, define and segment by commonality, such as:
  - Industry
  - Demographics
  - Installations/purchases
  - Behavior/psychographics
- How big is the market? How large are the segments?
- What research do you have currently that defines the market? How can it help the team better understand the needs and requirements of the target market?
  - Include any research that specifically links the marketplace and the product or service you will be promoting, as well as any competitive research.
  - For distribution and discussion, use an executive summary of any research. There's nothing to be gained from overwhelming people with volumes of market research, it is virtually guaranteed that it won't be read.

Sales Input from Day One

I've said it before and I'll say it again: Listen to your sales force. Everyone has an opinion on how to close a sale, but theirs is the only vote that counts. Their insight and experience is invaluable. Some of the important learnings fall into these areas:

Win/loss information provides a picture of the sales process. What are the types of customers or companies currently in the market for your kind of product or service? When do you win and from whom? When do you lose the sale, why, and with whom? Who was involved in the decision-making process and how long did the process take?

What is the field's initial view of the sales process for this marketing effort—by telephone, internal sales, third party? How do these avenues of distribution interact; what are roles and responsibilities? What's the average sale, time to sale, decision-making process, definable steps in the decision-making process, and requirements at each step? To find out specifics and verify this information, you'll need to supplement the sales force's information with depth research.

What are the criteria for a lead and how can leads be categorized? What determines whether a response is worth following up? How can marketing communicate with sales, reliably saying, "This is worth your time"?

Baselining to Establish a Starting Point

As discussed in Chapter 6, your baseline is a measure of the success of recent and current marketing efforts—and will help you measure the effectiveness of the IDM plan.

To obtain a baseline, look at the most recent marketing/communications to the market you'll be addressing. Include some samples in the information sent out to the team so that everybody is familiar with what's already been done. Supporting documentation should answer the following questions:

- Who was the target market and what was the timeframe?
- What were the goals and objectives?
- What strategies and tactics were deployed?
- What were the results?
- What factors contributed to the success of the program?
- What stood in its way?

Benchmarking

Include benchmarks whenever possible. Share information on "best of breed" companies in the same or similar industries. Examine their information, samples, and results to see what can be learned from their experience. Points of comparison may include:

- Telemarketing productivity
- Media contribution
- Database deployment
- Program results
- Customer satisfaction
- Processes and work flows

See Chapter 6 for a more detailed discussion of benchmarking.

Situation Analysis

Where does your product or service rank in the value/price grid in Exhibit 7-2? Your IDM plan will focus on moving your product, company or service into the upper right quadrant.

Exhibit 7-2. Commodities fall into the lower half, where price is the major factor in the customer's decision. Value-added products and services are in the upper two quadrants. The customer focuses on value, with price as secondary (or not even a concern).

Assessing Strengths and Weaknesses

The following charts (Exhibits 7-3 and 7-4) can be used to assess the strengths and weaknesses of your company, product or service. This establishes the position now—as the team believes the customer sees the world.

The assessment is completed by the team with only the information and insight that each member of the cross-functional team brings to the table. Remember that the results are based on opinions and should be verified through depth research.

What does the team perceive as strengths and corresponding weaknesses of:

- The corporation?
- The product or service?
- Value to the customer/prospect?
- The competition?

- Sales and distribution?
- Price?
- Post-sales support?
- Customer service?
- Sales channels?
- Marketing channels?
- Other areas as appropriate to your company or objectives?

Arrange the strengths and weaknesses in hierarchical order by importance to the customers. The most important should be on top. This maps out the territory you need to explore through your depth research. Then, as a team, complete the "What We'd Like to Know" form (Exhibit 7-4) to list topics and specific questions that should be included in the depth research interview guide.

Strengths	Confidence Level	Weaknesses	Confidence Level

Exhibit 7-3. Strengths and Weaknesses

Strengths		Weaknesses	
Topic	Specific Questions	Topic	Specific Questions

Exhibit 7-4. What We'd Like to Know

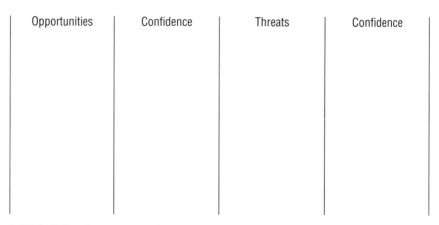

Exhibit 7-5. Opportunities/Threats

The team will then go through the same exercise to look at opportunities and threats. By opportunities, we mean opportunities to promote your product or service to the target market such as new customer needs, expertise of new sales channels, changing marketplace trends, competitor weaknesses, etc. Threats are defined as anything that could derail the planned promotion, as well as general threats to market share such as competitive pressure, economic climate, emerging technology, legislation, etc.

Once threats and opportunities are listed, it becomes clear what areas need further clarification. As a team, complete the "What We'd Like to Know" form once again, based on the identified (or suspected) opportunities and threats, and further the process of building the depth research interview guide.

Setting Goals and Objectives

The next critical success factor for the cross-functional team is setting the goals and objectives, and then refining the view of the target audience.

Goals are stated broadly, and encompass both program and business objectives. Multiple, complementary goals are recommended and may include:

- Awareness
- Maintenance or improvement of market share
- Relationship building
- Identification of current and future business.

Objectives should be stated more narrowly and should be clear, achievable, and measurable, and may include:

- Achieving double-digit response ($x\%$)
- $x\%$ response over the baseline

- x% increase in leads
- Cost per lead of $x
- Specific number of sales
- Cost per sale of x%
- Volume of overall sales (revenue)
- Specific E:R target.

Given the accomplishments and thinking of the team so far, what adjustments should be made to target market definitions or segmentation? In other words, where is the greatest opportunity? The team should ask themselves these questions:

- Do we need to redefine the target market?
- How should the target market be most effectively segmented (e.g., by SIC, product purchased, etc.)?
- Should certain segments be prioritized (because they represent greater opportunity)?
- Based on a preliminary view of the decision-making process and sales input, who are the decision makers and influencers, by title (as applicable), who should be on the database? What are the responsibilities and concerns of each? Are there definable steps in the decision-making process?
- What database work needs to be done to make sure that you are reaching this audience (e.g., outside list enhancements, outbound telemarketing list scrub, field review, etc.)?

Preliminary Strategies and Tactics

The purpose of this discussion is to state the possibilities and open the discussion for input and suggestions. Remember that this is still the first meeting, so the team will not have enough information to make decisions, but will be able to determine areas that need to be investigated, developed, and validated through depth research.

This discussion may include:

- *Potential messages to the audience.* Should there be different messages for different parts of the audience (the stratification of messages by decision maker, influencer, and gatekeeper, or by end-user, financial buyer, and technical specifier, for example)?
- *Appropriate offers.* What will have value to prospects/customers? How will they perceive your company's investment in the offer? How much does the customer need to do to respond and how does the offer prequalify the respondent? How do the offers/contacts move the customer/prospect along the buying cycle?
- *Initial media mix.* Consider past history with the customer or the market segment and what has worked and not worked in the past.

Refer to "do not call/do not mail" trending information. How many ways and times are you contacting the customer? What is the value of each contact?

- *Testing.* What variables should be tested to lay the groundwork for further improvements? Potential tests may include: pricing, communications design and content, lists, database segmentation, media mix, etc. Refer to Chapter 6 for a more detailed discussion of testing.
- *Ongoing communications.* What is the preliminary strategy to continue communications/contacts with the customers who are not yet ready to buy? How will these move decision makers along the buying cycle and increase penetration and yield?
- *Measurements.* How will you measure results? Refer to Chapter 6 for a detailed discussion of how to measure an IDM program.
- *Potential return.* Is the investment of time and money going to pay off? What can you expect in terms of sales and profitability? Refer to the Business Case discussion in Chapter 6.

Construct an Initial Calendar of Events

In each case history cited, the Calendar of Events (Exhibit 7-6) appears as a central, visual planning tool. Construct your own, based on these preliminary discussions.

A suggestion: Lay out the axes for the Calendar of Events on an overhead foil prior to the meeting. During the meeting, fill in the calendar with a grease pencil, so everyone can see the program form and take shape.

Have a professional graphic designer or desktop artist render the completed Calendar of Events, with clear, open typography and representative icons. Include it with the Initial Marketing Action Plan.

Timeframe
This axis is for time intervals, such as months.

Tactical Steps
This axis is for the tactical steps, such as

Sales force integration

Icons are used to indicate specific media deployments, tying tactics to timeframe

Focused print advertising

Initial direct mail

Exhibit 7-6. Format for Calendar of Events with example

Lining Up Resources

When planning an integrated marketing campaign, you will be drawing on internal resources across the company as well as numerous external resources. To keep the process on track and on time, it's important to have a clear idea now of what's needed and who will do it.

Make or Buy?   There are many arguments pro and con for using internal resources or buying outside. When making that decision, you'll need to balance expertise, availability, and cost of the one against the other. Here are some considerations when making your decision.

The integrated database (covered in detail in Chapter 2; following is a quick overview of considerations):

- The database must be market-driven, accurate, lean, and actionable
  - Older data may be warehoused in a larger database (Customer Information System) or sales contact report system
  - The database must be able to accept outside lists and enhancements
- You need the ability to continuously update as the program progresses and you get more information about customers and the market
- The database must be capable of driving the direct mail and be interactive with telemarketing, in order to
  - generate mail tapes
  - "load out" records on a daily basis for outbound telemarketing, cleaning the list of inbound responders
  - gather relevant response data from all media
- Systems must facilitate
  - the packaging of information for management reports, including all cost and all revenue
  - the input of information from field follow-up/the lead management process.

Telemarketing (covered in detail in Chapter 3, following is a quick overview of issues):

- Professional, well-trained resources for both inbound and outbound
- Technical capabilities to handle the expected volume
- Ability to interact electronically with the database
- Ability to conform with necessary methods and procedures (e.g., making and reporting a sale)

The selection of a telemarketing resource is a critical success factor, as this powerful channel will generate the vast majority of qualified response. Don't forget, telemarketing execution is a powerful leverage point for customer satisfaction or dissatisfaction, so evaluate the criteria and make your selection carefully. Refer to Appendix D, a Checklist for Decision Making about In-House versus Outside-Vendor Telemarketing Services for quick, actionable guidelines to the make or buy decision-making process concerning telemarketing.

Creative (covered in detail in Chapter 4, following is a quick overview of issues):

- Skill and track record of writers, designers, production staff
- Range of capabilities
- Turnaround time
- Ability to function as a "turn-key" operation—handling all creative services from initial discussions to camera-ready art to managing all production through placements, data processing, printing, lettershop, etc.

Testing.   Testing should be central to your plan. What are the major variables that can leverage success? For a complete discussion of testing, see Chapter 6. Here are some brief guidelines for building a test:

- Build a test matrix, so one can understand, at a glance, the cells that have been selected, which variables are being tested, and how the results can be read.
- Test one variable per cell.
- Make sure you have a control cell with a representative sampling of the general universe.
- Variables should be significant and worth the investment (a new creative approach or pricing strategy, for example).
- Test against widely held beliefs.
- Per Chapter 6, use a combination of logarithmic probability tables and practical guidelines to determine the size of your test.
- Populate the test cells with randomly selected names from the database. (Use care. If you have segmented the target market, names should come from the same segment. Going from segment to segment represents another variable).
- Be vigilant. Make sure that test cells are kept pure and that measurement is possible throughout media deployment. Names should be coded by test cell, with that code appearing on telemarketing files and on all printed pieces such as direct mail.

Building the Business Case

The Business Case is the financial justification of the marketing effort, executed prior to the expenditure of marketing dollars or sales resources. It details all projected expenses and all projected revenue, and arrives at the ratio of Expense to Revenue, or E to R percentage. The E to R equation reflects the viability of the pilot, program, or campaign.

Certainly, this is the initial draft: The Business Case must be refined per the results of depth research and the final marketing action plan.

Chapter 6 contains a complete discussion and direction for preparing the Business Case. Here is a brief overview of the process:

Step One.   Baseline. What happened before, in a like promotion. Make sure you're comparing apples to apples on the following key points:

- Target market
- Offer
- Response rate
- Leads (and did the field agree that they were leads?)
- Lead conversion to sale
- Number of sales
- Average sale
- Average time to sale
- Total cost

Step Two.   Develop the Expense Items. Expenses should be fully loaded and include the media expenditures as well as costs associated with:

- Events, as appropriate
- In-house costs of:
  - support personnel
  - sales representatives
  - resources

Step Three.   Projections for Response, Leads, and Sales. The basis of these projections should be:

- Baseline (promotional history)
- Industry averages
- Industry "best in class"
- Consultative or expert input
- Sales force input

Projections should include:

- % response by medium
- % leads (or qualified inquiries, as appropriate) from initial inbound and outbound
- % attendance (as applicable)
- % leads forwarded to field, per lead classification
- Close ratio (per field input)
- Expected average order
- Expected time to sale

Step Four.   Calculate E:R. Divide projected expense by projected revenue to arrive at the percentage or ratio of expense to revenue. (Guidelines for determining the potential viability of your program are contained in Chapter 6.)

Conclusion of Phase 1: The Initial Marketing Action Plan

Per the timeline, we've had one week of preparation, and 4 weeks for the development of Phase 1. We are now in Week 5.

The conclusion of Phase 1 is the publication of the Initial Marketing Action Plan. This document is the net result of all the work of the IDM Manager and the Cross-Functional Team. It is the centerpiece of your second formal meeting of the team. It is important to publish, present, and distribute this document to:

- Continue the momentum of the program and the communication with the Cross-Functional Team
- Provide a solid basis for moving into Phase 2
- Create a promotional history, so future marketing efforts can learn from and build upon this effort
- Demonstrate to management the process and the business viability of the program

Following is the suggested Table of Contents for the Initial Marketing Action Plan:

- Goals
- Target market
- Business issues
- Objectives
- Strategies
- Integrated database
- Sales process
  - Roles and responsibilities
  - Information that comprises a lead
  - Categorization of leads
  - Lead management process
- Tactics
  - Marketing programs
  - Testing
  - Integrated media mix
  - Managing customer contacts
  - Calendar of events
- Depth research
- Measurement
- Business case
- Timeline/status report

PHASE 2: CONDUCTING IDM DEPTH RESEARCH AND DEVELOPING THE FINAL MARKETING ACTION PLAN

As we discussed in Chapter 2, IDM depth research is a linchpin of the IDM campaign. This is where you validate your assumptions, test your theories and obtain clear information about those in your target market and what will have value to them.

Depth research is directional, qualitative sales and marketing research about the message and the offer. It is not, and was never meant to be, quantitative and is not a substitute for quantitative market research.

Here, step by step, is the process for conducting depth research:

Step One: Develop the Interview Guide

The interview guide should cover:

- Issues from Strengths/Weaknesses and Threats/Opportunities analysis (What We'd Like to Know)
- Competitive issues as identified by sales, marketing, and others on the team
  - How do decision makers currently view your company and product or service?
  - How do decision makers view your competition and their product or service?
  - How can your company gain competitive differentiation?
- Questions about the decision-making process
  - Who are the decision makers?
  - What are their titles, as appropriate?
  - Are there definable steps in the decision-making process?
  - What are the information needs at each step?
  - How long does the process, and each step, take?
- Sales coverage and process issues
  - What is their view of your sales process?
  - Where does the customer see, or need, value?
- Reactions to strategies and tactics
  - What other offers could you make that would earn their confidence and trust?
- Media preference
  - How should each medium be used; what are executional guide lines?

It's a good idea to begin the interview guide with broad questions to allow the interviewee to "warm-up" to the conversation. Once you have put together the questions in the interview guide, step back, reread it, and ask yourself whether these questions will yield actionable customer information and validation needed to move the initial Marketing Action Plan to the final Marketing Action Plan.

Ask the team to review the interview guide. Be sure to pass the questions by sales (who know the customers) and higher-level management (who have the big-picture view).

Make the appropriate changes and circulate the interview guide that will be used on the initial depth research interviews. This is only the first draft; expect to be revising it based on live interviews and emerging trends.

Step Two: Generating Names for Depth Research

Create the research matrix as the first step in determining your research sample, and how you will analyze results. In the sample below, we want to understand how to communicate with customer and prospects over three database segments (e.g., industry segments or demographic divisions). Use Exhibit 7-7 as a guideline when preparing your research matrix.

Populate the cells with decision makers:

- For business to business, determine which names/titles are decision makers (based on earlier market analysis and sales input).
- For consumer, decide who in the target market is the primary decision maker.

Most depth research will require 12 to 15 depth interviews, each lasting from 45 minutes to an hour. In the example above, 2 to 3 interviews per cell should give us the information we need. However, a more complex research matrix may require more interviews .

Per the timeline, we've allocated no more than three weeks for developing the interview guide, scheduling, and completing the interviews. We need to move quickly.

You'll find that scheduling the interviews is entirely dependent upon the schedules of the decision makers. Not everyone you approach will have the time or the interest to give you 45 minutes. Thus, some recommendations:

Names should be generated, as appropriate, by the sales force. They can contact and pre-screen decision makers. You will need a five-time multiplier

	Customer	Prospect
Segment 1		
Segment 2		
Segment 3		

Exhibit 7-7.

of names to interviews, to complete the process quickly. Thus, if you have targeted 12 to 15 interviews, you will need a pool of 60 to 75 decision makers to contact for scheduling.

Gathering Names. As stated, your sales reps are the prime source of names. If you don't have a sales force, use your database (but increase the multiplier; if names are not prescreened by sales, you will need 7 to 10 times more decision-maker names than targeted interviews). When requesting names, be specific about the information you need on each decision maker, including:

For Business to Business:

- Name
- Title
- Company
- Mailing address
- Telephone number
- Fax number
- Client rep
- Brief background information, which may include industry, size of company (e.g., annual sales, number of employees, number of branch offices, installation, customer satisfaction rating)
- Identification per research matrix

For consumer:

- Name
- Mailing address
- Telephone number
- Fax number
- Client rep, as appropriate
- Brief background information which may include demographics, purchasing history, customer satisfaction rating
- Identification per research matrix

As appropriate, the sales rep should make the first contact with the decision makers to let them know why they have been selected and what's expected of them, as well as to obtain agreement to participate. Arm your reps with a single-page synopsis of the basic research objectives and methodology.

Once we have the pool of decision makers who have consented to be interviewed, the scheduling process begins. Decision makers are contacted individually through high-quality, carefully scripted outbound telemarketing, making specific reference to the field contact, as appropriate. Outbound must be carefully managed, populating a central registration log, showing the dates and times of all interviews. When a decision maker agrees to a specific interview time, a confirming note with a copy of the interview guide is faxed out.

Once all interviews are scheduled, circulate a master list with names and times. Encourage team members to listen in and ask follow-on questions. Follow each interview with a brief analysis to discuss key points, trends, anomalies and points needing further clarification. This discussion will identify necessary revisions to the interview guide.

Share the in-progress information with the creative team to make sure that the link is made between what customers are saying and the creative message that is being crafted.

Step Three: Conducting the Interviews

Interviewing how-to:

- Interviewing is a skill that improves with training and experience. The effectiveness of the interviewing process relies on both speaking *and* listening.
- Consider using a professional organization the first time to help organize and phrase questions.
- Have team members sit in on the interviews to learn the process and to ask follow-on questions.
- The same members should stay with the process through completion to learn about analyzing the responses.
- Pick your interviewer carefully based on patience and the ability to get people to open up: It's as much a talent as a skill. Again, you may want to use a professional organization the first time out, to accelerate your learning curve.
- Stick to the structure of the interview guide, but stay alert, listen carefully. Go off script to probe issues that are not clear or to determine trends that may be emerging. Clarify decision makers' input so the direct voice of the customer may be heard.
- Ask decision makers for their permission to audio tape the interview. (Check with your legal representative to make sure you are conforming to all applicable legislation.) These tapes are invaluable in analysis. Promise the decision makers that they will be kept confidential, and will only be used in analysis—and keep your promise.

Step Four: Analysis

Analyze research results according to your research matrix. Within each cell, what were the comments and reactions of decision makers to the questions. Are the groups similar or dissimilar? What trends have emerged? What direction can be assumed?

Remember that this is qualitative research, designed to provide directional information on the decision-making process, messaging, offers, media preference, etc.

Finalizing the Marketing Action Plan

Based on the analysis of depth research interviews, you are ready to issue the Final Marketing Action Plan. The Major sections to the plan should cover:

Depth Research Results

- Executive summary of the research
- Methodology
- Detailed findings

Final Marketing Action Plan, with changes/additions as needed to:

- Goals
- Target market
- Business issues
- Objectives
- Strategies
- Integrated database
- Sales issues
    - Sales process, roles, and responsibilities
    - Information that comprises a lead
    - Categorization of leads
    - Lead management process
- Tactics
    - Marketing programs
    - Testing
    - Integrated media mix
    - Customer contacts
    - Calendar of events
        - Overlay relevant corporate publicity and advertising.
        - How is media and message synergy being managed?
          Sequence
          Timing
        - Are all target markets addressed?
          Number of customer-driven contacts
          Customer media synergy
        - Then, per contact management, generate and review an overview of all programs to this target market.
          What is the relevance and value of each contact?
          What synergies can be realized between programs?
- Business Case
- Timeline/status report

You may want to schedule some follow-up depth interviews with selected interviewees to validate any specific points about media selection, creative positioning and execution, event content, and logistics before finalizing implementation.

PHASE 3: IDM IMPLEMENTATION

It's time to take all the planning and turn it into action.

The timeline becomes your bible during this phase. Refer to it as you read this chapter. Copy it, make whatever changes are necessary per your program, and use it. Remember, as you get into Phase 3, you should be dealing with exact due dates and not "week of" due dates.

The calendar should include timing for each phase of the program, assigned responsibility, and an area to note the current status of any action. The status column should indicate whether the action has been taken and, if not, why not.

Implementation is problem intensive. There are many deliverables and many individuals with responsibilities for those deliverables. And all are being developed concurrently. The timeline we've provided is a proven tool, based on many years of experience, and will get you through implementation.

In your role as the IDM manager, the timeline is your quality tool, to make sure that everything is happening, and the program is progressing to budget and on schedule.

The sample timeline assumes the implementation of an information-sharing event as the strategic selling vehicle and a media mix that integrates advertising, mail, and telemarketing.

> When managing an IDM program, tight proactive management is the key to a successful program. Don't let deadlines slip. Don't assume that things are getting done. Use the timeline and status report as your quality-management tools.

Development of the Integrated Database

Research results and the efforts of the team in refining the Final Marketing Action Plan will result in new information about the target market. This information may fall into the following categories:

- The decision-making process
- Primary decision makers and influencers
- Information requirements

In light of this information, and the tactics and offers to be deployed, you should reevaluate the database with your subject-matter experts. How complete and actionable is the information? What information do we need and where do we get it? Per Chapter 2, some potential strategies for database enhancement include:

- Outside list enhancements
- Merge/purge, or the selective combining of information sources through technology
- Outbound telemarketing database list scrub.

Here are some timeline pointers:

- Outside lists may take 10 to 15 working days to arrive, once they are ordered.
- Budget at least a week (five working days) for merge/purge.
- It will take at least two weeks to get the database list scrub completed, depending on the size of your list, telemarketing capacity, and the complexity of the actual scrub script.
- No matter what you come out with at the end of this process, the final database must be reviewed by the field for corrections, additions, and deletions of sensitive accounts. The field must have confidence in the database, or they will not have confidence in the leads.

It is also time to assess the critical linkages between the database and:

Direct Mail.   Mailing tapes must be generated in a format easily used by the imaging and production vendor. As nixies and address corrections come in, further mailing tapes must be generated with the corrected information. Also, the database must "catch" business reply and fax responders to remove them from the outbound calling queue.

Telemarketing.   The database will "load out" or supply the telemarketing resource with names eligible for outbound calling. This list must be "cleaned" daily, with inbound responders removed from the outbound eligibility list. Ongoing analysis will enable the database to assist in prioritization of outbound.

Project Management.   All results must come back to the database, which then must generate regular and ad hoc reports for analysis.

Sales Channels.   The integrated database must be friendly and accessible to the field for:

- Database correction, additions, and deletions
- Results of lead follow-up
- Sales information

Implementation of Creative

The IDM manager must give strong creative direction per research results. It helps considerably if the creative team members have been involved in the depth research process. This provides the copy and design team with direct input on customer needs, wants, and preference and encourages the kind of thinking that leads to innovative, "out-of-the-box" solutions.

Copy and design need to work as a team to integrate the creative positioning, strategy, and message across all media—and to meet the timeframes established in the Marketing Plan.

> Since timing is so important, be aware of what approvals will be needed and schedule time with key people to move the process ahead as quickly as possible. Let them know what's coming, when it's coming, what their responsibility is, and what the ramifications are if the approval process is not completed to schedule.
>
> Legal can be your ally or your adversary. It's up to you. Lawyers are known as a notorious bottleneck, but if you keep them advised and informed from early in the process, establish timelines, and gain their concurrence to those timelines, we've found them to be an important asset.

Event Planning and Coordination

All logistics—dates, places, facilities, and catering—should be worked out as early as possible since availability of meeting facilities may be a deciding factor in your scheduling. And the event information drives the rest of the creative.

Timing. As you are booking locations and resources, to gain maximum registration and attendance, allow approximately four weeks between the arrival of the invitation and the date of the event.

Venue. If an event is important to your target market, should it be face-to-face or remote, as in an audio teleconference? Ask the staff in depth research. The face-to-face event has many advantages, such as time away from everyday distractions and peer networking. However, remote access venues, such as audio teleconferencing, have strong appeal. Teleconferencing requires no travel, allows multiple parties to attend via a speakerphone, and substantially lowers your cost.

Location. Consider including a question in your depth research about the distance that interviewees are willing to travel to an event. It will help you in your selection of location(s) for the event.

Speakers and Topics. The depth research should have given you an indication of what interests the market. Don't be afraid to ask for specific recommendations. People are happy to tell you whom they trust and want to hear.

You may also find that decision makers want to hear case histories. If these are important, depth research may help generate interested decision makers. At the end of the interview, if the decision maker has indicated a strong story, ask for his or her cooperation.

Rehearsing Speakers

Request a copy of each speech and all visuals in advance, and schedule at least two rehearsals prior to the event. Time the rehearsals so that speakers have a chance to modify their speeches as needed. The last thing you want at the event is a speech that's not appropriate, incoherent visuals, or a speaker who doesn't deliver as promised.

◆ IDM Validation Depth Research

The realities of event planning, coordination, and creative development may suggest the deployment of validation depth research. Development may cause the introduction of a new speaker or a change in focus; creative may suggest an unusual or dimensional package.

These additional interviews can provide great value by validating issues per customer needs prior to the expenditure of marketing dollars. However, it is essential that validation research be executed quickly and expertly. Here are some tips:

- At the end of the depth research interview, ask decision makers if we can recontact them to validate specific topics or creative executions.
- Schedule interviews with these previously interviewed decision makers.
- Approximately four to six interviews should be sufficient, depending on the complexity of the research matrix or program.
- Follow all guidelines for depth research.

Production

Production can cause the biggest headaches and poses an area ripe for possible delays and cost overruns. The job of managing multiple vendors to very exacting specifications and a tight timeline is a challenge—but an essential part of having the IDM program come off as planned.

It will help if you have lined up the best resources you can afford beforehand and obtained written commitments from them of specifications, delivery, schedules and cost estimates. This will eliminate large areas of potential misunderstanding.

Once production begins, issue purchase orders to each resource detailing all required quality-control procedures and reiterating specifications, costs, and expected dates for deliverables.

Advertising Placement.   Periodicals often have long lead times, so check when your materials are due to the publication. Also be sure that your production people are clear on exactly what is due—camera-ready art or film, as well as sizing or any unique specifications that, if not covered, will delay the insertion.

Direct Mail Production.   Creating a finished direct mail piece draws on many vendors—printers for brochures and letters, data processing for personalization, envelope suppliers, mailing houses/lettershops, etc. Timing and coordination are essential.

Proactive quality control is especially critical in direct mail. To detect problems early (and, trust me, there will be problems), have the supervisor on each production run, pull, inspect, and sign a sample at 15-minute intervals. This will catch errors early and head them off before they become major disasters. If an error does get through, you'll know the extent of the problem by inspecting the signed samples.

Fulfillment.   Fulfillment may be an industry term, but its purpose and importance are intuitive. Customers have responded and we have promised them something in return. This is the fulfillment of that promise. And because a promise is involved, timeliness and quality are of the utmost importance.

It's absolutely essential that the fulfillment materials are generated and sent out per plan (e.g., per the seven-step lead generation process: within 24 hours for the confirmation card, and 1.5 weeks before the event for the briefing package). The quality of the fulfillment has a direct impact on how the customer perceives your mailing.

> To test the quality of the fulfillment, include, or "seed" yourself and team members in database, so that you experience all media as if you were a member of the target market. Everyone should respond, via different media (800 number, outbound, business reply, fax) and test the fulfillment process multiple times.

Telemarketing.   Bring your telemarketing resource in early to determine capacity, staffing, and completion plans. As we have mentioned so many times before, telemarketing is the most powerful medium for generating qualified response, customer satisfaction, and dissatisfaction. Ensure good results. Plan on being on-site for training and call start.

Your telemarketing resource is likely to be well equipped and skilled in training on telemarketing skills. However, you, and selected team members, are the experts on your corporation, the target market, and the program.

Your assistance in training can make a big difference. Bring along any visual materials that are appropriate, especially samples of the publicity, ads, and direct mail. Your communicators need to see what the target market sees.

Measurement is critical and can be used to immediately improve results, through script development, list management, etc. It's very important to be on-site for the first few rounds of telemarketing—inbound and outbound. You're there to answer questions, provide direction and advice, analyze the key productivity metrics and work in partnership with your telemarketing resource to sharpen the script based on actual customer contact.

Lead Management.   This is where most companies fail. Start this process early and ensure field buy-in.

And a hint: The field is your customer; treat them to good customer service. To get things off to a good start, call a selection of reps the day before their first report is due. Offer to take the information over the phone. It will make them feel that their contribution is appreciated, and it ensures that the information will be captured.

Analyses.   A major responsibility of the IDM Manager is the interim analyses of key response and productivity data to fine tune the process. Have all resources format reports early in the process and send you copies for your approval. That way, you are assured that the systems are in place.

And be aggressive if interim metrics are not measuring up to baseline or projections. Small changes or adjustments along the way can add up to a big impact on results. If you see trouble, and it's not responding to traditional triage (e.g. scripting, list management), try something bold. One suggestion is a high impact "Western Union" communication to non-responders which says, "We've been trying to reach you with critical information."

The key to final analyses is not to add-up the interim analyses, it's to find how we can do better next time.

PHASE 4: ONGOING COMMUNICATIONS

IDM as a continuing, ongoing communication stream will increase your yield and penetration over time, bringing incremental response and sales. Therefore, make sure that you start the ongoing communications as soon as possible after the conclusion of the specific program (after the event, following response to the offer, etc.).

For starters, send a thank you and ask for feedback. Your responses will give you valuable information on wants, needs and preferences. IDM is a continuing loop of communications that brings you and the customer into ever closer partnership.

POSTSCRIPT

We've covered IDM in great detail, presenting results and examples to help you plan and implement IDM at your own operation. As we've said before, be prepared for bumps along the way because IDM requires a change in how people think about marketing. Since it is detailed and precise, some people are scared off by the thought of the time and resources needed to make IDM a reality. However, with strong leadership and by following the steps we've outlined here, you will be able to construct your own plans and achieve the magnitude of improvement in results that IDM can bring.

The results of a fully realized IDM program are well worth it—both for the immediate increase in qualified response and for the longer-term value of good, solid relationships with your customers. It's the long-term relationships that will solidify near-term and future sales and improve your bottom line.

IDM will help you navigate in rapidly changing markets. But more importantly, it encourages sharing of information across corporate "boundaries"—and the eventual dismantling of those boundaries—that benefits the entire enterprise.

Mike Lawrie, IBM US Vice President and Area General Manager, comments on IBM's experience with Integrated Direct Marketing:

> As we acquire a better understanding of buyer behavior and buyer intentions, as we better understand how people buy information technology, we will be better able to serve our customers at a lower cost with greater customer satisfaction. Once we broke out of the old industrial marketing mold and began to really listen to our customers—not just what they wanted to buy, but their overall reaction to IBM—it spurred us to take the ideas and accelerate our implementation. When we realized we could get to targeted portions of the market at reduced costs with increased response, we knew we were onto something. It opens up a whole new area in competitively reaching a marketplace.

POSTSCRIPT

Fine-tuning IDM Implementation— A Checklist

Scott Hornstein
Senior Partner, ERDM.

Many years of implementing IDM programs have given us perspective on how to fine-tune a program—how get the extra measure of performance. Following is our checklist of what to look for and what to do about it.

I. Integrated Database

- The database must reflect the decision-making process of your target market.
  - Consumer: Is the opportunity for response/sale by decision maker, or by household (i.e., is there one opportunity per household, or many)?
  - Business-to-business: Is your opportunity by decision maker, by enterprise, or by decision-making unit (d.m.u.)?
  - In either case, the database should contain both decision makers and influencers, their specific roles and information needs.
- Key list segments should be refreshed each time they are used through interactive communications and field review. Plan a comprehensive quarterly update including an outbound telemarketing scrub and outside enhancements, as required.
- Track your "nixies" (returned, undeliverable mail) and outbound telemarketing "bad" numbers (e.g., disconnected, out-of-business, etc.). Do not tolerate waste.

II. Advertising

- Rates are often negotiable. Even if you are testing, or aren't spending a lot now, try to negotiate a better deal. Don't focus your negotiations on price—position, size, and color may have more of an effect on qualified response.

III. Direct Mail

- Direct mail should be released in waves (subsets of the universe released at specific time intervals). Only release the mail that telemarketing can follow up within 24 to 72 hours.
- Personalize only the components necessary for the next mail drop. If possible, maintain the flexibility to increase or decrease the size

of a mail drop, to change copy as required to affect the current promotion. This strategy may cause additional cost, but may generate
incremental response and sales due to the flexibility this will give
you to better manage response compression and to address new customer concerns in letter copy.

- Reference the telemarketing in direct mail copy. Direct mail should
be a springboard for telemarketing response, both inbound and outbound. Provide solid business and customer satisfaction reasons for
calling the 800 number. Tell your customers the value-add of the outbound call.
- Personalization can increase qualified response by as much as 10 to
15 percent. However, database accuracy is a strong variable in the
performance of personalization. Check your database carefully.
- First Class mail works. The increase in qualified response usually
more than pays for the additional cost.

IV. Inbound Telemarketing

- Plan for capacity. Where possible, avoid generating peaks of response
that will "max out" your capabilities and drive up blockage and abandon rates. Stagger your promotions, if possible, to ensure that every
call, every opportunity, is answered.

V. Outbound Telemarketing

- Achieving Response Compression (24 to 72 hours from mail receipt
to outbound call) will maximize qualified response/sales.
- Improve TQC (Total Quality Control) by instituting a standard qualitative and quantitative monitoring procedure. All members of the
cross-functional team (subject matter experts and internal clients)
should be required to monitor.
- If you are not meeting your goals for outbound completed calls per
hour, look deeper. Is the answer in the current attempts (dials) per
hour? Is the list dirty (a large number of disconnects, out of business)? Is talk time longer than anticipated?
- Scripts are constantly evolving. We must learn and improve. Monitoring, communicator feedback sessions, and "reasons for not interested" reports provide good information for script changes.
- Create early exit points in the script to allow "not interesteds" to get
off the phone—improving both customer satisfaction and productivity.
- Clean all outbound calling lists of inbound responders and direct
mail nixies daily.
- If "do not call" requests escalate, consider discontinuing outbound
telemarketing.

VI. Response

- Focus on qualified response. Measure casual interest, such as free literature requests from suspects, separately.
- Plot your response curve. Use this as a "predictive" tool for future promotions.

VII. Lead Management

- While a closed loop lead management system is essential to long-term success, most companies fail in their attempts to implement such systems because communications between marketing and sales is so badly fractured. To succeed:
  - Involve field sales in both the planning and implementation of the system—make sure it is not perceived as a "police action".
  - Make sure you are providing the information field sales needs for qualified leads. Some of the information that should be tracked:
    - When did marketing contact the customer/prospect, and with what offer?
    - When did the customer/prospect respond, and by what medium?
    - What were the customer's/prospect's responses to qualifying questions (as applicable)?
    - What else do we know about the customer/prospect? (Previous response? Previous purchases?)
    - How has this response met the field's definition of a lead and criteria for qualification of a lead?
    - When did sales first contact the lead? What were the results?
    - What were the results of the first substantive conversation with the lead?
      - Part of the covenant between marketing and sales must be that marketing will not take up the fields' time unless a lead meets their predetermined criteria, and sales, in turn, will follow up highly qualified leads within 24 hours, even if it's only a phone call.
      - Should the lead be reclassified? What should the new classification be?
      - What was sold? In what time frame?
      - If no sale, why not?

Use these battle tested hints, clues, and guidelines to keep your IDM plan flexible and responsive to changing needs. Maximize your response, customer satisfaction, and return on investment by using the IDM quality and performance metrics to refine and improve your customer communications.

Congratulations on having completed this book. We hope you found the marketing journey exciting and full of useful ideas.

We realize that we have presented you with a lot of material. Don't feel overwhelmed. By simply following the IDM process we have detailed, you will achieve significant increases in results.

Some final pointers for you:

- Don't underestimate the magnitude of sales and marketing change required in most companies.
  Therefore, structure manageable, well-conceived IDM pilots to prove your case through powerful results.
- You can't change your company in one day. Plan a logical, manageable sequence of events.
- Communicate openly and frequently with allies and potential resistors; include the key players from the beginning.
- Secure both senior management (aerial cover) and grassroots support. Keep validating and reinforcing their support.
- Be careful: Just using different media is not IDM! Precision deployment of the right media to the right people at the right time is IDM.

We wish you the best of luck on your marketing journey. If, as you implement your own IDM programs, you'd like to call us for ideas or advice, we'd be happy to make the time to speak with you. You can reach us at 718/225-4151.

Working-Week Calendar for IDM Program Implementation

Following is a sample calendar for implementation of an IDM lead generation program deploying information-sharing events as the strategic selling vehicles.

Working-Week Calendar for IDM Program Implementation

PHASE 1: Developing the Initial Marketing Action Plan

Week	Action	Responsibility	Status
1	• Cross-Functional Creative Team Is Established	IDM Manager	
	• Roles and responsibilities are reviewed		
	• Deliverables for First Meeting		
	• IDM process overview	IDM Manager	
	• Initial view of target market	Team	
	• Sales input	Sales Force	
	- Definition of a lead		
	- Criteria for categorization of leads		
	• Baselining	IDM Manager/Marketing	
	- Overview by promotion		
	- Samples		
	- Results analysis		
	• Benchmarking	IDM Manager/Marketing	
	- "Best in class" benchmarks		
	• Situational analyses	Team	
	- "Value/price" grid		
	- Strengths and weaknesses		
	- Opportunities and threats		
	• Goals and objectives	Team	
	- Broadly stated goals		
	- Specific objectives		

- Audience
  - Further segmentation/prioritization
  - What database work must be done
- Preliminary strategies and tactics
  - Ongoing communications
  - IDM quality and performance metrics

Team

Database Team

2–3
- Construct an Initial Calendar of Events
- Overlay corporate advertising or publicity that may support this effort, as appropriate

IDM Manager/Marketing/ Marketing Support

- Make or Buy: What Resources Are Required
- Develop the Testing Matrix
- Build the Initial Business Case
  - Step One: Baseline
  - Step Two: Develop the expense items
  - Step Three: Projections
  - Step Four: Calculate E:R
    - Most likely case
    - Conservative
    - Aggressive

IDM Manager/Team
IDM Manager/Team
IDM Manager/Team

4
- Develop and Issue the Initial Marketing Action Plan
  - Goals
  - Target market
  - Business issues
  - Objectives
  - Strategies

IDM Manager

Working-Week Calendar for IDM Program Implementation

Week	Action	Responsibility	Status
	• Relationship information systems/database		
	• Sales issues		
	- Sales process, roles and responsibilities		
	- Information that comprises a lead		
	- Categorization of leads		
	- Lead management process		
	- Tactics		
	- Marketing programs		
	- Testing		
	- Integrated media mix		
	- Customer contacts		
	- Calendar of events		
	• Depth research		
	• Business case		
	• Timeline/status report		

PHASE 2: Conducting IDM Depth Research and Development of the Final Marketing Action Plan

Week	Action	Responsibility	Status
5	• Customer and Prospect Names for Depth Research Are Generated by the Field (as appropriate)	Field	
	• Depth Research Interviews Are Scheduled	Research	
	• Draft of Interview Guide Is Reviewed by Team and Research Resource	Team/Research	
	• Final draft of interview guide is issued		

		Research
5-7	• Depth Research Interviews Are Conducted	
7-8	• Depth Research Results Are Analyzed	
8	• Depth Research Results and Final Marketing Action Plan	

- Depth Research Results and Final Marketing Action Plan
  • Research executive summary
  • Methodology
  • Detail findings
  • Final marketing action plan, with changes/additions to:
    - Goals
    - Target market
    - Business issues
    - Objectives
    - Strategies
    - Relationship information systems/database
    - Sales issues
      • Sales Process, roles, and responsibilities
      • Information that comprises a lead
      • Categorization of leads
      • Lead-management process

| 8 | • Depth Research Results and Final Marketing Action Plan | |

- Tactics
  - Marketing programs
  - Testing

Working-Week Calendar for IDM Program Implementation

Week	Action	Responsibility	Status
	- Integrated media mix		
	- Customer contacts		
	- Calendar of events		
	• Per contact management, generate and review an overview of all programs to this target market		
	- What is the relevance and value of each contact?		
	- What synergies can be realized between programs?		
	• Business case		
	• Timeline/status report		

PHASE 3: Implementation

Week	Action	Responsibility	Status
9	• Outside List Enhancements Are Identified and Secured	Database	
	• Specifications for Telemarketing Database Scrub	Team	
	• Titles and information to be built		
	• IDM list scrub script is developed	Telemarketing Team	
	• Team approval (72-hour turnaround)		
	• Training begins	Telemarketing	

Week	Task	Responsible
10	• All Required Resources Have Been Determined	IDM Manager/ Marketing Support
	• P.O.s/service agreements are issued	
	• IDM List Scrub of Database Begins	Telemarketing
	• Performance/productivity metrics issued and analyzed daily	
	• Creative for Advertisements Is Circulated and Reviewed	Team
	• Fast approval is required	
11	• Validation Depth Research (as required)	Research
	• Camera-Ready Art for Advertisements Is Released	Creative
	• Copy and Design for Initial Mail Package and Confirmation Card Are Circulated	Creative
	• Team suggestions/comments (72-hour turnaround)	Team
12	• All Outside List Enhancements, As Appropriate, Arrive	Database
	• All Logistics for Each Event (Dates/Times/Places) Are Determined	Marketing Support
	• Merge/Purge Specifications Are Developed	Database
	• Script and Visuals for Each Presentation and Case History	Marketing Support
	• Script and visuals are circulated to team for approval	

Working-Week Calendar for IDM Program Implementation

Week	Action	Responsibility	Status
	• Camera-Ready Art for the Initial Mail Package and Confirmation Card Are Released to the Printer	Creative	
	• Telemarketing Staffing and Resources Are Finalized	Telemarketing	
13	• Initial Telemarketing Script Is Circulated	Telemarketing	
	• Two Complete Rehearsals Are Scheduled for Each Event	Marketing Support	
	• Merge/purge Is Complete		
	• List of All Eligible Customers and Prospects Is Sent to Field for Update/Review	Database/Field	
14	• Magnetic Tape of All Names to be Mailed Arrives at Service Bureau	IMI	
15	• Advertising Appears in Selected Publications	Marketing Support	
	• Magnetic Tape of All Names Eligible for Outbound Telemarketing Arrives at Telemarketing	Database	
	• Final Script for Initial Inbound and Outbound Telemarketing	Telemarketing	
16	• Briefing Package Is Developed	Creative Team	
	• Ongoing Communications Strategies Are Finalized		

Task	Responsibility
• Telemarketing Script for Confirmation Calls Circulated	Marketing Support
• Team approves (24-hour turnaround)	Team
• Telemarketing Training	Telemarketing/Team
• Field "Kick-Off" Event (i.e., Audio Teleconference)	IDM Manager

• Lettershop/First Week of Mailing
  • Release to USPS
  • Daily mail release report
  • Inbound/BRC/Fax Response
	Marketing Support

• Outbound Telemarketing Follow-Up to Initial Mailing
  • Per principles of response compression - 24 to 72 hours after mail receipt
  • IDM performance/productivity metrics issued daily
	Telemarketing

• IDM metrics analyzed daily - Real time improvements	Telemarketing/IDM Manager
• Communicator feedback to further refine script	Telemarketing
• Confirmation Cards Are Completed and Mailed Within 24 Hours of Receipt of Registration	Telemarketing
• Central Registration Log Is Kept and Updated Daily	Marketing Support

Calculating the Lifetime Value of a Customer

Richard J. Courtheoux,
President, Precision Marketing Corporation

Accurate calculation of lifetime value requires considerable thought, effort, and serves as a base of information on customer performance. The methodology described below attempts to project future customer performance using historical patterns as a base. In changing businesses, these patterns should be adapted to reflect current expectations.

Lifetime value can be computed by executing the following steps:

1. Segment customers into a manageable number of cells. These cells can be based on recency of last purchase, frequency (number of purchases), dollar amount of purchases, merchandise purchase categories, or other criteria appropriate to a business. Alternate cells may represent customers with similar formula scores from a statistical technique such as multiple regression. The number of cells should be:
   - Enough so that genuine differences in customer responsiveness can be represented.
   - Not so many that the amount of work explodes and the accuracy of the statistics for each cell deteriorates.

   Accurate lifetime value calculations typically use 25–100 cells.
2. Choose a time period for tracking results. Six-month seasons are a good balance between too much and too little detail.
3. Estimate the contributions to overhead and profit which are derived from the starting period of the customers in a cell. For example,
   - Track all the revenues and costs which can be associated with those customers during the period.
   - Tracking cell performance by medium (or offer) for each cell is not advisable by itself, since some customers move from one cell to another within any given time period.
4. Describe the movements of customers among cells from the beginning of one time period to the next. For example, a cell may have 1000 customers at the start of one season, and have those identical 1000 customers at the outset of the next season. This is often the most sensitive and complicated part of the analysis.
5. Project the movement of 1000 new customers over a number of periods into the future, using the customer-movement patterns

described in Step 4. The projection should be planned far enough into the future so that only a small amount of discounted contribution is being observed.

6. Use the number of customers in each cell for each period projected in Step 5, along with the financial performance information from Step 3, to calculate contribution per period.
7. Apply a cost of capital (or discount rate) which represents the rate of interest that your company needs to justify an investment. The cost of capital is a means of equalizing current and future cash flows. It reflects both the time value of money and the uncertainty of future cash flows. For example:
   - A company with a 12 percent annual cost of capital will require a $112 return next year for a $100 investment this year.
   - If no projected number is used in your company, an annual real rate of 12 percent (which covers inflation) is a reasonable number to apply.

Projected cash flows in all seasons after the initial one are adjusted to their equivalent in season one dollars. An example illustrates how these steps can be executed.

1. Segment customers by recency of last purchase. Group in 6-month intervals all customers who have purchased in the last 3 months.
2. Use 6-month seasons as the time period for the analysis.
3. For each cell:
   - Identify the customers in the cell at the start of the season.
   - Add up all the revenues obtained during the season from these customers.
   - Compute the costs for these customers during the season, including promotion, merchandise and fulfillment.
   - The contribution is the difference between total revenues and total costs.

The total contribution should be divided by the number of customers in the cell at the start of the season in order to produce a contribution per customer. A typical table might look like this:

Recency Group	Contribution per Customer
0-6	$4.39
7-12	2.20
13-18	1.02
19-24	.57
25-30	.07
31-36	(.09)
37+	–

4. At the end of the season, movements of customers among cells can be summarized as follows:

Start Cell	End Cell	Probability
0-6	0-6	0.25
	7-12	0.75
7-12	0-6	0.17
	13-18	0.83
13-18	0-6	0.12
	19-24	0.88
19-24	0-6	0.09
	25-30	0.91
25-30	0-6	0.06
	31-36	0.94
31-36	0-6	0.03
	37+	0.97
37+	37+	1.00

5. The calculations displayed in Table B-1 show the movements and financial contributions from 1000 customers in a recency group 0-6 at the start of the season. A cost of capital of 6 percent per season (12 percent per year) is used for discounting future season contributions. The key figure is the cumulative discounted contribution of $2,590 from the 1000 new starting customers.

The calculation shows a lifetime value per new customer of $12.59 (= $12,590/1000 customers). This could be expanded to include:

- Acquisition season contribution. The analysis shown ignores all first order revenues and costs, in effect allocating them to the customer acquisition process.
- More time periods. However, the additional discounted contribution by period 10 is quite small. Carrying the analysis to more periods will only add slightly to the estimated lifetime value for this business. In many firms, the projection should extend as much as 10 years.
- Detailed financial calculations. Contribution could be broken down to show revenue, list rental income, cost of goods, fulfillment cost, etc.
- Loss of some customers from the file due to attrition.

This analysis becomes a base case which can be modified to evaluate various business options.

This is, admittedly, a complex calculation. It demands not only the financial sophistication to carry out the calculations but also database records sufficiently completed and organized to provide the fodder for the figuring. Still, whether you follow the procedure outlined above or simplify it to deal with only a few individual market segments (tracking buying behavior over

TABLE B-1. New Customer Lifetime Value Calculation

Customers					Season					
	1	2	3	4	5	6	7	8	9	10
0–6 months	1000	250	190	154	130	108	86	62	48	37
7–12 months	0	750	187	142	115	98	81	64	46	36
13–18 months	0	0	622	155	118	95	81	67	53	38
19–24 months	0	0	0	547	136	104	84	71	59	47
25–30 months	0	0	0	0	498	124	94	76	65	54
31–36 months	0	0	0	0	0	468	117	89	72	61
37+ months	0	0	0	0	0	0	454	568	654	724
Contribution	4390	2743	1877	1458	1060	818	685	521	401	310
Discounted contribution	4390	2588	1671	1224	840	611	482	346	251	183
Cumulative discounted contribution	4390	6978	8649	9873	10714	11325	11808	12155	12406	12590

SOURCE: Reprinted from DMA Mail Order Manual, Release No. 620.4, with permission from Direct Marketing Association, Inc., New York, 1986.

time and factoring in the net present value of the revenues produced), deriving a quantitative figure for the lifetime value of a customer is critical.

Of course, the process doesn't stop with the presentation of a neat figure on paper. Once you can identify the long-term value of a customer, this must become a key element in top management decision making. The purpose of IDM is to create an ongoing relationship between company and customer. For virtually all sellers of goods or services, it is repeat business over time that not only provides the bulk of the profit but also brings in new customers through referrals. By identifying the key segments of the marketplace and pinpointing their continuing value to the company, we can accurately apply the resources of IDM at appropriate levels. For a particularly active segment of the customer base, or a segment that has the potential for becoming very active, more frequent contact employing a greater diversity of media may be warranted. For less frequent but still steady buyers, less intensive but regular contact through a single medium may be cost justified. It is up to the IDM manager to put together the market-segmentation data with an eye toward establishing acceptable marketing expenditures for each segment, and to make program recommendations to senior management on the basis of this rationale.

APPENDIX C

Outbound and Inbound Telemarketing

Outbound Telemarketing Daily Productivity Report: Telemarketing Database Scrub

(Today's Date)   (Time Period Covered by This Report)   (Total Records/% Complete)

	Mon. (date)	Tues. (date)	Wed. (date)	Thurs. (date)	Fri. (date)	Week Total	MTD Total	PTD Total
Calling Hours								
Training Hours								
Completed Surveys								
Disconnect/OOB								
Do Not Call								
Duplicate								
Refused								
No Listing								
Unavailable*								
Not Qualified								
Total Completed Records								
No Answer								
Call Back								
Busy								
Total Attempts								
Attempts/Hr.								
Completed Records/Hr.								
Demographics Updated								

*Unavailable after X attempts.

Inbound Telemarketing Daily Productivity Report: Response/Registration Generation

(Today's Date)   (Time Period Covered by This Report)   (Total Records/% Complete)

	Mon. (date)	Tues. (date)	Wed. (date)	Thurs. (date)	Fri. (date)	Week Total	MTD Total	PTD Total
Calling Hours								
Training Hours								
Registration:								
Total Business Registrations:								
Total Executive Registrations:								
Total No. Registrations								
Total Calls to ACD								
# Blocked								
% Blocked								
# Abandon								
% Abandon								
# Misdirect								
% Misdirect								
Total Contacts:								

Outbound Telemarketing Daily Productivity Report: Registration Generation

(Today's Date)   (Time Period Covered by This Report)   (Total Records/% Complete)

	Mon. (date)	Tues. (date)	Wed. (date)	Thurs. (date)	Fri. (date)	Week Total	MTD Total	PTD Total
Calling Hours								
Training Hours								
Registration:								
Total Business Registrations:								
Total Executive Registrations:								
Total No. Registrations								
Total Contacts:								
Disconnect/OOB								
Do Not Call								
Duplicate								
Refused								
Unavailable*								
Not Qualified								
Total Attempts:								
Total Completed Records:								
Attempts/Hr.								
Contacts/Hr.								
Completed Records/Hr.								

*Unavailable after X attempts.

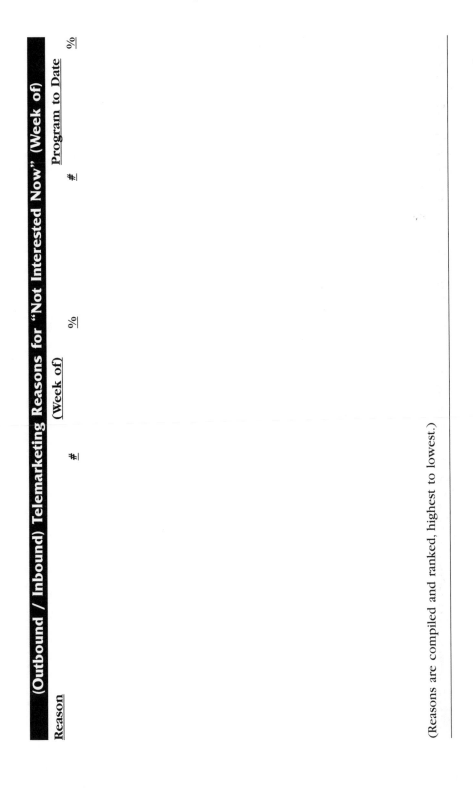

(Outbound / Inbound) Telemarketing Reasons for "Not Interested Now" (Week of)

Reason

(Week of) # %

Program to Date # %

(Reasons are compiled and ranked, highest to lowest.)

City	Outbound Reg.	Inbound Reg.	Fax Reg.	BRC Reg.	Field Reg.	Total Execs.	Total D.M.U.s
Total							

Central Response/Registration Log As of (date)

Checklist for Decision Making about In-House versus Outside-Vendor Services

A brief rundown of the considerations involved in choosing either in-house or outside-vendor direct marketing services is given below.

Advantages of In-House Operation

Control. The major advantage of developing an in-house operation is the level of control which can be exercised over its functioning. In some instances this is absolutely critical, as in transactions in which salespeople must be licensed by a government authority. Even if there is no licensing requirement, the individuals involved in writing copy, answering telephones, or even fulfilling orders can be more intensively trained and, hence, more knowledgeable about the company's product or service if they are employees of that company rather than an outside agency or service bureau.

Database access. It is easier to draw from, or add to, an ongoing central database from within a single corporate facility than to spread information-gathering and dispersal over several vendor companies. This is not to say that it is impossible to enter data from a service bureau into your central files, or to provide ongoing data updates to field operations. However, a centralized operation is more convenient and up-to-the-minute in its database functions.

Employee commitment. If properly structured, an in-house operation can produce higher levels of employee enthusiasm and involvement than can an outside vendor. This assumes that the employees in the direct-response departments are fully integrated with the company as a whole, receive adequate compensation, and see the opportunity for advancement.

Learning-curve effects. In an in-house operation, the individuals involved develop a unique level of experience working with the distinctive concerns of the company. Their efficiency and productivity increase over time, as does their value to their employer. The same is true of the operation as a whole: As it continues over time, whether as the long program or as individual campaigns, efficiency and productivity increase, with resulting improvements in profitability. The company develops a special-purpose tool, shaped to meet its own marketing requirements, which can be applied to a wide range of direct response opportunities, often on short notice.

Advantages of Vendor Services

Expert capabilities. The rapid growth of direct marketing in the recent past has created a shortage of professionals with the expertise and experience required to design and manage direct marketing operations. Even companies with the desire to start in-house operations and the willingness to offer substantial salaries to managers may find it difficult to hire the necessary personnel. However, an established agency or service bureau will have a team of experts in place, thoroughly trained and experienced in a variety of programs conducted for many clients.

Minimal capital outlay. The start-up expense involved in setting up facilities and hiring personnel for a direct marketing operation can be enormous. An in-house telemarketing facility involves real estate, furniture, telephone lines and equipment, hiring, training, and more. Fulfillment operations are also labor- and space-intensive. By using a service organization, the company avoids these up-front expenses, and the overhead expenses involved in running a direct marketing operation are spread by the vendor over a range of concurrent programs.

Faster start-up. Clearly an existing direct marketing vendor will have systems and people in place, eliminating the substantial lag time involved in initially setting up operations.

Easier shutdown. If a direct marketing program is not going well, it is relatively simple to call a vendor and have operations suspended. In a facility staffed with your own employees, even a temporary hold on a program can mean layoffs and extra expenses.

Staffing considerations. While in-house or outside marketing executives are generally well-paid professionals, there are several areas in direct marketing operations that require less skilled labor in fairly large quantity. The expense involved in hiring telemarketing personnel, or additional warehouse help to handle single-item fulfillment, will prove exorbitant unless your facility is running at near-peak load on a regular basis. Unusual hours (such as 24-hour operator service) and peak-period staffing requirements (pre-Christmas shipping, for instance) also make direct marketing labor requirements distinctively demanding.

Union versus nonunion labor. Finally, there is the question of union versus nonunion labor. If additional personnel hired by your firm would be union members with the associated benefits and expenses, it may well prove less costly to farm out the work.

In general, it is wise to rely on outside resources as much as possible in the initial phases of involvement with direct marketing. Up-front investment is minimized; experienced, talented individuals are available at all levels of the operation; and the program can be started, stopped, and restarted more or less at will. Once direct marketing has proven itself as a valuable tool within your marketing plans, then serious consideration should be given to bringing some or all of the functions involved in-house, perhaps drawing on vendors who have proven their abilities in the role of consultants.

Selecting Outside Vendors

Someday there may be a direct-response agency that truly brings together all the services required for integrated direct marketing under one roof—but it doesn't exist today, and creating a single source of that sort would be a massive undertaking. Consider the breadth of media encompassed under the IDM umbrella, ranging from broadcast media through direct mail, print advertising, inbound and outbound telemarketing, audio and video teleconferencing, to the creation of premiums and incentives. And that only covers the media mix: additional specialty services include marketing research, database management, fulfillment, and consulting services to help bring order and direction to the program as a whole.

It is clear that in a program of any size, you will have to work with several vendors. A primary criterion for selecting these vendors for an integrated direct marketing program is an understanding of, appreciation of, and enthusiasm for the synergistic nature of the program being undertaken.

Some companies—even many with unquestioned expertise and a superb track record in their chosen field—find it extremely difficult to integrate their operations effectively with other media practitioners. The problem may be attitudinal. *There is no "star" medium in an IDM media mix; everyone is a supporting player.* The marketer gains from this ensemble approach, but the agency demanding an individual spotlight loses out.

Rigid internal systems may also spell trouble for a vendor working in an IDM environment. We demand a free flow of information between vendors, so that the strengths of each medium and service function can be appropriately employed, and the response generated through each medium can be used to fine-tune the use of the other media in the mix. This does not imply a loss of confidentiality, since the client supervises this interchange, and no information goes beyond those with a "need to know." However, the number of individuals who do need to know is greater in IDM than in traditional marketing, and a vendor unable or unwilling to engage in an open interchange of information and ideas will only impede the process.

Above all, look for a sense of enthusiasm about the project at hand. There are two very good reasons that a vendor who understands the IDM concept should demonstrate an intense level of interest in your program: it's a matter of dollars and sense. The demonstrated potential of IDM as a major distribution channel for goods and services makes an IDM program a good bet for rapid growth, and with growth comes program expansion, increased use of the vendor services, and greater profits.

Second, integrating resources into complementary, synergistic programs is clearly the direction our industry will be following for the foreseeable future. Every opportunity to undertake a program on behalf of a client interested in pursuing this approach represents the chance to build up the knowledge base in this area. Experience and expertise in meeting the unique requirements of an IDM program are an increasingly important aspect of any agency's offer to a potential client. Now is the time to build up credentials in this regard, and it makes sense to devote extra time and energy to clients who wish to pursue this methodology today.

Checklist for Selecting an Agency or Service Bureau

Exhibit D-1 is an adaptation of a questionnaire developed to help clients choose outside marketing vendors. It can help you to organize the wealth of choices available so that you will be able to select the agency or service bureau that best meets your needs. We have included both general areas to be considered in assessing the capabilities of any direct marketing service supplier, and specific criteria involved in choosing a direct marketing agency, telemarketing service, or fulfillment operation.

This checklist is presented in a format that makes it ready to be photocopied and filled in during the selection process.

Exhibit D-1.

Agency name _____ Telephone number _____

Address _____

Name and title of agency contact

_____

(1) Corporate affiliation _____

(2) Length of time in business _____

(3) Current clients _____

_____

(4) Clients competitive with your company

_____

(5) Past clients _____

(6) Current or previous experience with your company

_____

_____

(7) Previous experience with similar product or service

_____

_____

(8) Previous experience with IDM campaigns

_____

_____

(9) Membership in Direct Marketing Association

_____

(10) References:
    Three current clients _____

    _____

    _____

    Three past clients   _____

    _____

    _____

FOR DIRECT MARKETING AGENCIES

Areas of media expertise

_____

_____

Level of executives to be assigned to your account

_____

Organizational structure

_____

Assessment of creative samples

_____

Adequacy of resources

_____

FOR TELEMARKETING AGENCIES AND SERVICE BUREAUS

Communicator training and turnover _____

_____

Number of communicators

_____

Ratio of supervisors to communicators

_____

Organizational structure

_____

Capacity (hours per month)

_____

Scripting (structured scripting versus call guides)

_____

Automation (What is automated? Scripting? MIS? Telecommunications?)

_____

MIS (Manual or automated? How detailed?)

_____

Security of clients' names and other information

_____

Creative thinking (creative or strategic versus operations shop)

_____

_____

IDM Quality and Performance Metrics

Print

- Universe/circulation
- Gross response/registration (by company, by executive, by source)
  - BRC
  - FAX
  - Inbound
- Qualified response (by company, by executive, by source)
- Reasons for not interested now (by source)
- Net attendance (by company, by executive, by source)
- Qualified leads (by company, by executives, by source)
- Sales (by source)
- Average sale (by source)
- Time to sale (by source)
- Reasons for no sale (by source)

Direct Mail

- Timing relative to electronic or print advertising
- Universe of list(s)
- Gross count by list(s) with selections
- Counts by list(s) after merge/purge, suppression
- Net count of list(s) by test cell
- Net count/multi-buyers
- Gross response/registration (by company, by executive, by source)
  - BRC
  - FAX
  - Inbound
- Qualified response (by company, by executive, by source)
- Reasons for not interested now (by source)
- Net attendance (by company, by executive, by source)
- Qualified leads (by company, by executives, by source)

- Sales (by source)
- Average sale (by source)
- Time to sale (by source)
- Reasons for no sale (by source)

Telemarketing

- Training
  - Test results
    - Product knowledge
    - Computer skills
    - Telemarketing skills
- inbound
  - Blockage before, during and after hours
  - # calls during regular hours
    - by source code
  - Staffing
  - # calls/communicator/hour
    - By source code
  - # Misdirects by extension (media)
  - Reason/misdirect
  - # abandon
  - # rings to answer
  - Average speed to answer
  - Wait time
  - Talk time
  - After-call work
  - Monitoring
    - Product knowledge
    - Telemarketing skills
    - Customer satisfaction rating
  - Gross response/registration (by company, by executive, by source)
  - Qualified response (by company, by executive, by source)
  - Reasons for not interested now (by source)
  - Net attendance (by company, by executive, by source)
  - Qualified leads (by company, by executives, by source)
  - Sales (by source)
  - Average sale (by source)
  - Time to sale (by source)
  - Reasons for no sale now (by source)
- outbound
  - Net names
    - By test cell
    - Geographical representation

- Staffing
- Response compression plan
- Completion plan
- # dials/attempts per hour
- # disconnect
  - By list
- # wrong numbers
  - By list
- # "not available"—scheduled call back
- # decision maker Requested Call Back (RCB)
- # contacts
- # completed calls
- New names to database
- Wait time
- Talk time
- After-call work
- Monitoring
  - Product knowledge
  - Telemarketing skills
  - Customer satisfaction rating
- Gross response/registration (by company, by executive, by source)
- Qualified response (by company, by executive, by source)
- Reasons for not interested now (by source)
- Net attendance (by company, by executive, by source)
- Qualified leads (by company, by executive, by source)
- Sales (by source)
- Average sale (by source)
- Time to sale (by source)
- Reasons for no sale (by source)

Index

A/B test, 9, 44
Adept Technology, Inc., 135, 140
    case history, 11
Advertising, 81, 141, 185
    measurement, 130-31
    placement, 182
Aftermarket, 134
Analysis
    interim, 183
    of research results, 176
Andino, Peter, 119
Anton, Ramona, 79, 82, 98
Assessment, 164-66
Association list, 30
AT&T, 54, 67, 127
Audio track capability, 68

Back test, 148
Bang tail envelope, 70
Baseline, 128, 163, 170
    establishing, 145
Behavioral information, 41
Bell Atlantic, 62, 149
Benchmarking, 126-53, 163-64
Beyond 2000: The Future of Direct Marketing, 3
Billing, 26
    insert, 70, 103
Brandon, Yvonne, 113-14
BRC (Business reply card), 62, 64, 130, 151
Briefing package, 93
Broadcast media, 53. See also Television, Radio
Budget, 48, 135-40, 157
    allocation, 24, 46
    guidelines by medium, 140-45
Bulletin board, 68
Business case, 145-50, 170-72
Business reply card (BRC), 62, 64, 130, 151

Business-to-business, 9, 18, 23, 174, 185
    direct response advertising, 45
    buying cycle, 18, 65, 123

Cable television, 68
Calendar of events, 168
    for implementation, 178
Call center, 70
Call monitoring, 61
Call Report System, 27-28
Campaign, for IDM, 73-77
Catalog company, 52
Catalog copy, 52
Change agent, 13
Change leader, 14
Citibank (Citicorp), 56-57, 60
    case history, 10
Citicorp. *See* Citibank
Closed loop lead management
    system, 132, 187
Closed market, 119
Closure rate, 6
Cluster Plus, 33
Cluster system, 33, 42
Columbia House, 149
Communication
    process, 3, 19, 122
    strategy, 17
    ongoing, 66, 146, 155, 158, 168
Compensation plan, 8, 123
Compiled list, 30
Computer
    effect on direct mail, 54
    synchronization, 121
    intelligence, 31
Conference call, 155
Confirmation
    call, 93
    card, 93, 182
Consensual database, 124

Consultant, 12
  role of IDM manager as, 157
Consumer marketing, 9, 23, 173, 185
Controlled circulation, 30
Conversion, 9
  to lead, 130
  to sale, 130
Cook, Terry, 123
Coordination, during implementation,
  181
Corporate culture, 50, 120
Cost efficiency, 112
Cost per lead 9, 11, 132
Cost per response, 145
Cost per sale, 48, 56, 132
Coverage, 30
Creative, 7, 170
  implementation of, 180
  strategy, 98
  team, 82-83, 105
Creative process, 72-76, 108
  case histories, 77-104
  key points, 106
Credibility, 103
Credit, 103
Cross-functional team, 73, 158, 172
  assembling, 159
Cross-reference, 26, 34, 41
Cultural resistance, 119
Customer, 5
  categories, 19
  contact, 28, 109-25
  life cycle, 7, 15, 63
  relations, 2, 15
  satisfaction, 95, 134, 150
Customer contact management, 28,
109-22
  strategic issues, 122-25
Customer-oriented response, 2

D&B, 31
Data
  hierarchy, 35
  verification, 28
Database, 4, 26, 74-75, 89, 158, 167
  in depth research, 175-76
  financial, 21
  infrastructure, 122

integrated, 178-79, 185
list scrub, 28, 35, 41, 179
Database resource, as member of team,
  160-61
Dawson, Garry, 157
Decision cycle, 24
Decision maker, 19, 25, 30, 35, 78, 157,
  173-76
Decision-making unit (d.m.u.), 23
Demographic profile, 17, 18, 30
Deployment of media, 49
Depth Research,5, 25, 29, 52, 63,
  74-76, 132, 155, 172
  interview, 77, 81
  study, 21, 106
Desktop artist, 168
Desktop publishing, 142
Direct mail, 20, 45, 70, 141, 179,
  185-86
  increasing effectiveness of, 55
  computer and, 54
  measurements, 130
  production, 181
Direct Marketing Association, 17, 41
Direct response media, 107, 151
Direct response television (DRTV),
  68
Direct, J. Walter Thompson, 40
Distribution, 51
Downturn, 12
Drive time, 69

Early out, 129
Editor, 52
Electronic mail, 68
Electronic media, 51
Enhancement, of list, 30, 32
Envelope
  bang tail, 70
  outer, 55
Equifax, 31
ER. *See* Expense to revenue
ERDM. *See* Ernan Roman Direct Market-
  ing Corporation.
Ernan Roman Direct Marketing Corpo-
  ration (ERDM), 2, 36
Event planning, 180-81
Exchange, list, 32. *See also* List

Expense item, 146
  in business case, 171
Expense-to-revenue (ER), 9, 134, 146, 172
Extended information, 22

Face-to-face selling, 16
Farber, Barry A., 12
Fax, 65, 130
  option, 45
Field criteria, 132
Field sale(s), 40, 41, 187
  call report system, 27-28
  force, 5-6
  as member of team, 159
  process, 163
Financial record(s), 26
First class mail, 55, 186
Focus group, 24
Follow up, 16, 48, 83, 132
Ford, 48
Free standing insert (F.S.I.), 44, 45, 151
Frequency, 112
F.S.I. *See* Free standing insert.
Fulfillment, 182

Garwood, Dave, 118
Geographic pocket, 33
Gibbens, Dan, 101, 120, 121, 122
Gillespie, Brian M., 157
Gillespie, Curt, 8, 101, 118
GM/Saturn, 67
Goal, 50, 128
  setting, 166-67
Graphic designer, 168
Guideline, for IDM program, 154-87

Halo effect, 65
Hewlett-Packard (H-P), 38, 106-7, 126, 132
  case history, 9, 35-37
Home shopping network(s), 53
  Home Shopping Network, 68
Hornstein, Scott, 18, 51, 52, 124, 185

IBM, 48, 50, 113, 118, 126-27
  case history, 10
  depth research, 74-101

IDM (Integrated Direct Marketing)
  calendar, 137-38
  creative process of, 72-108
  customer relationship in, 15-42, 109-25
  five basic principles, 5-8, 11-12
  marketing blend of, 43-71
  measuring results, 126-54
  overview, 1-12
  worksheets and guidelines, 154-87
Image, 50
Implementation, of program, 155, 156, 178-83
Inbound telemarketing, 44, 46, 70-71, 128-30, 186
Infomercial, 53, 68
Information system (IS), 17, 38-39, 41
Insert
  free standing or perforated, 69
Integrated database, 16-19, 185
Integrated media, 59
Integration, 40
Interactive communication, 16
Interactive scripting, 61
Interim analysis, 183
Interviewing, 176
  guide, 173-74
IS. *See* Information system

J.Walter Thompson Direct, 40
Johnson & Johnson, 67
JWT (J.Walter Thompson) Direct, 40

Lakin, Greg, 62, 66
Lawrie, Mike, 50, 118, 150, 184
Lead, 132
  follow-up, 9, 11
Lead generation process, 24, 38, 77-104
  program, 115
  seven steps of, 182
Lead management, 20, 183
  closed loop, 132, 187
Lead time, 51
Leadership, 155
Lifecycle event, 101
Lifestyle information, 41
Lifetime value, 63, 66, 133
Lindbeck, Asar, 126

List
  broker, 31
  ecology, 29
  enhancement, 179
  financially based, 31
  rental, 32, 142
  scrub, 178
Location, of event, 180
Logo, 83, 84

Magazine, 69
Mail, 51, 151
  release, 61
Mailing tape, 179
Majkowski, Dan, 106, 155
Management
  expectations of, 158-61
  IDM, 157
  as member of team, 159
Market evaluation, 24
Market evolution, 2
Marketing
  action plan, 155, 172-78
  in creative process, 75
  goals and measurement, 2
  mass, 3-4
  as member of team, 161
Mass media path, 68
Master's Tour, 68
MCI, 67
Measurement, 126, 128-53, 158, 168,
    183
  qualitative, 127
Media
  contribution, 58
  performance, 46
  preference, 29, 56
Media integration, 43, 57, 106
  flow chart of, 64
Media mix, 4, 46, 167-68, 178
Medical IDM pilot, 80
Membership list, 30
Merge/purge, 33, 35-36, 42, 141, 179
Message impact, 112
Metric(s)
  interim, 183
  quality and performance, 128-31
  types of, 129

Micro-marketing, 4
MIS (Marketing Information System),
    35, 36
Misdirect, 46-47
Modeling, 42
Monetary value, 112
Multi-media, 105, 108

NCOA (National Change of Address), 31
NDL/Lifestyle Selector, 33
Needs assessment, 24
Negotiation, 24
Neiger, Judie, 36, 126, 132
Networking, 81
Neuenschwander, Donald, 37
New York Times, The, 110
News story, 67
Newspaper, 69
Niche product, 69
Nixie, 28, 179, 185, 186

Objective, 157
  setting, 79-81, 166-67
"One organization" thinking, 123
Open market, 120
Orfuss, Mitchell A., 40, 107
Organizational integration, 49-50
Outbound call, 6
Outbound telemarketing, 44, 46, 70-71,
    95, 128-30, 186
Outer envelope, 55
Outside list, 30
Outsourcing, 39

Paterson, Mike, 113, 119-20, 122
Percent response, 130
Personalization, 4
  in direct mail, 186
Personalized engagement, 95
Planning process, 6, 155
Point of sale scanner, 4
Postage, 143
Postcard, 151
Preannouncement, 47
Predictive database, 124
Predictive model, 20
Pre-sale, 3
Print advertising, 51, 52, 54, 151

Print media, 46, 51, 69, 108
Printing cost, 142-43
Prizm, 33
Probability table, 149
Product, 8
Product management, as member of team, 160
Product search, 65
Production
    cost, 142-43
    during implementation, 181-83
Productivity, 129
Program implementation process, 155, 156, 178-83
Project management, 179
Projection, in business case, 171
Proofreading, 141
Prospect, categories of, 19
Psychographic, 18, 41
Public relations, 51, 67, 108
Publication
    controlled circulation, 30
    vertical, 45, 54
Publicity, 51, 67
Purchase, 24

Qualified lead, 36, 81-82
Qualified opportunity, 132
Quality, 129
    control, 99
QVC, 68

Radio, 46, 51, 69, 108, 151
Rapp, Stan, 8
Reach, 45
Reader's Digest, 110, 123
Recency, 112
Relationship marketing, 120
Reply device, 35, 55
Research, 174-76, 180-81. See also Depth research
    matrix, 174
    technique, 4
Resource, 169-70
Responder list, 30
Response, 16
    compression, 47, 55, 61-62, 65, 76, 186

media, 45, 130
projection, 146
qualified, 187
rate, 11, 56
Results analysis, 61
Retail television, 68
Ries, Al, 109, 110, 112
Rollout, 148
Roman, Ernan, Direct Marketing Corporation (ERDM). See Ernan Roman Direct Marketing Corporation
Run time, 68
Russell, Pam, 154, 158

Sales
    channel, 179
    cycle, 7
    force, 175
    integration, 49
Salutation, of letter, 55
Sarason, S.B., 14
Scanner, point of sale, 4
Schultz, Don, 3, 8
Script, 88-92
    exit point in telemarketing, 186
    in publicity release, 52
Service bureau, 39
Shopping channel, 68
Situation analysis, 164
Sort, 31
Speaker, for event, 181
Specialist, 52
Specialization, 2
Sporting event, 68
Spot television, 68
Sprint, 67
St. Amant, Bryan, 135-36, 140
Stone, Bob, 154
Strategy, 114, 167
Subscription list, 30
Systems checklist, 39

Tactic, 167
Target market, defining, 162
Target Marketing, 17-18
Team meeting, initial, 161-62
Teleconference, 36

Telemarketing, 20, 51, 118, 136, 140, 151, 169, 179, 182-83
  cost, 143
  database scrub, 28
  inbound and outbound, 44, 46, 70-71, 95, 128-30, 186
  problems with, 6, 56-62
  script, 10, 28, 35, 88-92
  scripted vs. nonscripted, 28, 59-61
  scrub, 36
  three-step formula, 144
Telephone, 151
Television, 45-46, 51, 53, 67, 108, 152
  retail, 68
Testimonial, 97
Testing, 168, 170
  matrix, 148-50, 170
Timeline, 155, 158, 174
  for implementation, 178
Timing, 94, 127, 180
Toll-free 800 number, 55. *See also* Telemarketing, inbound
  increase in usage, 62

Topic, for event, 181
Total Quality Control (TQC), 10, 60, 186
TRW, 31

UPC code, 4
USAA, 101-5, 119
  case history, 10
USPS (United States Postal Service), 31

Validation depth research, 181
Value-added, 134, 141
Venue, for event, 180
Vertical publication, 45, 54

Warner Plumbing, 69
Washington Post, 69
Working-week calendar, 156
Worksheet(s), 154-87
Writer, 52
Wunderman, Lester, 1, 43, 54

Yellow Pages, 31

Ernan Roman, President of Ernan Roman Direct Marketing Corporation (ERDM), is acknowledged as the pioneer of the Integrated Direct Marketing (IDM^{sm}) methodology. In 1983, he founded his New York-based consulting firm to implement the IDM process for clients.

With ERDM, Mr. Roman has developed IDM programs on behalf of an impressive roster of corporations, including numerous divisions of AT&T, Hewlett-Packard, IBM, Bell Atlantic, Motorola, and Citibank.

His first book was published in 1988. *Integrated Direct Marketing: Techniques and Strategies for Success* explained the foundations of IDM and provided case histories of early results from blue chip clients. It has become a landmark book on reengineering the sales and marketing process.

His new book, *Integrated Direct Marketing: The Cutting-Edge Strategy for Synchronizing Advertising, Direct Mail, Telemarketing, and Field Sales,* explains critical aspects of the battle-tested IDM process, including detailed results, financial analyses, and guidelines for how to implement IDM at your company.

Mr. Roman has published numerous articles in a variety of business and marketing publications, including *Inc., Business Marketing, Direct, Ad Age,* and *Sales and Marketing Management.* A renowned speaker, he has presented at major marketing conferences and seminars throughout North America, Europe, and Asia. In 1979, Mr. Roman was the recipient of the first Telemarketing Leader Award, presented by the Direct Marketing Association for outstanding contributions to the telemarketing field. He is also a two-time winner of the prestigious DMA Echo Award for direct marketing excellence.